Hockings'

SOUTH AMERICAN CUPS

**A statistical history of
South American football
since 1893**

by Ron Hockings

Other books by Ron Hockings

Statistical History of Chelsea FC 1905-85
2nd Edition 1905-86
3rd Edition 1905-88

Chelsea FC Players Who's Who 1905-89

European Cups 2nd Edition

© Ron Hockings 1991

Published by Articulate
12a North Street, Emsworth, Hampshire PO10 7DQ, England

ISBN 0-951 7533-0-4

Typesetting and artwork by Articulate Studio, Hampshire
Printed and bound by Hartnolls, Bodmin, Cornwall

CONTENTS

DEDICATION

To Jean, my wife, for being so patient and understanding about all the time I have spent watching and computing football over the past 35 years.

ACKNOWLEDGEMENTS

My thanks to World Soccer and Keir Radnedge; Michael Parr from Newcastle under Lyme; Jorgen Nielson from Randers, Denmark.

FOREWORD

I believe that the information in this book has never before been published in Europe. I have tried to be as accurate as possible but I know that in the Copa America section for example, there are some half-time scores, attendances and goal scorers missing, particularly from Ecuador and Bolivia. If any reader can help with these omissions or has any additional information on international line-ups or the like, I should be pleased to hear from them.

In the Copa Libertadores all the results are correct according to the South American Confederation, but the first result may not always be the home result.

I hope you will find this book entertaining and informative.

Ron Hockings

1977 **Boca Juniors** (Argentina)

COPA LIBERTADORES

The South American Club Championships
Copa Libertadores de America

The first championship was held in 1960, both as a direct result of the success of the European Champions Cup and because of the interest and finance it generated. However it was some time before the South American counterpart reached the same heights as the European Cup. On several occasions it was nearly abandoned, with many winners on the edge of bankruptcy, matches finishing in full scale riots and loss of interest in the South American Championships.

The competition is organised differently from the European Championship. The Champion Cup and (from 1965) the runners-up in each country are entitled to enter. The format is being constantly changed. At first it was on a knock-out basis, then in groups, some of them with as many as seven teams having to play 12 matches in the first round; the 1967 competition went to 114 matches. Apart from in the first two seasons, the previous year's winners automatically advance to the semi-finals of the next season's competition. Which means that some countries could have three entries.

In recent years, some countries have run a play-off mini league with the top clubs to select entries for the following year's competition. The Copa Libertadores cup winners go on to play the European Champions for the World Cup Championship. The final is held every December in Tokyo.

1973 **Independiente** (Argentina)

COPA AMERICA

South American Championships
"Copa America"

This championship started in 1916 with an unofficial competition held in Argentina. (Although I have included a series of matches played in 1910 which it has been suggested were a championship.) It is now the oldest running international team competition in the world since the end of the British Championships in the early 1980's. The championships have not been held on a regular basis, only 27 of the 34 so far played have been deemed to be official, the others being 'extraordinarios', the last of these being in 1959.

Of the eligible countries, many have entered irregularly and it was not until 1975 that all ten teams finally appeared when Uruguay, the then holders, joined the competition at the semi-finals. Prior to this the competition was treated with some disdain, some countries not entering, sending weak teams without their European stars, 'B' and even youth teams. For some years the championship was held in the same country, but loss of interest and financial instability finally forced a change.

From 1975 the matches were played on a home and away basis. This lasted for three championships, until 1987 when once again they were held in just one country, Argentina, in 1989 the venue was Brazil. This year, 1991, will see the championships taking place in Chile, although the Chileans have been banned because of the troubles that took place in the 1990 World Cup qualifying match against Brazil.

1960 **Penarol** (Uruguay)

1967 **Racing** (Argentina)

THE WINNERS

LIBERTADORES CUP FINALS

Date	Home/Match		H/T	F/T	Venue	Attend
12-6-60	**Penarol, Uruguay** *A Spencer*	v Olimpia, Paraguay	0-0	1-0	Montevideo	
19-6-60	Olimpia, Paraguay *H Recalde*	v **Penarol Uruguay** *L Cubilla*	1-0	1-1	Asuncion	35,000
9-6-61	**Penarol, Uruguay** *A Spencer*	v Palmeiras Sao Paulo, Brazil	0-0	1-0	Montevideo	50,000
11-6-61	Palmeiras Sao Paulo, Brazil *L Colella*	v **Penarol, Uruguay** *J Sasia*	0-1	1-1	Sao Paulo	40,000
28-7-62	Penarol, Uruguay *A Spencer*	v **Santos FC Sao Paulo, Brazil** *Coutinho 2*		1-2	Montevideo	50,000
2-8-62	**Santos FC Sao Paulo, Brazil** *Dorval, Mengalvio*	v Penarol, Uruguay *A Spencer 2, J Sasia*		2-3	Santos	30,000
30-8-62	**Santos FC Sao Paulo, Brazil** *Coutinho, Pele 2*	v Penarol, Uruguay	1-0	3-0 po	Buenos Aires	36,540
4-9-63	**Santos FC Sao Paulo, Brazil** *Coutinho 2, Lima*	v Boca Juniors, Argentina *Sanfilippo*	3-1	3-2	Rio de Janeiro	55,000
11-9-63	Boca Juniors, Argentina *Sanfilippo*	v **Santos FC Sao Paulo, Brazil** *Pele, Coutinho*	0-0	1-2	Buenos Aires	50,000
6-8-64	Nacional, Uruguay	v **Independiente, Argentina**		0-0	Montevideo	
12-8-64	Independiente, Argentina *Mario Rodriguez*	v **Nacional, Uruguay**	1-0	1-0	Avellaneda	
9-4-65	**Independiente, Argentina** *R Bernao*	v Penarol, Uruguay	0-0	1-0	Avellaneda	
12-4-65	Penarol, Uruguay *Goncalvez, Reznik, Rocha*	v **Independiente, Argentina** *De la Mata*	2-0	3-1	Montevideo	
15-4-65	**Independiente, Argentina** *Perez, Bernao, Avallay, Mura*	v Penarol, Uruguay *J Joya*	3-1	4-1 po	Santiago	
12-5-66	**Penarol, Uruguay** *Abaddie, Joya*	v River Plate, Argentina	0-0	2-0	Montevideo	49,400
18-5-66	River Plate, Argentina *Daniel Onega, Sarnari, Ermindo Onega*	v **Penarol, Uruguay** *Rocha, Spencer*	1-1	3-2	Buenos Aires	60,400
20-5-66	**Penarol, Uruguay** *Spencer 2, Matosas own goal, Rocha*	v River Plate, Argentina *Daniel Onega, Solari*	0-2	4-2 po aet	Santiago	39,200
15-8-67	**Racing Club Avellaneda, Argentina**	v Nacional, Uruguay		0-0	Avellaneda	54,704
25-8-67	Nacional, Uruguay	v **Racing Club Avellaneda, Argentina**		0-0	Montevideo	62,000
29-8-67	**Racing Club Avellaneda, Argentina** *Cardoso, Raffo*	v Nacional, Uruguay *Esparrago*	2-0	2-1 po	Santiago	25,000
2-5-68	**Estudiantes La Plata, Argentina** *Veron, Flores*	v Palmeiras Sao Paulo, Brazil *Servilio*	0-1	2-1	La Plata	
7-5-68	Palmeiras Sao Paulo, Brazil *Tupazinho 2, Rinaldo*	v **Estudiantes La Plata, Argentina** *Veron*		3-1	Sao Paulo	
16-5-68	**Estudiantes La Plata, Argentina** *Ribaudo, Veron*	v Palmeiras Sao Paulo, Brazil	1-0	2-0 po	Montevideo	

11

THE WINNERS

Date	Home team		Away team	HT	FT	Venue	Attendance
15-5-69	Nacional, Uruguay	v	Estudiantes La Plata, Argentina *E Flores*	0-0	0-1	Montevideo	50,000
21-5-69	Estudiantes La Plata, Argentina *E Flores, Conigliaro*	v	Nacional, Uruguay	2-0	2-0	La Plata	30,000
20-5-70	Estudiantes La Plata, Argentina *N Togneri*	v	Penarol, Uruguay	0-0	1-0	La Plata	36,500
27-5-70	Penarol, Uruguay	v	Estudiantes La Plata, Argentina		0-0	Montevideo	50,000
26-5-71	Estudiantes La Plata, Argentina *D Romeo*	v	Nacional, Uruguay	1-0	1-0	La Plata	32,000
2-6-71	Nacional, Uruguay *J Masnik*	v	Estudiantes La Plata, Argentina	0-0	1-0	Montevideo	62,000
9-6-71	Nacional, Uruguay *Esparrago penalty, Artime*	v	Estudiantes La Plata, Argentina	1-0	2-0 po	Lima	42,000
17-5-72	Universitario Lima, Peru	v	Independiente, Argentina		0-0	Lima	45,500
24-5-72	Independiente, Argentina *Maglioni 2*	v	Universitario Lima, Peru *P Rojas*	1-0	2-1	Avellaneda	65,750
22-5-73	Independiente, Argentina *Mendoza*	v	Colo Colo, Chile *Sa own goal*	0-0	1-1	Avellaneda	65,600
29-5-73	Colo Colo, Chile	v	Independiente, Argentina		0-0	Santiago	77,600
6-6-73	Independiente, Argentina *Giachello, Mendoza*	v	Colo Colo, Chile *C Caszelly*	1-1	2-1 po	Montevideo	45,000
12-10-74	Sao Paulo FC, Brazil *Rocha, Mirandinha*	v	Independiente, Argentina *Saggioratto*	0-1	2-1	Sao Paulo	51,600
16-10-74	Independiente, Argentina *Bochini, Balbuena*	v	Sao Paulo FC, Brazil	1-0	2-0	Avellaneda	48,750
19-10-74	Independiente, Argentina *Pavoni penalty*	v	Sao Paulo FC, Brazil	1-0	1-0 po	Santiago	27,650
18-6-75	Union Espanola, Chile *S Ahumada*	v	Independiente, Argentina	0-0	1-0	Santiago	43,200
25-6-75	Independiente, Argentina *P Rojas, Pavoni penalty, Bertoni*	v	Union Espanola, Chile *De Las Heras penalty*	0-0	3-1	Avellaneda	52,000
29-6-75	Independiente, Argentina *Ruiz Moreno, Bertoni*	v	Union Espanola, Chile	1-0	2-0 po	Asuncion	45,000
21-7-76	Cruzeiro Belo Horizonte, Brazil *Nelinho, Palinha 2, Valdo*	v	River Plate, Argentina *O Mas penalty*	3-0	4-1	Belo Horizonte	58,700
28-7-76	River Plate, Argentina *Juan Jose Lopez, Gonzales*	v	Cruzeiro Belo Horizonte, Brazil *Palinha*	1-0	2-1	Buenos Aires	45,000
30-7-76	Cruzeiro Belo Horizonte, Brazil *Joaozinho, Nelinho pen, Ronaldo*	v	River Plate, Argentina *O Mas penalty, Urquiza*	1-0	3-2 po	Santiago	35,200
6-9-77	Boca Juniors, Argentina *Veglio*	v	Cruzeiro Belo Horizonte, Brazil	1-0	1-0	Buenos Aires	50,000
11-9-77	Cruzeiro Belo Horizonte, Brazil *Nelinho*	v	Boca Juniors, Arginata	0-0	1-0	Belo Horizonte	55,850
14-9-78	Boca Juniors, Argentina	v	Cruzeiro Belo Horizonte, Brazil		0-0 5-4p	Montevideo	45,000
23-11-78	Deportivo Cali, Colombia	v	Boca Juniors, Argentina		0-0	Cali	
28-11-78	Boca Juniors, Argentina *Perotti 2, Mastrangelo, Salines*	v	Deportivo Cali, Colombia	1-0	4-0	Buenos Aires	
22-7-79	Olimpia, Paraguay *Aquino, Piazza*	v	Boca Juniors, Argentina	2-0	2-0	Asuncion	45,000
27-7-79	Boca Juniors, Argentina	v	Olimpia, Paraguay		0-0	Buenos Aires	50,000
30-7-80	Internacional Porto Alegre, Brazil	v	Nacional, Uruguay		0-0	Porto Alegre	80,000
16-8-80	Nacional, Uruguay *Victorino*	v	Internacional Porto Alegre, Brazil	1-0	1-0	Montevideo	75,000
13-11-81	Flamengo Rio de Janeiro, Brazil *Zico 2, 1 penalty*	v	Cobreloa Calama, Chile *Merello penalty*	2-0	2-1	Rio de Janeiro	114,000

12

Date	Home/Team		Away/Team			Venue	Attendance
20-11-81	Cobreloa Calama, Chile *Merello*	v	**Flamengo Rio de Janeiro, Brazil**	0-0	1-0	Santiago	61,700
23-11-81	**Flamengo Rio de Janeiro, Brazil** *Zico 2*	v	Cobreloa Calama, Chile	1-0	2-0 po	Montevideo	35,000
26-11-82	**Penarol, Uruguay**	v	Cobreloa Calama, Chile		0-0	Montevideo	70,000
30-11-82	Cobreloa Calama, Chile	v	**Penarol, Uruguay** *Morena*	0-0	0-1	Santiago	70,000
22-7-83	Penarol, Uruguay *F Morena*	v	**Gremio Porto Alegre, Brazil** *Tita*	1-1	1-1	Montevideo	65,000
28-7-83	**Gremio Porto Alegre, Brazil** *Caio, Cesar*	v	Penarol, Uruguay *Morena*	1-0	2-1	Porto Alegre	75,000
24-7-84	Gremio Porto Alegre, Brazil	v	**Independiente, Argentina** *J Burruchaga*	0-1	0-1	Porte Alegre	55,000
27-7-84	**Independiente, Argentina**	v	Gremio Porto Alegre, Brazil		0-0	Avellaneda	75,000
17-10-85	**Argentinos Juniors, Argentina** *Commisso*	v	America de Cali, Colombia	1-0	1-0	Buenos Aires	50,000
22-10-85	America de Cali, Colombia *W Ortiz*	v	**Argentinos Juniors, Argentina**	1-0	1-0	Cali	50,000
24-10-85	**Argentinos Juniors, Argentina** *Commisso*	v	America de Cali, Colombia *Gareca penalty*	1-1	1-1 5-4p	Asuncion	35,000
22-10-86	America de Cali, Colombia *R Cabanas*	v	**River Plate, Argentina** *Funes, Alonso*	0-2	1-2	Cali	55,000
29-10-86	**River Plate, Argentina** *Funes*	v	America de Cali, Colombia	0-0	1-0	Buenos Aires	85,000
21-10-87	America de Cali, Colombia *Bataglia, Cabanas*	v	**Penarol, Uruguay**	2-0	2-0	Cali	45,000
28-10-87	**Penarol, Uruguay** *D Aguirre, Villar*	v	America de Cali, Colombia *Cabanas*	0-1	2-1	Montevideo	70,000
31-10-87	**Penarol, Uruguay** *D Aguirre*	v	America de Cali, Colombia	0-0	1-0 po aet	Santiago	30,000
19-10-88	**Newells Old Boys Rosario, Argentina** *Gabrich*	v	**Nacional, Uruguay**	0-0	1-0	Rosario	45,000
26-10-88	**Nacional, Uruguay** *Vargas, S Ostolaza, De Leon pen*	v	Newells Old Boys Rosario, Argentina	2-0	3-0 aet	Montevideo	75,000
24-5-89	Olimpia, Paraguay *Bobadilla, Sanabria*	v	**Nacional Medellin, Colombia**	1-0	2-0	Asuncion	50,000
31-5-89	**Nacional Medellin, Colombia** *Mano own goal, Uzurriaga*	v	Olimpia, Paraguay	1-0	2-0 aet 5-4 pens	Bogota	50,000
3.10.90	**Olimpia, Paraguay** *R V Amarilla, A Samaniego*	v	Barcelona Guayaquil, Ecuador	0-0	2-0	Asuncion	35,000
10.10.90	Barcelona Guayaquil, Ecuador *M A Trobbiani*	v	**Olimpia, Paraguay** *R V Amarilla*	0-0	1-1	Guayaquil	70,000

ARGENTINA
Independiente 1964, 1965, 1972, 1973, 1974, 1975, 1984
Racing Club Avellaneda 1967
Estudiantes la Plata 1968, 1969, 1970
Boca Juniors 1977, 1978
Argetninos Juniors 1985
River Plate 1986

BRAZIL
Santos FC Sao Paulo 1962, 1963
Cruzeiro Belo Horizonte 1976
Flamengo Rio de Janeiro 1981
Gremio Porto Alegre 1983

PARAGUAY
Olimpia 1979, 1990

URUGUAY
Penarol 1960, 1961, 1966, 1982, 1987
Nacional 1971, 1980, 1988

COLOMBIA
Naconal Medellin 1989

THE WINNERS

SOUTH AMERICAN PLAYER OF THE YEAR

1971 Tostao (Brazil)	**1980** Diego Maradona
1972 Teofillo Cubillas (Peru)	(Argentina)
1973 Pele (Brazil/Santos)	**1981** Zico (Brazil)
1974 E.Figueroa (Chile)	**1982** Zico (Brazil)
1975 E.Figueroa (Chile)	**1983** Socrates (Brazil)
1976 E.Figueroa (Chile)	**1984** Enzo Francescoli
1977 Zico (Brazil)	(Uruguay)
1978 Mario Kempes	**1985** Cesar Romero
(Argentina)	Paraguay)
1979 Diego Maradona	**1986** Antonio Alzamendi
(Argentina)	(Uruguay)
	1987 Carlos Valderama
	(Colombia)
	1988 Ruben Paz (Uruguay)
	1989 Bebeto (Brazil)

1990 Raul Amarilla (Paraguay)

INTER-AMERICA CUP

For winners of Copa Libertadores and CONCACAF Champions Cup (Central American Confederation of Clubs)

1968 1st Edition

			H/T	F/T	Venue	Attend
13-2-69	Club Deportivo Toluca, Mexico *Linares*	v **Estudiantes La Plata, Argentina** *Conigliaro, Bilardo*		1-2	Mexico City	
19-2-69	**Estudiantes La Plata Argentina** *Veron*	v Club Deportivo Toluca, Mexico *Linares, Albino*		1-2	La Plata	
21-2-69	**Estudiantes La Plata Argentina** *Conigliaro 2, E.Flores*	v Club Deportivo Toluca, Mexico		3-0 po	Montevideo	

1969 Not Played

1970 Not Played

1971 2nd Edition

15-7-72	Cruz Azul, Mexico *Pulido*	v **Nacional, Uruguay** *Mamelli*		1-1	Mexico City	
7-11-72	**Nacional, Uruguay** *Mamelli, B.Castro*	v Cruz Azul, Mexico *Bustos*		2-1	Montevideo	

1972 3rd Edition

17-3-73	Olimpia, Honduras *Brand*	v **Independiente, Argentina** *Semenewicz, Maglioni*	0-1	1-2	San Pedro Lugo	
20-6-73	Olimpia, Honduras	v **Independiente, Argentina** *Balbuena, Maglioni*	0-1	0-2	Tegucigalpa	

1973 4th Edition

24-11-74	Deportivo Municipal, Guatemala *Bochini*	v **Independiente, Argentina**	0-1	2-4p	Guatemala City	
26-11-74	**Independiente, Argentina** *Mitrovich*	v Deportivo Municipal, Guatemala		1-0	Guatemala City	

1974 Not Played

1975 5th Edition

26-8-76	**Independiente, Argentina** *Bochini, Villaverde*	v Atletico Espanol, Mexico *Rameriz, Borbolla*		2-2	Caracas, Venezuela	
29-8-76	Atletico Espanol, Mexico *(Ramirez, Rivero penalties)*	v **Independiente, Argentina** *(Pavoni, Bertoni, Soria, Arroyo penalties)*		0-0 2-4p	Caracas, Venezuela	

14

1976 Not Played

1977 6th Edition

28-3-78	Boca Juniors, Argentina *Salinas 2, Mastrangelo*	v	**America, Mexico**		3-0	Buenos Aires
17-4-78	**America, Mexico** *Kiese*	v	Boca Juniors, Argentina		1-0	Mexico City
19-4-78	**America, Mexico** *Aceves, Reynoso*	v	Boca Juniors, Argentina *Pavon*		2-1 aet	Mexico City

1978 Not Played

1979 7th Edition

18-2-80	F.A.S. El Salvador *Casadei 2, Abraham penalty*	v	**Olimpia, Paraguay** *Solalinde, Yaluk, Isasi*	0-2	3-3	San Salvador
17-3-80	**Olimpia, Paraguay** *Aquino, Michelagnoli 2, Ortiz 2*	v	F.A.S. El Salvador	2-0	5-0	Asuncion

1980 8th Edition

25-3-81	**Universidad Autonoma de Mexico, Mexico** *Hugo Sanchez 2, Ferreti*	v	Nacional, Uruguay *Esparrago*	1-0	3-1	Mexico City
8-4-81	Nacional, Uruguay *J Cabrera 2, W Cabrera*	v	**Universidad Autonoma de Mexico, Mexico** *Vargas*	0-0	3-1	Montevideo
14-5-81	**Universidad Autonoma de Mexico, Mexico** *Ferreti, Vargas*	v	Nacional, Uruguay *J Cabrera*	0-0	2-1	Los Angeles

1982 Not Played

1983 Not Played

1984 Not Played

1985 9th Edition

11-12-86	Defence Force, Trinidad & Tobago	v	**Argentinos Juniors, Argentina** *Dely Valdez*		0-1	Trinidad

1986 10th Edition

21-7-87	Liga Deportivo Alajuelense, Costa Rica	v	**River Plate, Argentina**		0-0	Alajuele	16,000
16-8-87	**River Plate, Argentina** *Villazan, Funes, H.Enrique*	v	Liga Deportivo Alajuelense, Costa Rica		1-0	3-0	Buenos Aires	20,000

1987 Not Played

1988 11th Edition

5-3-89	Olimpia, Honduras *Rivera penalty*	v	**Nacional, Uruguay** *Fonseca*	0-1	1-1	Tegucigalpa	30,000
30-3-89	**Nacional, Uruguay** *Fonseca, Ostolaza, Noe 2*	v	Olimpia, Honduras	2-0	4-0	Montevideo	30,000

1989 12th Edition

25-7-90	**Nacional Medellin, Colombia** *L A Fajardo, O Galeano*	v	Universidad de Autonoma de Mexico	0-0	2-0	Medellin	26,000
1-8-90	Universidad Autonoma de Mexico *Negrete penalty*	v	**Nacional Medellin, Colombia** *Nava own goal, O Galeano, J Arango, Restrepo*	0-1	1-4	Mexico City	2,500

THE WINNERS

RECOPA

For winners of Libertadores and Super Cups

1988 1st Edition

31-1-89	Nacional, Uruguay	v Racing Club Avellaneda, Argentina	0-0	1-0	Fonseca	
6-2-89	Racing Club Avellaneda, Argentina	v Nacional, Uruguay		0-0		

1989 2nd Edition

17.3.90	Boca Juniors, Argentina *Diego Latorre*	v Nacional Medellin, Colombia	1-0	1-0	Orange Bowl, Miami	9,000

1990 3rd Edition
Awarded to Nacional Medellin, Colombia as reward for winning Libertadores and Havelange Super Cup

HAVELANGE SUPER CUP

For Libertadores Cup Winners

1988 1st			H/T	F/T	Round	Attend
2-3-88	Boca Juniors, Argentina *Comas*	v Gremio Porto Alegre, Brazil	1-0	1-0	1st	
16-3-88	Gremio Porto Alegre *Lima, Cuca*	v Boca Juniors, Argentina	2-0	2-0	1st	
24-2-88	Racing Club Avellaneda, Argentina *Iglesias, Colombatti*	v Santos FC Sao Paulo, Brazil	1-0	2-0	1st	
3-3-88	Santos FC Sao Paulo, Brazil	v Racing Avellaneda, Argentina		0-0	1st	5,000
30-3-88	Estudiantes de la Plata, Argentina *Gissi*	v Flamengo Rio de Janeiro, Brazil	1-0	1-1	1st	6,000
5-4-88	Flamengo Rio de Janeiro, Brazil	v Estudiantes de la Plata, Argentina	1-0	3-0	1st	
13-4-88	Olimpia, Paraguay *Ramirez, Mendoza*	v River Plate, Argentina	2-0	2-0	1st	
20-4-88	River Plate, Argentina *Alzamendi 2, Da Silva 2*	v Olimpia, Paraguay		4-0	1st	
6-4-88	Penarol, Uruguay *Herrera*	v Argentinos Juniors, Argentina	0-0	1-0	1st	
15-4-88	Argentinos Juniors, Argentina *Espindola, Batista*	v Penarol, Uruguay	0-0	2-0	1st	
10-2-88	Independiente, Argentina *Merlini*	v Cruzeiro Belo Horizonte, Brazil *Vilmar, Hamilton*	0-0	1-2	1st	
25-2-88	Cruzeiro Belo Horizonte, Brazil *Heribeto*	v Independiente, Argentina	1-0	1-0	1st	
	Nacional, Uruguay	bye				
24-4-88	Nacional, Uruguay *Lemos, Olivera 2*	v Flamengo Rio de Janeiro, Brazil	1-0	3-0	qf	18,000
4-5-88	Flamengo Rio de Janeiro, Brazil *Castro 2*	v Nacional, Uruguay	0-1	0-2	qf	67,000
3-5-88	Gremio Porto Alegre, Brazil *Valdo*	v River Plate, Argentina	1-0	1-0	qf	
11-5-88	River Plate, Argentina *Palma, Alzamendi 2*	v Gremio Porto Alegre, Brazil *Lima*	1-0	3-1	qf	
5-5-88	Cruzeiro Belo Horizonte, Brazil *Ramon*	v Argentinos Juniors, Argentina	0-0	1-0	qf	
18-5-88	Argentinos Juniors, Argentina	v Cruzeiro Belo Horizonte, Brazil *Heriberto*	0-0	0-1	qf	
	Racing Club Avellaneda, Argentina	bye		qf		
30-5-88	Nacional, Uruguay *Olivera 2, Vargas*	v Cruzeiro Belo Horizonte, Brazil *Careca, Heraldo*	1-0	3-2	sf	10,000
4-6-1988	Cruzeiro Belo Horizonte, Brazil *Robson*	v Nacional, Uruguay	0-0	1-0	sf	91,000

25-5-88	Racing Club Avellaneda, Argentina	v	River Plate, Argentina	0-1	2-1	sf	30,000
	Fernandez 2, 1 penalty		Borelli				
1-6-88	River Plate, Argentina	v	Racing Club Avellaneda, Argentina	1-0	1-1	sf	
	Gutierrez penalty		Fabbri				
13-6-88	Racing Club Avellaneda, Argentina	v	Cruzeiro Belo Horizonte, Brazil	1-1	2-1	Final	50,000
	Fernandez, Colombatti		Robson				
18-6-88	Cruzeiro Belo Horizonte, Brazil	v	Racing Club Avellaneda, Argentina	0-1	1-1	Final	
	Robson		Catalan				
1989 2nd							
3-10-89	Flamengo Rio de Janeiro, Brazil	v	Argentinos Juniors, Argentina	0-0	0-1	1st	16,000
			Rudman				
10-10-89	Argentinos Juniors, Argentina	v	Flamengo Rio de Janeiro, Brazil	0-1	2-1	1st	5,000
	Airez, Vidal Gonzalez		Nando				
4-10-89	Olimpia, Paraguay	v	Cruzeiro Belo Horizonte, Brazil	2-0	2-0	1st	10,000
	Samamiego, Neffa						
11-10-89	Cruzeiro Belo Horizonte, Brazil	v	Olimpia, Paraguay		3-0	1st	
4-10-89	Nacional, Uruguay	v	Nacional Medellin, Colombia	1-1	2-1	1st	25,000
	Dely Valdez, Revelez		Uzurriaga				
11-10-89	Nacional Medellin, Colombia	v	Nacional, Uruguay	2-0	2-0	1st	24,000
	Arango, Trellez						
4-10-89	Santos FC Sao Paulo, Brazil	v	Independiente, Argentina	0-2	1-2	1st	3,000
	Ditinho		Alfaro Moreno, Insua				
11-10-89	Independiente, Argentina	v	Santos FC Sao Paulo, Brazil	1-0	2-0	1st	
	Insua, Monzon						
5-10-89	River Plate, Argentina	v	Gremio Porto Alegre, Brazil	2-1	2-1	1st	20,000
	Centurion, Borrelli		Helcio				
11-10-89	Gremio Porto Alegre, Brazil	v	River Plate, Argentina	1-1	2-1	1st	
	Kita, Adilson Heleno		Centurion				
3-10-89	Estudiantes de la Plata, Argentina	v	Penarol, Uruguay	0-0	3-0	1st	12,000
	MacAllister 2, Di Carlo						
10-10-89	Penarol, Uruguay	v	Estudiantes de la Plata, Argentina	1-0	1-0	1st	
	Carrasco, Silvera						
18-10-89	Nacional Medellin, Colombia	v	Independiente, Argentina	2-1	2-2	2nd	22,000
	Trellez 2		Luduena, Giusti				
25-10-89	Independiente, Argentina	v	Nacional Medellin, Colombia	1-0	2-0	2nd	
	Alfaro Moreno, Monzon						
19-10-89	Boca Juniors, Argentina	v	Racing Club Avellaneda, Argentina		0-0	2nd	17,000
26-10-89	Racing Club Avellaneda, Argentina	v	Boca Juniors, Argentina	1-1	1-2	2nd	30,000
	Fabbri		Ponce penalty, Caciuffo				
26-10-89	Gremio Porto Alegre, Brazil	v	Estudiantes de la Plata, Argentina	0-0	0-1	2nd	15,000
			Cariaga				
1-11-89	Estudiantes de la Plata, Argentina	v	Gremio Porto Alegre, Brazil	0-1	0-3	2nd	
26-10-89	Cruzeiro Belo Horizonte, Brazil	v	Argeninos Juniors, Argentina	1-0	1-1	2nd	27,000
	Hamilton		Airez				
1-11-89	Argentinos Juniors, Argentina	v	Cruzeiro Belo Horizonte, Brazil	0-0	2-0	2nd	5,000
	Airez, Caceres						
9-11-89	Argentinos Juniors, Argentina	v	Independiente, Argentina	0-1	0-1	sf	20,000
			Giusti				
15-11-89	Independiente, Argentina	v	Argentinos Juniors, Argentina	0-0	2-1	sf	25,000
	Insua, Reggiardo		Caceres				
9-11-89	Gremio Porto Alegre, Brazil	v	Boca Juniors, Argentina		0-0	sf	28,400
16-11-89	Boca Juniors, Argentina	v	Gremio Porto Alegre, Brazil	2-0	2-0	sf	45,000
	Marangoni, Cuciuffo						
23-11-89	Boca Juniors, Argentina	v	Independiente, Argentina		0-0	Final	23,000
29-11-89	Independiente, Argentina	v	Boca Juniors, Argentina		0-0 5-3p	Final	60,000
1990 3rd							
31-10-90	River Plate, Argentina	v	Olimpia, Paraguay	0-0	3-0	1st	22,000
	S Berti, R Median Bello 2						
7-11-90	Olimpia, Paraguay	v	River Plate, Argentina	2-0	3-0 4-3 p	1st	15,000
	A Samaniego, L Monzon,						
	R Amarilla pen						
31-10-90	Gremio Porto Alegre, Brazil	v	Estudiantes la Plata, Argentina	0-0	1-0	1st	20,000
	E Pratola own goal						
8-11-90	Estudinates la Plata, Argentina	v	Gremio Porto Alegre, Brazil	1-0	2-0	1st	10,000
	R Trotta, D Peinado						
14-10-90	Penarol, Uruguay	v	Santos FC Sao Paulo, Brazil	0-0	1st		15,000

17

THE WINNERS

8-11-90	Santos FC Sao Paulo, Brazil *Mendonca 2*	v	Penarol, Uruguay *V Lopez, A Baran*	2-1	2-2 2-4p	1st	10,000
24-10-90	Independiente, Argentina *R Insua penalty*	v	Nacional, Uruguay *J Dely Valdez*	0-1	1-1	1st	16,000
8-11-90	Nacional, Uruguay *W Cabrera, Y Lemos*	v	Independiente, Argentina *L Artime*	1-0	2-1	1st	10,000
25-10-90	Argentinos Juniors, Argentina *O Coloccini, W Perazzo, H Cejas*	v	Flamengo Rio, Brazil *Luis Antonio penalty*	2-0	3-1	1st	5,000
9-11-90	Flamengo Rio, Brazil *Nelo, Renato, Gaucho*	v	Argentinos Juniors, Argentina *P Hernandez*	1-1	3-1 3-4p	1st	5,000
26-10-90	Cruzeiro Belo Horizonte, Brazil *Heyder*	v	Racing Avellaneda, Argentina	1-0	1-0	1st	17,000
7-11-90	Racing Avellaneda, Argentina *H Perez penalty*	v	Cruzeiro Belo Horizonte, Brazil	1-0	1-0 4-2p	1st	13,000
	Boca Juniors, Argentina				bye	1st	
14-11-90	Penarol, Uruguay	v	Boca Juniors, Argentina *B Giunta*	0-1	0-1	2nd	20,000
21-11-90	Boca Juniors, Argentina	v	Penarol, Uruguay *C Silvera, J Villar penalty*	0-1	0-2	2nd	50,000
14-11-90	Olimpia, Paraguay *F Franco*	v	Racing Avellaneda, Argentina *N Ortega Sanchez*	0-0	1-1	2nd	30,000
21-11-90	Racing Avellaneda, Argentina	v	Olimpia, Paraguay *J Guasch, R Amarilla, A Samaniego*	0-1	0-3	2nd	25,000
16-11-90	Argentinos Juniors, Argentina *S Perez, J Ortega*	v	Nacional, Uruguay *J Dely Valdez*	2-1	2-1	2nd	12,000
21-11-90	Nacional, Uruguay *E Vargas, F Revelez, W Cabrera*	v	Argentinos Juniors, Argentina *J Ortega*	0-0	3-1	2nd	25,000
	Estudiantes la Plata, Argentina					2nd	
28-11-90	Estudiantes la Plata, Argentina	v	Nacional, Uruguay		0-0	sf	14,000
5-12-90	Nacional, Uruguay	v	Estudiantes la Plata, Argentina		0-0 5-3p	sf	
28-11-90	Penarol, Uruguay *A Paz, C Silvera*	v	Olimpia, Paraguay *R Amarilla*	1-0	2-1	sf	40,000
19-12-90	Olimpia, Paraguay *G Gonzalez 2, R Amarilla 2, S Suarez*	v	Penarol, Uruguay	2-0	6-0	sf	14,000
5-1-91	Nacional, Uruguay	v	Olimpia, Paraguay *G Gonzalez, R Amarilla, Samaniego*	0-0	0-3	Final	45,000
11-1-90	Olimpia, Paraguay *Sameniego, R Amarilla, Luis Monzon*	v	Nacional, Uruguay *Jose Garcia, Hector Moran, Wilson Nunez*	1-2	3-3	Final	40,000

WORLD CLUB CHAMPIONSHIP FINALS

				H/T	F/T	Venue	Attend
3-7-60	Penarol, Uruguay	v	**Real Madrid, Spain**		0-0	Montevideo	71,872
4-9-60	**Real Madrid, Spain** *Puskas 2, Di Stefano, Herrera, Gento*	v	Penarol, Uruguay	4-0	5-1	Madrid	125,000
4-9-61	Benfica, Portugal *Coluna*	v	**Penarol, Uruguay**	0-0	1-0	Lisbon	55,000
17-9-61	**Penarol, Uruguay** *Sasia penalty, Joya 2, Spencer 2*	v	Benfica, Portugal	4-0	5-0	Montevideo	56,358
19-9-61	**Penarol, Uruguay** *Sasia 2, 1 penalty*	v	Benfica, Portugal *Eusebio*	2-1	2-1	Montevideo	60,241
19-9-62	**Santos, Brazil** *Pele 2, Coutinho*	v	Benfica, Portugal *Santana 2*	1-0	3-2	Rio	90,000
11-10-62	Benfica, Portugal *Eusebio, Santana*	v	**Santos, Brazil** *Pele 3, Coutinho, Pepe*	0-2	2-5	Lisbon	75,000
16-10-63	AC Milan, Italy *Trapattoni, Amarildo 2, Mora*	v	**Santos, Brazil** *Pele 2, 1 penalty*	2-0	4-2	Milan	80,000
14-11-63	**Santos, Brazil** *Pepe 2, Almir, Amarildo, Lima*	v	AC Milan, Italy *Altafini, Mora*	0-2	4-2	Rio	135,000
16-11-63	**Santos, Brazil** *Dalmo penalty*	v	AC Milan, Italy	1-0	1-0 play off	Rio	121,000

Date	Team		Team			Venue	Attendance
9-9-64	Independiente, Argentina Rodriguez	v	**Inter Milan, Italy**	0-0	1-0	Buenos Aires	70,000
23-9-64	**Inter Milan, Italy** Mazzola, Corso	v	Independiente, Argentina	2-0	2-0	Milan	70,000
26-9-64	**Inter Milan, Italy** Corso	v	Independiente, Argentina	0-0	1-0 aet	Madrid	45,000
8-9-65	**Inter Milan, Italy** Peiro, Mazzola 2	v	Independiente, Argentina	2-0	3-0	Milan	70,000
15-9-65	Independiente, Argentina	v	**Inter Milan, Italy**		0-0	Buenos Aires	70,000
12-10-66	**Penarol, Uruguay** Spencer 2	v	Real Madrid, Spain	1-0	2-0	Montevideo	58,324
26-10-66	Real Madrid, Spain	v	**Penarol, Uruguay** Rocha penalty, Spencer	0-2	0-2	Madrid	70,000
18-10-67	Glasgow Celtic, Scotland McNeill	v	**Racing Clube BA, Argentina**	0-0	1-0	Glasgow	103,000
1-11-67	**Racing Clube BA, Argentina** Raffo 2	v	Glasgow Celtic, Scotland Gemmell penalty	1-1	2-1	Buenos Aires	80,000
4-11-67	**Racing Clube BA, Argentina** Cardenas	v	Glasgow Celtic, Scotland	0-0	1-0	Montevideo	65,172
25-9-68	**Estudiantes, Argentina** Conigliaro	v	Manchester United, England	1-0	1-0	Buenos Aires	50,120
16-10-68	Manchester United, England Morgan	v	**Estudiantes, Argentina** Veron	0-1	1-1	Manchester	63,428
8-10-69	**AC Milan, Italy** Sormani 2, Combin	v	Estudiantes, Argentina	2-0	3-0	Milan	60,675
22-10-69	Estudiantes, Argentina Aguirre, Suarez, Conigliaro	v	**AC Milan, Italy** Rivera	2-1	2-1	Buenos Aires	65,000
26-8-70	Estudiantes, Argentina Echecopar, Veron	v	**Feyenoord Rotterdam, Holland** Kindvall, van Hanegem	2-1	2-2	Buenos Aires	50,000
9-9-70	**Feyenoord Rotterdam, Holland** van Daele	v	Estudiantes, Argentina	0-0	1-0	Rotterdam	67,000
15-9-71	Panathinaikos, Greece * Filakouris	v	**Nacional, Uruguay** Artime	0-0	1-1	Athens	60,000
29-12-71	**Nacional, Uruguay** Artime 2	v	Panathinaikos, Greece * Filakouris	1-0	2-1	Montevideo * replaced Ajax	70,000
6-9-72	Independiente, Argentina Sa	v	**Ajax Amsterdam, Holland** Cruyff	0-1	1-1	Buenos Aires	65,000
28-9-72	**Ajax Amsterdam, Holland** Neeskens, Rep 2	v	Independiente, Argentina	1-0	3-0	Amsterdam	65,000
28-11-73	Juventus, Italy	v	**Independiente, Argentina** Bochini	0-0	0-1 one game	Rome	35,000
11-3-75	Independiente, Argentina Balbuena	v	**Atletico Madrid, Spain ***	1-0	1-0	Buenos Aires	60,000
10-4-75	Atletico Madrid, Spain * Irureta, Ayala	v	Independiente, Argentina	1-0	2-0	Madrid * Bayern Munich replaced	45,000
1975	Independiente, Argentina	v	Bayern Munich, Germany			could not agree dates.	
23-11-76	**Bayern Munich, Germany** Muller, Kapellmann	v	Cruzeiro, Brazil	0-0	2-0	Munich	22,000
21-12-76	Cruzeiro, Brazil	v	**Bayern Munich, Germany**		0-0	Belo Horizonte	114,000
21-3-78	**Boca Juniors, Argentina** Mastrangelo, Ribolzi	v	Borussia Monchengladbach, Germany Hannes, Bonhof	1-1	2-2	Buenos Aires	50,000
6-9-78	Borussia Monchengladbach, Germany	v	**Boca Juniors, Argentina** Felman, Mastrangelo, Salinas	0-3	0-3	Karlsruhe	21,500
1978	not played						
18-11-79	Malmo FF, Sweden *	v	**Olimpia, Paraguay** Isasi	0-1	0-1	* replaced Notts Forest	4,811
3-3-80	**Olimpia, Paraguay** Solalinde penalty, Michelagnoli	v	Malmo FF, Sweden * Earlandsson	1-0	2-1	Asuncion	35,000
11-2-81	**Nacional, Uruguay** Victorino	v	Nottingham Forest, England	1-0	1-0	Tokyo	62,000
13-12-81	**Flamengo, Brazil** Nunes 2, Adilio	v	Liverpool, England	3-0	3-0	Tokyo	62,000
12-12-82	**Penarol, Uruguay** Jair, Silva	v	Aston Villa, England	1-0	2-0	Tokyo	62,000
11-12-83	**Gremio Porto Alegre, Brazil** Renato Gaucho 2	v	Hamburger SV, Germany Schroder	1-0	2-1	Tokyo	62,000

19

THE WINNERS

Date	Winner		Opponent	H/T	F/T	Venue	Attend
9-12-84	**Independiente, Argentina** *Percudani*	v	Liverpool, England	1-0	1-0	Tokyo	62,000
8-12-85	**Juventus, Italy** *Platini penalty, Laudrup*	v	Argentinos Juniors, Argentina *Ereros, Castro*	0-0	2-2 aet 4-3 pens	Tokyo	62,000
14-12-86	**River Plate, Argentina** *Alzamendi*	v	Steaua Bucharest, Romania	1-0	1-0	Tokyo	62,000
13-12-87	**FC Porto, Portugal** *Gomes, Madjer*	v	Penarol, Uruguay *Viera*	1-0	2-1 aet	Tokyo	45,000
11-12-88	**Nacional, Uruguay** *Ostolaza 2*	v	PSV Eindhoven, Holland *Romario, Ron Koeman penalty*	1-0	2-2 aet 7-6 pens	Tokyo	62,000
17-12-89	**AC Milan, Italy** *A Evani*	v	Nacional Medellin, Columbia	0-0	1-0	Tokyo	62,000

ARTEMIO FRANCHI CUP

Between the winners of the European Championship and Copa America

Date				H/T	F/T	Venue	Attend
21.08.85	FRANCE *D Rochateau, J Toure*	v	URUGUAY	(1-0)	2-0	Paris	20,405

1961 **Penarol** (Uruguay)

FULL RESULTS OF BERTADORES COPA

1960 I

		Home	Playoff	Away	Rnd
San Lorenzo, Argentina	v Esporte Clube Bahia Salvador, Brazil	3-0		2-3	1
Penarol, Uruguay	v Jorge Wilsterman Cochabamba, Bolivia	7-1		1-1	1
Millonarios Bogota, Colombia	v Universidad de Chile, Chile	1-0		6-0	1
Penarol, Uruguay	v San Lorenzo, Argentina	0-0	2-1*	1-1	sf
Olimpia, Paraguay	v Millonarios Bogota, Colombia	5-1		0-0	sf
Penarol, Uruguay	v Olimpia, Paraguay	1-0		1-1	Final

1961 II

		Home	Playoff	Away	Rnd
Independiente Santa Fe, Colombia	v Barcelona Sporting Guayaquil, Ecuador	2-2		3-0	1
Olimpia, Paraguay	v Colo Colo, Chile	5-2		1-2	2
Penarol, Uruguay	v Universitario Lima, Peru	5-0		0-2	2
Independiente Santa Fe, Colombia	v Jorge Wilsterman Cochabamba, Bolivia	1-0	ot	2-3	2
Palmeiras Sao Paulo, Brazil	v Independiente, Argentina	1-0		2-0	2
Penarol, Uruguay	v Olimpia, Paraguay	3-1		2-1	sf
Palmeiras Sao Paulo, Brazil	v Independiente Santa Fe, Colombia	4-1		2-2	sf
Penarol, Uruguay	v Palmeiras Sao Paulo, Brazil	1-0		1-1	Final

1962 III

		Home	Playoff	Away	Rnd
Group 1					
Santos FC Sao Paulo, Brazil	v Deportivo Municipal La Paz Bolivia	4-3		6-1	
Cerro Porteno, Paraguay	v Santos FC Sao Paulo, Brazil	1-1		1-9	
Deportivo Municipal La Paz, Bolivia	v Cerro Porteno, Paraguay	1-2		2-3	

Santos FC	4	3	1	0	20-6	7
Cerro Porteno	4	2	1	1	7-13	5
Municipal	4	0	0	4	7-15	0

		Home	Playoff	Away	Rnd
Group 2					
Racing Club Avellaneda, Argentina	v Sporting Cristal, Peru	2-1		1-2	
Racing Club Avellaneda, Argentina	v Nacional, Uruguay	2-2		2-3	
Sporting Cristal, Peru	v Nacional, Uruguay	0-1		1-2	

Nacional	4	3	1	0	9-6	7
Racing Club	4	1	1	2	7-8	3
Sporting Cristal	4	1	0	3	5-7	2

		Home	Playoff	Away	Rnd
Group 3	Universidad Catolica, Chile	v Millonarios Bogota, Colombia	4-1		1-1	
	Emelec Guayaquil, Ecuador	v Universidad Catolica, Chile	7-2		0-3	
	Millonarios Bogota, Colombia	v Emelec Guayaquil, Ecuador	3-1		2-4	

Catolica	4	2	1	1	10-9	5
Emelec	4	2	0	2	12-10	4
Millonarios	4	1	1	2	7-10	3

		Home	Playoff	Away	Rnd
Penarol, Uruguay	v Nacional, Uruguay	3-1	1-1	1-2	sf
Santos FC Sao Paulo, Brazil	v Universidad Catolica, Chile	1-0		1-1	sf
Santos FC Sao Paulo, Brazil	v Penarol, Uruguay	2-3	3-0*	2-1	Final

LIBERTADORES RESULTS

1963 IV

			Home	Playoff	Away	Rnd
Group 1	Alianza Lima, Peru	v Millonarios Bogota, Colombia	0-0		1-0	
	Botafogo Rio de Janeiro, Brazil	v Alianza Lima, Peru	2-1		1-0	
	Botafogo Rio de Janeiro, Brazil	v Millonarios Bogota, Colombia	2-0		2-0	

Botafogo	4	4	0	0	5-1	8
Alianza	4	1	1	2	2-3	3
Millonarios	4	0	1	3	0-3	1

			Home		Away	
Group 2	Penarol, Uruguay	v Everest, Ecuador	9-1		5-0	

Penarol	2	2	0	0	14-1	4
Everest	2	0	0	2	1-14	0

			Home		Away	
Group 3	Boca Juniors, Argentina	v Olimpia, Paraguay	5-3		0-1	
	Boca Juniors, Argentina	v Universidad de Chile, Chile	1-0		3-2	
	Universidad de Chile, Chile	v Olimpia, Paraguay	4-1		1-2	

Boca Juniors	4	3	0	1	9-6	6
Olimpia	4	2	0	2	7-10	4
Universidad	4	1	0	3	7-7	2

			Home		Away	Rnd
	Santos FC Sao Paulo, Brazil	v Botafogo Rio de Janeiro, Brazil	1-1		4-0	sf
	Boca Juniors, Argentina	v Penarol, Uruguay	1-0		2-1	sf
	Santos FC Sao Paulo, Brazil	v Boca Juniors, Argentina	3-2		2-1	Final

1964 V

			Home	Playoff	Away	Rnd
Group 1	Cerro Porteno, Paraguay	v Aurora Cochabamba, Bolivia	7-0		2-2	
	Nacional, Uruguay	v Aurora Cochabamba, Bolivia	2-0		3-0	
	Nacional, Uruguay	v Cerro Porteno, Paraguay	2-0		2-2	

Nacional	4	3	1	0	9-2	7
Cerro Porteno	4	1	2	1	11-6	4
Aurora	4	0	1	3	2-14	1

			Home		Away	
Group 2	Independiente, Argentina	v Millonarios Bogota, Colombia	5-1		disq	
	Independiente, Argentina	v Alianza Lima, Peru	4-0		2-2	
	Alianza Lima, Peru	v Millonarios Bogota, Colombia	1-2		2-3	

Independiente	4	3	1	0	11-3	7
Millonarios	4	2	0	2	6-8	4
Alianza	4	0	1	3	5-11	1

			Home		Away	Rnd
Group 3	Italia Caracas, Venezuela	v Esporte Clube Bahia Salvador, Brazil	0-0		2-1	prel
	Italia Caracas, Venezuela	v Barcelona Sporting Guayaquil, Ecuador	3-0		0-1	
	Colo Colo, Chile	v Italia Caracas, Venezuela	4-0		2-1	
	Colo Colo, Chile	v Barcelona Sporting Guayaquil, Ecuador	0-4		3-2	

Colo Colo	4	3	0	1	9-7	6
Barcelona	4	2	0	2	7-6	4
Italia	4	1	0	3	4-7	2

			Home		Away	Rnd
	Independiente, Argentina	v Santos FC Sao Paulo, Brazil	2-1		3-2	sf
	Nacional, Uruguay	v Colo Colo, Chile	4-2		4-2	sf
	Independiente, Argentina	v Nacional, Uruguay	1-0		0-0	Final

1965 VI

			Home	Playoff	Away	Rnd
Group 1	Boca Juniors, Argentina	v Deportivo Quito, Ecuador	4-0		2-1	
	Boca Juniors, Argentina	v The Strongest, Bolivia	2-0		3-2	
	The Strongest, Bolivia	v Deportivo Quito, Ecuador	2-2		1-0	

Boca Juniors	4	4	0	0	11-3	8
The Strongest	4	1	1	2	5-7	3
Deportivo Quito	4	0	1	3	3-9	1

			Home		Away	
Group 2	Santos FC Sao Paulo, Brazil	v Universidad de Chile, Chile	1-0		5-1	
	Santos FC Sao Paulo, Brazil	v Universitario Lima, Peru	2-1		2-1	
	Universidad de Chile, Chile	v Universitario Lima, Peru	5-2		0-1	

Santos FC	4	4	0	0	10-3	8
Universidad	4	1	0	3	6-9	2
Universitario	4	1	0	3	5-9	2

Group 3	Guarani, Paraguay	v Galicia Caracas, Venezuela	2-0		2-1
	Guarani, Paraguay	v Penarol, Uruguay	2-1*		0-2
			* tie awarded to Penarol for player ineligability of Guarani		
	Galicia Caracas, Venezuela	v Penarol, Uruguay	0-0		0-2

Penarol	4	2	1	1	5-2	5
Guarani	4	3	0	1	6-4	6
Galicia	4	0	1	3	1-6	1

Santos FC Sao Paulo, Brazil	v Penarol, Uruguay	5-4	1-2	2-3	sf
Independiente, Argentina	v Boca Juniors, Argentina	2-0	0-0gd	0-1	sf
Independiente, Argentina	v Penarol, Uruguay	1-0	4-1*	1-3	Final
					* in Santiago

1966 VII			**Home**	**Playoff**	**Away**	**Rnd**
Group 1	River Plate, Argentina	v Boca Juniors, Argentina	2-1		0-2	
	River Plate, Argentina	v Lara Basquimento, Venezuela	3-0		2-1	
	Boca Juniors, Argentina	v Lara Basquimento, Venezuela	2-1		3-0	
	River Plate, Argentina	v Italia Caracas, Venezuela	3-0		2-1	
	Boca Juniors, Argentina	v Italia Caracas, Venezuela	5-2		2-1	
	River Plate, Argentina	v Universitario Lima, Peru	5-0		1-1	
	Boca Juniors, Argentina	v Universitario Lima, Peru	2-0		1-2	
	Boca Juniors, Argentina	v Alianza Lima, Peru	0-1		1-0	
	River Plate, Argentina	v Alianza Lima, Peru	3-2		2-0	
	Lara Basquimento, Venezuela	v Alianza Lima, Peru	2-1		0-3	
	Lara Basquimento, Venezuela	v Universitario Lima, Peru	0-0		0-1	
	Italia Caracas, Venezuela	v Alianza Lima, Peru	3-1		2-1	
	Italia Caracas, Venezuela	v Universitario Lima, Peru	2-2		2-1	
	Universitario Lima, Peru	v Alianza Lima, Peru	2-0		1-1	
	Lara Basquimento, Venezuela	v Italia Caracas, Venezuela	1-0		1-1	

River Plate	10	8	1	1	21-8	17
Boca Juniors	10	7	0	3	19-9	14
Italia Caracas	10	4	2	4	15-16	10
Universitario	10	3	4	3	10-14	10
Alianza	10	2	1	7	10-16	5
Lara Basquimento	10	1	2	7	5-17	4

Group 2	Guarani, Paraguay	v Olimpia, Paraguay	2-0	2-1*	3-3
			* play off for semi final place		
	Guarani, Paraguay	v Universidad Catolica, Chile	2-1		0-2
	Universidad de Chile, Chile	v Olimpia, Paraguay	1-2		0-2
	Olimpia, Paraguay	v Universidad Catolica, Chile	0-0		0-4
	Guarani, Paraguay	v Universidad de Chile, Chile	1-1		0-2
	Universidad de Chile, Chile	v Universidad Catolica, Chile	0-0		2-2

Universidad Catolica	6	2	3	1	9-4	7
Guarani	6	2	2	2	8-9	6
Olimpia	6	2	2	2	7-10	6
Univ de Chile	6	1	3	2	6-7	5

Group 3	Deportivo Municipal La Paz, Bolivia	v Penarol, Uruguay	1-3		1-2
	Jorge Wilsterman Cochabamba, Bolivia	v Deportivo Municipal La Paz, Bolivia	1-1		1-1
	Jorge Wilsterman Cochabamba, Bolivia	v Emelec Guayaquil, Ecuador	2-1		1-3
	Deportivo Municipal La Paz, Bolivia	v Nueve de Octubre Guayaquil, Ecuador	5-1		4-3
	Penarol, Uruguay	v Nueve de Octubre Guayaquil, Ecuador	2-0		2-1
	Jorge Wilsterman Cochabamba, Bolivia	v Nueve de Octubre Guayaquil, Ecuador	4-1		2-3
	Deportivo Municipal La Paz, Bolivia	v Emelec Guayaquil, Ecuador	4-1		1-2
	Penarol, Uruguay	v Nacional, Uruguay	0-4		3-0
	Penarol, Uruguay	v Jorge Wilsterman Cochabamba, Bolivia	2-0		0-1
	Nacional, Uruguay	v Deportivo Municipal La Paz, Bolivia	4-1		2-3
	Nacional, Uruguay	v Jorge Wilsterman Cochabamba Bolivia	3-0		0-0
	Emelec Guayaquil, Ecuador	v Nueve de Octubre Guayaquil, Ecuador	2-1		5-0

LIBERTADORES RESULTS

		Home	Away
Emelec Guayaquil, Ecuador	v Nacional, Uruguay	0-1	0-2
Nacional, Uruguay	v Nueve de Octubre Guayaquil, Ecuador	3-1	3-2
Penarol, Uruguay	v Emelec Guayaquil, Ecuador	4-1	2-1

Penarol	10	8	0	2	20-10	16
Nacional	10	7	1	2	22-10	15
Municipal la Paz	10	4	2	4	22-20	10
Jorge Wilsterman	10	3	3	4	12-15	9
Emelec	10	4	0	6	16-18	8
Nueve de Octubre	10	1	0	9	13-32	2

Group 1	Independiente, Argentina	v River Plate, Argentina	1-1	1-2*	2-4	sf
					* play off for place in the Final	
	River Plate, Argentina	v Guarani, Paraguay	3-1		3-1	sf
	River Plate, Argentina	v Boca Juniors, Argentina	2-2		0-1	sf
	Independiente, Argentina	v Guarani, Paraguay	2-1		2-0	sf
	Boca Juniors, Argentina	v Independient, Argentina	0-2		0-0	sf
	Boca Juniors, Argentina	v Guarani, Paraguay	1-1		3-1	sf

River Plate	6	3	2	1	13-8	8
Independiente	6	3	2	1	9-6	8
Boca Juniors	6	2	3	1	7-6	7
Guarani	6	0	1	5	5-14	1

Group 2	Penarol, Uruguay	v Nacional, Uruguay	3-0	1-0	sf
	Universidad Catolica, Chile	v Penarol, Uruguay	1-0	0-2	sf
	Universidad Catolica, Chile	v Nacional, Uruguay	1-0	2-3	sf

Penarol	4	3	0	1	5-2	6
Univ Catolica	4	2	0	2	5-4	4
Nacional	4	1	0	3	3-7	2

Penarol, Uruguay	v River Plate, Argentina	2-0	4-2*	2-3	Final
					* in Santiago

1967 VIII

Group 1			Home	Playoff	Away
Italia Caracas, Venezuela	v Galicia Caracas, Venezuela		1-0		0-0
Universitario Lima, Peru	v Italia Caracas, Venezuela		3-0		1-0
Galicia Caracas, Venezuela	v Sport Boys Callao, Peru		2-1		0-2
Cruzeiro Belo Horizonte Brazil	v Italia Caracas, Venezuela		3-0		4-0
Cruzeiro Belo Horizonte Brazil	v Galicia Caracas, Venezuela		3-1		1-0
Universitario Lima, Peru	v Sport Boys Callao, Peru		1-0		1-0
Sport Boys Callao, Peru	v Italia Caracas, Venezuela		5-2		0-0
Cruzeiro Belo Horizonte, Brazil	v Universitario Lima, Peru		4-1		2-2
Sport Boys Callao, Peru	v Cruzeiro Belo Horizonte Brazil		1-2		1-3
Universitario Lima, Peru	v Galicia Caracas, Venezuela		2-0		0-2

Cruzeiro	8	7	1	0	22-6	15
Universitario	8	5	1	2	11-8	11
Sports Boys Callao	8	2	1	5	10-11	5
Galacia Caracas	8	2	1	5	5-10	5
Italia Caracas	8	1	2	5	3-16	4

Group 2	Independiente Santa Fe, Colombia	v Independiente Medellin, Colombia	2-0	0-4
	Bolivar La Paz, Bolivia	v 31 de Octubre, Bolivia	1-0	2-2
	Racing Club Avellaneda, Argentina	v River Plate, Argentina	2-0	0-0
	Racing Club Avellaneda, Argentina	v 31 de Octubre, Bolivia	0-3	6-0
	River Plate, Argentina	v Bolivar La Paz, Bolivia	3-3	2-0
	River Plate, Argentina	v 31 de Octubre, Bolivia	4-0	7-0
	Racing Club Avellaneda, Argentina	v Independiente Medellin, Colombia	2-0	5-2
	Racing Club Avellaneda, Argentina	v Independiente Santa Fe, Colombia	4-1	2-1
	Independiente Santa Fe, Colombia	v River Plate, Argentina	2-2	0-4
	River Plate, Argentina	v Independiente Medellin, Colombia	6-2	1-0
	Racing Club Avellaneda, Argentina	v Bolivar La Paz, Bolivia	6-0	2-0
	Bolivar La Paz, Bolivia	v Independiente Medellin, Colombia	0-2	2-2
	Bolivar La Paz, Bolivia	v Independiente Santa Fe, Colombia	2-2	2-1
	31 de Octubre, Bolivia	v Independiente Medellin, Colombia	1-2	0-3
	31 de Octubre, Bolivia	v Independiente Santa Fe, Colombia	6-2	0-2

LIBERTADORES RESULTS

Racing Club	10	8	1	1	29-7	17
River Plate	10	6	3	1	29-9	15
Independ Medellin	10	4	1	5	17-19	9
Bolivar	10	2	4	4	12-22	8
Independ Santa Fe	10	2	2	6	13-26	6
31 de Octubre	10	2	1	7	12-29	5

Group 3					
Emelec Guayaquil, Ecuador	v Barcelona Sporting Guayaquil, Ecuador	3-0		1-2
Cerro Porteno, Paraguay	v Guarani, Paraguay	1-0		2-1
Nacional, Uruguay	v Emelec Guayaquil, Ecuador	4-1		3-0
Barcelona Sporting Guayaquil Ecuador	v Nacional, Uruguay	2-1		0-2
Universidad Catolica, Chile	v Colo Colo, Chile	5-2		2-4
Emelec Guayaquil, Ecuador	v **Cerro Porteno, Paraguay**	2-1		1-1
Barcelona Sporting Guayaquil Ecuador	v Guarani, Paraguay	2-1		1-4
Emelec Guayaquil, Ecuador	v Guarani, Paraguay	0-2		0-3
Barcelona Sporting Guayaquil Ecuador	v Cerro Porteno, Paraguay	1-2		2-1
Colo Colo, Chile	v Guarani, Paraguay	1-0		2-4
Colo Colo, Chile	v Cerro Porteno, Paraguay	5-1		1-0
Universidad Catolica, Chile	v **Guarani, Paraguay**	1-1		1-1
Universidad Catolica, Chile	v Cerro Porteno, Paraguay	3-1		0-1
Universidad Catolica, Chile	v Nacional, Uruguay	0-0		0-3
Colo Colo, Chile	v Nacional, Uruguay	3-2		2-5
Emelec Guayaquil, Ecuador	v Universidad Catolica, Chile	2-1		2-5
Colo Colo, Chile	v Barcelona Sporting Guayaquil, Ecuador	3-2		1-1
Universidad Catolica, Chile	v **Barcelona Sporting Guayaquil, Ecuador**	2-1		2-0
Colo Colo, Chile	v Emelec Guayaquil, Ecuador	3-2		3-4
Nacional, Uruguay	v Guarani, Paraguay	3-1		1-0
Nacional, Uruguay	v Cerro Porteno, Paraguay	4-1		6-2

Nacional	12	9	1	2	34-12	19
Colo Colo	12	7	1	4	30-28	15
Univ Catolica	12	5	3	4	22-18	13
Guarani	12	4	2	6	18-15	10
Barcelona	12	4	1	7	14-23	9
Emelec	12	4	1	7	18-28	9
Cerro Porteno	12	4	1	7	14-26	9

Semi Finals

Group 1		Home	Playoff	Away	
Universitario Lima, Peru	v Colo Colo, Chile	3-0		1-0	sf
River Plate, Argentina	v Racing Club Avellaneda, Argentina	0-0		1-3	
Colo Colo, Chile	v River Plate, Argentina	1-0		1-1	
Universitario Lima, Peru	v Racing Club Avellaneda, Argentina	1-2	1-2*	2-1	

* play off for place in the Final

River Plate, Argentina	v Universitario Lima, Peru	0-1		2-2
Colo Colo, Chile	v Racing Club Avellaneda, Argentina	1-3		0-2

Racing Club	6	4	1	1	11-5	9
Universitario Lima	6	4	1	1	10-5	9
River Plate	6	0	3	3	4-8	3
Colo Colo	6	1	1	4	3-10	3

Group 2			
Nacional, Uruguay	v Penarol, Uruguay	1-0	2-2
Cruzeiro Belo Horizonte, Brazil	v Nacional, Uruguay	2-1	0-2
Cruzeiro Belo Horizonte, Brazil	v Penarol, Uruguay	1-0	2-3

Nacional	4	2	1	1	6-4	5
Cruzeiro	4	2	0	2	5-6	4
Penarol	4	1	1	2	5-6	3

Final				
Racing Club Avellaneda, Argentina	v Nacional, Uruguary	0-0	2-1*	0-0

* in Santiago

1968 IX

Group 1		Home	Playoff	Away
Independiente, Argentina	v Estudiantes La Plata, Argentina	2-4		0-2
Independiente, Argentina	v Millonarios Bogota, Colombia	3-1		2-1
Independiente, Argentina	v Deportivo Cali, Colombia	1-1	3-2*	0-1

* play off for quarter final place

Estudiantes La Plata, Argentina	v Millonarios Bogota, Colombia	0-0		1-0

25

LIBERTADORES RESULTS

Estudiantes La Plata, Argentina	v	Deportivo Cali, Colombia					3-0	2-1
Millonarios Bogota, Colombia	v	Deportivo Cali, Colombia					4-2	0-1

Team	P	W	D	L	F-A	Pts
Estudiantes	6	5	1	0	12-3	11
Independiente	6	2	1	3	8-10	5
Deportivo Cali	6	2	1	3	6-10	5
Millonarios	6	1	1	4	6-9	3

Group 2

Jorge Wilsterman Cochabamba, Bolivia	v	Sporting Cristal, Peru	0-1	0-2
Jorge Wilsterman Cochabamba, Bolivia	v	Always Ready La Paz, Bolivia	3-0	np
Jorge Wilsterman Cochabamba, Bolivia	v	Universitario Lima, Peru	0-0	5-1
Always Ready La Paz, Bolivia	v	Sporting Cristal, Peru	1-4	1-1
Always Ready La Paz, Bolivia	v	Universitario Lima, Peru	0-3	0-6
Universitario Lima, Peru	v	Sporting Cristal, Peru	1-1	2-2

Team	P	W	D	L	F-A	Pts
Universitario Lima	6	3	3	0	17-4	9
Sporting Cristal	6	3	3	0	11-5	9
Jorge Wilsterman	6	1	1	3	4-8	3
Always Ready	6	0	1	4	2-17	1

Group 3

Universidad Catolica, Chile	v	Universidad de Chile, Chile	2-1	3-2
Universidad Catolica, Chile	v	Nacional Quito, Ecuador	2-0	1-2
Universidad Catolica, Chile	v	**Emelec Guayaquil, Ecuador**	1-1	2-1
Universidad de Chile, Chile	v	Emelec Guayaquil, Ecuador	0-0	1-2
Emelec Guayaquil, Ecuador	v	Nacional Quito, Ecuador	0-0	1-0
Universidad de Chile, Chile	v	Nacional Quito, Ecuador	1-0	1-3

Team	P	W	D	L	F-A	Pts
Univ Catolica	6	4	1	1	11-7	9
Emelec	6	2	3	1	5-4	7
Nacional Quito	6	2	1	3	5-6	5
Univ de Chile	6	1	1	4	6-10	3

Group 4

Guarani, Paraguay	v	Libertad, Paraguay	1-1	2-0
Guarani, Paraguay	v	Penarol, Uruguay	1-1	0-2
Guarani, Paraguay	v	**Nacional, Uruguay**	2-1	2-2
Libertad, Paraguay	v	Penarol, Uruguay	1-0	0-4
Libertad, Paraguay	v	Nacional, Uruguay	0-2	0-4
Penarol, Uruguay	v	Nacional, Uruguay	1-0	0-0

Team	P	W	D	L	F-A	Pts
Penarol	6	3	2	1	8-2	8
Guarani	6	2	3	1	8-7	7
Nacional	6	2	2	2	9-5	6
Libertad	6	1	1	4	2-13	3

Group 5

Palmeiras Sao Paulo, Brazil	v	Nautico Recife, Brazil	0-0	3-1
Palmeiras Sao Paulo, Brazil	v	Portugues Caracas, Venezuela	3-0	2-1
Palmeiras Sao Paulo, Brazil	v	**Galicia Caracas, Venezuela**	2-0	2-1
Nautico Recife, Brazil	v	Portugues Caracas, Venezuela	3-2	1-1
Nautico Recife, Brazil	v	Galicia Caracas, Venezuela	1-0	1-2
Portugues Caracas, Venezuela	v	Galicia Caracas, Venezuela	1-0	0-2

Team	P	W	D	L	F-A	Pts
Palmeiras	6	5	1	0	12-3	11
Portugues Caracas	6	2	1	3	5-11	5
Galicia	6	2	0	4	5-7	4
Nautico Recife	6	1	2	3	7-8	4

Quarter finals

Group 1

Estudiantes La Plata, Argentina	v	Universitario Lima, Peru	1-0	0-1
Estudiantes La Plata, Argentina	v	**Independiente, Argentina**	1-0	2-1
Universitario Lima, Peru	v	Independiente, Argentina	0-3	0-3

Team	P	W	D	L	F-A	Pts
Estudiantes	4	3	0	1	4-1	6
Independiente	4	2	0	2	7-3	4
Universitario	4	1	0	3	1-7	2

Group 2

Sporting Cristal, Peru	v	Portugues Caracas, Venezuela	2-0	1-1
Sporting Cristal, Peru	v	Penarol, Uruguay	0-0	1-1

			Home	Playoff	Away
	Portugues Caracas, Venezuela	v Penarol, Uruguay	0-3		0-4
	Penarol, Uruguay	v Emelec Guayaquil, Ecuador	2-0		1-0
	Emelec Guayaquil, Ecuador	v Sporting Cristal, Peru	0-2		1-0
	Portugues Caracas, Venezuela	v Emelec Guayaquil, Ecuador	2-0		0-2

Penarol	6	4	2	0	11-1	10
Sporting Cristal	6	2	3	1	6-3	7
Emelec	6	2	0	4	3-7	4
Portugues Caracas	6	1	1	4	3-12	3

			Home		Away
Group 3	Universidad Catolica, Chile	v Guarani, Paraguay	4-2		1-2
	Guarani, Paraguay	v Palmeiras Sao Paulo, Brazil	2-0		1-2
	Palmeiras Sao Paulo, Brazil	v Universidad Catolica, Chile	4-1		1-0

Palmeiras	4	3	0	1	7-4	6
Guarani	4	2	0	2	7-7	4
Univ Catolica	4	1	0	3	6-9	2

Semi-finals

				Playoff	
	Estudiantes La Plata, Argentina	v Racing Club Avellaneda, Argentina	3-0	1-1*	0-2
				* Estudiantes won on goal difference in Buenos Aires
	Palmeiras Sao Paulo, Brazil	v Penarol, Uruguay	1-0		2-1

				Playoff	
Final	Estudiantes La Plata, Argentina	v Palmeiras Sao Paulo, Brazil	2-1	2-0*	1-3
					in Montevideo

1969 X

			Home	Playoff	Away
Group 1	Deportivo Cali, Colombia	v Union Magdalena Santa Marta, Colombia	2-2		3-1
	Deportivo Cali, Colombia	v Italia Caracas, Venezuela	3-0		1-2
	Deportivo Cali, Colombia	v Union Deportivo Canarias, Venezuela	2-0		1-1
	Union Magdalena Santa Marta, Colombia	v Italia Caracas, Venezuela	3-0		0-2
	Union Magdalena Santa Marta, Colombia	v Union Deportivo Canarias, Venezuela	1-0		0-1
	Italia Caracas, Venezuela	v Union Deportivo Canarias, Venezuela	2-0		1-1

Deportivo Cali	6	3	2	1	12-6	8
Italia Caracas	6	3	1	2	7-8	7
Union Magdalena	6	2	1	3	7-8	5
Deportivo Canarias	6	1	2	3	3-7	4

			Home	Playoff	Away
Group 2	Juan Aurich de Chiclana, Peru	v Sporting Cristal, Peru	3-3		2-2
	Juan Aurich de Chiclana, Peru	v Universidad Catolica, Chile	2-1	1-4*	2-4
	Juan Aurich de Chiclana, Peru	v Santiago Wanderers, Chile	3-1	0-1*	1-4
	Sporting Cristal, Peru	v Universidad Catolica, Chile	2-0	1-2*	2-3
	Sporting Cristal, Peru	v Santiago Wanderers, Chile	2-1	1-1*	0-2
	Santiago Wanderers, Chile	v Universidad Catolica, Chile	3-1		2-3
					* play off Round

Santiago Wanderers	6	3	0	3	13-10	6
Sporting Cristal	6	2	2	2	11-6	6
Univer Catolica	6	3	0	3	12-13	6
Juan Aurich	6	2	2	2	13-15	6

			Home	Playoff	Away
Group 3	Cerro Porteno, Paraguay	v Olimpia, Paraguay	4-1		2-1
	Cerro Porteno, Paraguay	v Litoral La Paz, Bolivia	1-0		6-0
	Cerro Porteno, Paraguay	v Bolivar La Paz, Bolivia	1-1		1-2
	Olimpia, Paraguay	v Litoral La Paz, Bolivia	3-0		2-0
	Olimpia, Paraguay	v Bolivar La Paz, Bolivia	0-4	2-1*	1-1
					* play off for Quarter Final place
	Bolivar La Paz, Bolivia	v Litoral La Paz, Bolivia	1-0		1-1

Cerro Porteno	6	4	1	1	15-5	9
Olimpia	6	3	1	2	12-7	7
Bolivar	6	2	3	1	6-8	7
Litoral	6	0	1	5	1-14	1

			Home		Away
Group 4	Penarol, Uruguay	v Nacional, Uruguay	1-1		2-2
	Penarol, Uruguay	v Barcelona Sporting Guayaquil, Ecuador	2-0	v	5-2

27

								Home		Away
Penarol, Uruguay	v	Deportivo Quito, Ecuador						5-2		1-1
Nacional, Uruguay	v	Barcelona Sporting Guayaquil, Ecuador						2-0		1-1
Nacional, Uruguay	v	Deportivo Quito, Ecuador						0-0		4-0
Barcelona Sporting Guayaquil, Ecuador	v	Deportivo Quito, Ecuador						0-0		0-1

Penarol	6	3	3	0	16-8	9
Nacional	6	2	4	0	10-4	8
Deportivo Quito	6	1	3	2	4-10	5
Barcelona	6	0	2	4	3-11	2

Quarter finals

Group 1

Italia Caracas, Venezuela	v	Cerro Porteno, Paraguay	0-0	0-1
Universidad Catolica, Chile	v	Italia Caracas, Venezuela	4-0	2-3
Cerro Porteno, Paraguay	v	Universidad Catolica, Chile	0-0	0-1

Univ Catolica	4	2	1	1	7-3	5
Cerro Porteno	4	1	2	1	1-1	4
Italia Caracas	4	1	1	2	3-7	3

Group 2

Santiago Wanderers, Chile	v	Nacional, Uruguay	1-1	0-2
Nacional, Uruguay	v	Deportivo Cali, Colombia	2-0	5-1
Deportivo Cali, Colombia	v	Santiago Wanderers, Chile	5-1	3-3

Nacional	4	3	1	0	10-2	7
Deportivo Cali	4	1	1	2	9-11	3
Santiago Wanderers	4	0	2	2	5-11	2

Group 3

Penarol, Uruguay	v	Olimpia, Paraguay	1-1	1-0

Semi-finals

Nacional, Uruguay	v	Penarol, Uruguay	0-0	2-0
Estudiantes La Plata, Argentina	v	Universidad Catolica, Chile	3-1	3-1

Final

Estudiantes La Plata, Argentina	v	Nacional, Uruguay	2-0	1-0

1970 XI

			Home	Playoff	Away
Group 1	Boca Juniors, Argentina	v Universitario La Paz, Bolivia	0-0		4-0
	Boca Juniors, Argentina	v River Plate, Argentina	2-1		3-1
	Boca Juniors, Argentina	v Bolivar La Paz, Bolivia	3-2		2-0
	Universitario La Paz, Bolivia	v River Plate, Argentina	0-2		0-9
	Universitario La Paz, Bolivia	v Bolivar La Paz, Bolivia	0-2		2-2
	Bolivar La Paz, Bolivia	v River Plate, Argentina	1-1		0-1

Boca Juniors	6	5	1	0	14-4	11
River Plate	6	3	1	2	15-6	7
Bolivar	6	1	2	3	7-9	4
Universitario La Paz	6	0	2	4	2-19	2

Group 2

Nacional, Uruguay	v	Penarol, Uruguay	1-1	0-0
Nacional, Uruguay	v	Galicia Caracas, Venezuela	2-0	4-0
Nacional, Uruguay	v	Valencia FC Acarigua, Venezuela	1-0	5-2
Penarol, Uruguay	v	Galicia Caracas, Venezuela	1-0	4-1
Penarol, Uruguay	v	Valencia FC Acarigua, Venezuela	0-0	11-2
Valencia FC Acarigua, Venezuela	v	Galicia Caracas, Venezuela	2-0	3-1

Nacional	6	4	2	0	13-3	10
Penarol	6	3	3	0	18-4	9
Valencia FC	6	2	1	3	9-19	5
Galicia Caracas	6	0	0	6	2-16	0

Group 3

Defensor Arica, Peru	v	America de Quito, Ecuador	0-1	1-1
Defensor Arica, Peru	v	Liga Dep Universitaria, Ecuador	0-0	2-1
Defensor Arica, Peru	v	Universitario Lima, Peru	1-1	1-2
America de Quito, Ecuador	v	Liga Dep Universitaria, Ecuador	1-3	1-4
America de Quito, Ecuador	v	Universitario Lima, Peru	0-3	0-3
Liga Dep Universitaria, Ecuador	v	Universitario Lima, Peru	2-0	0-2

Universitario Lima	6	4	1	1	11-4	9
LD Universitaria	6	3	1	2	10-6	7
Defensor Arica	6	1	3	2	5-6	5
America de Quito	6	1	1	4	4-14	3

Group 4				Home	Away
Guarani, Paraguay	v	Olimpia, Paraguay		1-0	0-0
Guarani, Paraguay	v	Rangers de Talca, Chile		2-0	1-0
Guarani, Paraguay	v	Universidad de Chile, Chile		1-0	0-0
Guarani, Paraguay	v	Deportivo Cali, Colombia		1-1	0-0
Guarani, Paraguay	v	America de Cali, Colombia		2-2	4-1
Olimpia, Paraguay	v	**Rangers de Talca, Chile**		**5-1**	**4-4**
Olimpia, Paraguay	v	Universidad de Chile, Chile		1-2	1-1
Olimpia, Paraguay	v	Deportivo Cali, Colombia		1-0	5-1
Olimpia, Paraguay	v	America de Cali, Colombia		1-1	1-0
Rangers de Talca, Chile	v	Universidad de Chile, Chile		1-7	1-2
Rangers de Talca, Chile	v	Deportivo Cali, Colombia		0-2	2-3
Rangers de Talca, Chile	v	**America de Cali, Colombia**		2-0	0-1
America de Cali, Colombia	v	Universidad de Chile, Chile		2-2	1-2
America de Cali, Colombia	v	Deportivo Cali, Colombia		2-4	2-4
Deportivo Cali, Colombia	v	Universidad de Chile, Chile		2-0	1-3

Guarani	10	5	5	0	11-4	15
Univ de Chile	10	5	3	2	19-11	13
Olimpia	10	4	4	2	19-11	12
Deportivo Cali	10	5	2	3	18-16	12
America de Cali	10	1	3	6	12-22	5
Rangers de Talca	10	1	1	8	11-26	3

Quarter finals

Group 1				Home	Away
Boca Juniors, Argentina	v	Universitario Lima, Peru		1-0	3-1
Boca Juniors, Argentina	v	River Plate, Argentina		0-1	1-1
River Plate, Argentina	v	Universitario Lima, Peru		5-3	2-1

River Plate	4	3	1	0	9-5	7
Boca Juniors	4	2	1	1	5-3	5
Universitario Lima	4	0	0	4	5-11	0

Group 2				Home	Away
Guarani, Paraguay	v	Penarol, Uruguay		2-0	0-1
Penarol, Uruguay	v	**Liga Dep Universitaria, Ecuador**		2-1	3-1
Guarani, Paraguay	v	Liga Dep Universitaria, Ecuador		1-1	0-1

Penarol	4	3	0	1	6-4	6
Guarani	4	1	1	2	3-3	3
LD Universitaria	4	1	1	2	4-6	3

Group 3						
Universidad de Chile, Chile	v	Nacional, Uruguay		3-0	2-1*	0-2

* play off for semi final place in Porto Alegre

Semi-finals

Penarol, Uruguay	v	Universidad de Chile, Chile		2-0	2-2ae	0-1
Estudiantes La Plata, Argentina	v	River Plate, Argentina		1-0		3-1

Final					
Estudiantes La Plata, Argentina	v	Penarol, Uruguay		1-0	0-0

1971 XII				**Home**	**Playoff**	**Away**
Group 1						
Universitario Lima, Peru	v	Sporting Cristal, Peru		0-0		3-0
Universitario Lima, Peru	v	Rosario Central, Argentina		3-2		2-2
Universitario Lima, Peru	v	Boca Juniors, Argentina		0-0		wo*
						* Boca Juniors withdrew
Sporting Cristal, Peru	v	Rosario Central, Argentina		1-2		0-4
Sporting Cristal, Peru	v	Boca Juniors, Argentina		2-0		2-2
Boca Juniors, Argentina	v	Rosario Central, Argentina		2-1		wo*

Universitario	6	3	3	0	8-4	9
Rosario Central	6	3	1	2	11-8	7
Boca Juniors	6	1	2	3	4-4	4
Sporting Cristal	6	1	2	3	5-11	4

LIBERTADORES RESULTS

Group 2									
Chaco Petrolero La Paz, Bolivia	v Penarol, Uruguay					1-1		0-1	
The Strongest, Bolivia	v Chaco Petrolero La Paz, Bolivia					2-1		1-3	
The Strongest, Bolivia	v Penarol, Uruguay					1-2		0-9	
The Strongest, Bolivia	v Nacional, Uruguay					1-1		0-5	
Chaco Petrolero La Paz, Bolivia	v Nacional, Uruguay					0-1		0-3	
Nacional, Uruguay	v Penarol, Uruguay					2-1		2-0	

Nacional	6	5	1	0	14-2	11
Penarol	6	3	1	2	14-6	7
Chaco Petrolero	6	1	1	4	5-9	3
The Strongest	6	1	1	4	5-21	3

Group 3									
Galicia Caracas, Venezuela	v Italia Caracas, Venezuela					0-0		5-6	
Galicia Caracas, Venezuela	v Fluminense Rio de Janeiro, Brazil					1-4		1-3	
Galicia Caracas, Venezuela	v Palmeiras Sao Paulo, Brazil					2-3		0-3	
Fluminense Rio de Janeiro, Brazil	v Palmeiras Sao Paulo, Brazil					2-0		1-3	
Fluminense Rio de Janeiro, Brazil	v Italia Caracas, Venezuela					6-0		0-1	
Italia Caracas, Venezuela	v Palmeiras Sao Paulo, Brazil					0-3		0-1	

Palmeiras	6	5	0	1	13-5	10
Fluminense	6	4	0	2	16-6	8
Italia Caracas	6	2	1	3	7-15	5
Galicia Caracas	6	0	1	5	9-19	1

Group 4									
Cerro Porteno, Paraguay	v Guarani, Paraguay					1-1		2-2	
Cerro Porteno, Paraguay	v Colo Colo, Chile					0-0		0-1	
Cerro Porteno, Paraguay	v Union Espanola, Chile					2-1		0-0	
Guarani, Paraguay	v Union Espanola, Chile					1-1		1-2	
Guarani, Paraguay	v Colo Colo, Chile					2-0		2-3	
Union Espanola, Chile	v Colo Colo, Chile					2-1		1-1	

Union Espanola	6	2	3	1	7-6	7
Colo Colo	6	2	2	2	6-7	6
Cerro Porteno	6	1	4	1	5-5	6
Guarani	6	1	3	2	9-9	5

Group 5									
Junior Barranquilla, Colombia	v Deportivo Cali, Colombia					2-1		0-2	
Junior Barranquilla, Colombia	v Emelec Guayaquil, Ecuador					0-0		1-1	
Junior Barranquilla, Colombia	v Barcelona Sporting Guayaquil, Ecuador					0-2		1-3	
Deportivo Cali, Colombia	v Barcelona Sporting Guayaquil, Ecuador					3-1		0-1	
Deportivo Cali, Colombia	v Emelec Guayaquil, Ecuador					1-0		1-3	
Emelec Guayaquil, Ecuador	v Barcelona Sporting Guayaquil, Ecuador					1-0	0-3*	1-1	

* play off for semi final place

Barcelona	6	3	1	2	8-6	7
Emelec	6	2	3	1	6-4	7
Deportivo Cali	6	3	0	3	8-7	6
Junior Barranquilla	6	1	2	3	5-9	4

Semi finals

Group 1									
Universitario Lima, Peru	v Palmeiras Sao Paulo, Brazil					1-2		0-3	
Universitario Lima, Peru	v Nacional, Uruguay					0-0		0-3	
Nacional, Uruguay	v Palmeiras Sao Paulo, Brazil					3-1		3-0	

Nacional	4	3	1	0	9-1	7
Palmeiras	4	2	0	2	6-7	4
Universitario Lima	4	0	1	3	1-8	1

Group 2									
Estudiantes La Plata, Argentina	v Barcelona Sporting Guayaquil, Ecuador					0-1		1-0	
Estudiantes La Plata, Argentina	v Union Espanola, Chile					2-1		1-0	
Barcelona Sporting Guayaquil, Ecuador	v Union Espanola, Chile					1-0		1-3	

Estudiantes	4	3	0	1	4-2	6
Barcelona	4	2	0	2	3-4	4
Union Espanola	4	1	0	3	4-5	2

Final					
Nacional, Uruguay	v Estudiantes La Plata, Argentina	1-0	2-0*	0-1	

* in Lima

LIBERTADORES RESULTS

1972 XIII

								Home	Playoff	Away
Group 1	Rosario Central, Argentina	v Independiente, Argentina						2-2		0-2
	Rosario Central, Argentina	v Independiente Santa Fe, Colombia						2-0		0-0
	Rosario Central, Argentina	v Nacional Medellin, Colombia						1-0		3-0
	Independiente Santa Fe, Colombia	v Independiente, Argentina						0-2		2-4
	Independiente Santa Fe, Colombia	v **Nacional Medellin, Colombia**						1-1		1-0
	Nacional Medellin, Colombia	v Independiente, Argentina						1-1		0-2

Independiente	6	4	2	0	13-5	10
Rosario Central	6	3	2	1	8-5	8
Independ Santa Fe	6	1	2	3	4-9	4
Nacional Medellin	6	0	2	4	2-9	2

								Home	Playoff	Away
Group 2	Oriente Petrolero Santa Cruz, Bolivia	v Chaco Petrolero La Paz, Bolivia						5-0		0-1
	Oriente Petrolero Santa Cruz, Bolivia	v Barcelona Sporting Guayaquil, Ecuador						0-0		1-1
	Oriente Petrolero Santa Cruz, Bolivia	v America de Cali, Colombia						4-2		0-3
	Barcelona Sporting Guayaquil, Ecuador	v America de Quito, Ecuador						3-1		0-0
	Barcelona Sporting Guayaquil, Ecuador	v Chaco Petrolero La Paz, Bolivia						3-0		2-1
	America de Quito, Ecuador	v Chaco Petrolero La Paz, Bolivia						1-0		2-1

Barcelona	6	3	3	0	8-3	9
America de Quito	6	3	1	2	9-7	7
Oriente Petrolero	6	2	2	2	10-7	6
Chaco Petrolero	6	1	0	5	3-13	2

								Home	Playoff	Away
Group 3	Atletico Mineiro Belo Horizonte, Brazil	v Sao Paulo Fc, Brazil						2-2		0-0
	Atletico Mineiro Belo Horizonte, Brazil	v Olimpia, Paraguay						0-0		2-2
	Atletico Mineiro Belo Horizonte, Brazil	v Cerro Porteno, Paraguay						1-1		0-1
	Sao Paulo FC, Brazil	v Olimpia, Paraguay						3-1		1-0
	Sao Paulo FC, Brazil	v Cerro Porteno, Paraguay						4-0		2-3
	Olimpia, Paraguay	v Cerro Porteno, Paraguay						1-1		3-1

Sao Paulo FC	6	3	2	1	12-6	8
Olimpia	6	2	2	2	7-8	6
Cerro Porteno	6	2	2	2	7-11	6
Atletico Mineiro	6	0	4	2	5-6	4

								Home	Playoff	Away
Group 4	Union San Felipe, Chile	v Universidad de Chile, Chile						3-2		1-2
	Union San Felipe, Chile	v Alianza Lima, Peru						0-0		0-1
	Union San Felipe, Chile	v Universitario Lima, Peru						0-0		1-3
	Universidad de Chile, Chile	v Alianza Lima, Peru						2-3		4-3
	Universidad de Chile, Chile	v Universitario Lima, Peru						1-0		1-2
	Universitario Lima, Peru	v Alianza Lima, Peru						2-1		2-2

Universitario Lima	6	3	2	1	9-6	8
Univ de Chile	6	3	0	3	12-12	6
Alianza	6	2	2	2	10-10	6
Union San Felipe	6	1	2	3	5-8	4

								Home	Playoff	Away
Group 5	Valencia FC Acarigua, Venezuela	v Italia Caracas, Venezuela						1-1		0-2
	Valencia FC Acarigua, Venezuela	v Penarol, Uruguay						1-4		1-2
	Italia Caracas, Venezuela	v Penarol, Uruguay						1-5		0-1

Penarol	4	4	0	0	12-3	8
Italia Caracas	4	1	1	2	4-7	4
Valencia Fc	4	0	1	3	3-9	1

Semi-finals

								Home	Playoff	Away
Group 1	Penarol, Uruguay	v Universitario Lima, Peru						1-1		3-2
	Penarol, Uruguay	v **Nacional, Uruguay**						0-3		1-1
	Universitario Lima, Peru	v Nacional, Uruguay						3-0		3-3

Universitario	4	1	2	1	9-7*	4
	* qualified on goal difference					
Nacional	4	1	2	1	7-7	4
Penarol	4	1	2	1	5-7	4

LIBERTADORES RESULTS

Group 2				Home	Playoff	Away
	Independiente, Argentina	v	Barcelona Sporting Guayaquil, Ecuador	1-0		1-1
	Independiente, Argentina	v	Sao Paulo FC, Brazil	2-0		0-1
	Barcelona Sporting Guayaquil, Ecuador	v	Sao Paulo FC, Brazil	0-0		1-1

Independiente	4	2	1	1	4-2	5
Sao Paulo FC	4	1	2	1	2-3	4
Barcelona	4	0	3	1	2-3	3

Final					
	Independiente, Argentina	v	Universitario Lima, Peru	2-1	0-0

1973 XIV

Group One				Home	Playoff	Away
	River Plate, Argentina	v	Oriente Petrolero Santa Cr, Bolivia	3-1		7-1
	River Plate, Argentina	v	San Lorenzo, Argentina	0-4		0-1
	River Plate, Argentina	v	Jorge Wilsterman Cochabamb, Bolivia	2-2		0-1
	Oriente Petrolero Santa Cr, Bolivia	v	San Lorenzo, Argentina	0-4		0-2
	Oriente Petrolero Santa Cr, Bolivia	v	Jorge Wilsterman Cochabamb, Bolivia	3-1		0-1
	Jorge Wilsterman Cochabamb, Bolivia	v	San Lorenzo, Argentina	1-0		0-3

San Lorenzo	6	5	0	1	15-1	10
Jorge Wilsterman	6	3	1	2	6-8	7
River Plate	6	2	1	3	12-10	5
Oriente Petrolero	6	1	0	5	5-19	2

Group 2				Home	Playoff	Away
	Nacional, Uruguay	v	Penarol, Uruguay	2-0		1-1
	Nacional, Uruguay	v	Botafogo Rio de Janeiro, Brazil	1-2		2-3
	Nacional, Uruguay	v	Palmeiras Sao Paulo, Brazil	1-2		1-1
	Penarol, Uruguay	v	Botafogo Rio de Janeiro, Brazil	2-2		1-4
	Penarol, Uruguay	v	Palmeiras Sao Paulo, Brazil	0-2		0-2
	Palmeiras Sao Paulo, Brazil	v	Botafogo Rio de Janeiro, Brazil	3-2	1-2*	0-2

* play off for semi final place

Botafogo	6	4	1	1	14-8	9
Palmeiras	6	4	1	1	10-6	9
Nacional	6	1	2	3	8-9	4
Penarol	6	0	2	4	3-12	2

Group 3				Home		Away
	Emelec Guayaquil, Ecuador	v	Nacional Quito, Ecuador	2-0		0-1
	Emelec Guayaquil, Ecuador	v	Union Espanola, Chile	1-0		1-1
	Emelec Guayaquil, Ecuador	v	Colo Colo, Chile	1-5		1-0
	Nacional Quito, Ecuador	v	Colo Colo, Chile	1-1		1-5
	Nacional Quito, Ecuador	v	Union Espanola, Chile	1-0		1-2
	Colo Colo, Chile	v	Union Espanola, Chile	5-0		0-0

Colo Colo	6	3	2	1	16-4	8
Emelec	6	3	1	2	6-6	7
Nacional Quito	6	2	1	3	5-10	5
Union Espanola	6	1	2	3	3-10	4

Group 4				Home		Away
	Millonarios Bogota, Colombia	v	Deportivo Cali, Colombia	6-2		0-0

Group 5				Home		Away
	Universitario Lima, Peru	v	Sporting Cristal, Peru	2-2		0-1
	Universitario Lima, Peru	v	Cerro Porteno, Paraguay	0-1		0-2
	Universitario Lima, Peru	v	Olimpia, Paraguay	2-1		0-1
	Cerro Porteno, Paraguay	v	Olimpia, Paraguay	4-2		1-2
	Cerro Porteno, Paraguay	v	Sporting Cristal, Peru	1-1		5-0
	Sporting Cristal, Peru	v	Olimpia, Paraguay	1-0		0-1

Cerro Porteno	6	4	1	1	14-5	9
Olimpia	6	3	0	3	7-8	6
Sporting Cristal	6	2	2	2	5-9	6
Universitario Lima	6	1	1	4	4-8	3

Semi-finals

Group 1				Home		Away
	Millonarios Bogota, Colombia	v	Independiente, Argentina	1-0		0-2
	Millonarios Bogota, Colombia	v	San Lorenzo, Argentina	0-0		0-2
	Independiente, Argentina	v	San Lorenzo, Argentina	2-2		1-0

	Independiente	4	2	1	1	5-3	5
	San Lorenzo	4	1	2	1	4-3	4
	Millonarios	4	1	1	2	1-4	3

Group 2

Colo Colo, Chile	v Botafogo Rio de Janeiro, Brazil	3-3		2-1
Colo Colo, Chile	v Cerro Porteno, Paraguay	4-0		1-5
Botafogo Rio de Janeiro, Brazil	v Cerro Porteno, Paraguay	2-0		2-3

	Colo Colo	4	2	1	1	10-9	5
	Cerro Porteno	4	2	0	2	8-9	4
	Botafogo	4	1	1	2	8-8	3

Final

Independiente, Argentina	v Colo Colo, Chile	1-1	2-1*	0-0
				* Montevid

1974 XV

Group 1

		Home	Playoff	Away
Rosario Central, Argentina	v Huracan, Argentina	1-0	0-4*	0-1
				* play off for semi final place
Union Espanola, Chile	v Colo Colo, Chile	2-1		2-0
Huracan, Argentina	v Union Espanola, Chile	3-1		5-1
Huracan, Argentina	v Colo Colo, Chile	2-1		2-0
Rosario Central, Argentina	v Colo Colo, Chile	2-0		3-1
Rosario Central, Argentina	v Union Espanola, Chile	1-0		4-0

	Huracan	6	5	0	1	13-4	10
	Rosario Central	6	5	0	1	11-2	10
	Union Espanola	6	2	0	4	6-14	4
	Colo Colo	6	0	0	6	3-13	0

Group 2

Sao Paulo FC, Brazil	v Palmeiras Sao Paulo, Brazil	2-0	2-1
Sao Paulo FC, Brazil	v Municipal La Paz, Bolivia	1-1	3-3
Jorge Wilsterman Cochabamba, Bolivia	v Palmeiras Sao Paulo, Brazil	1-0	0-2
Jorge Wilsterman Cochabamba, Bolivia	v Sao Paulo FC, Brazil	0-1	0-5
Palmeiras Sao Paulo, Brazil	v Municipal La Paz, Bolivia	1-0	3-0
Jorge Wilsterman Cochabamba, Bolivia	v Municipal La Paz, Bolivia	1-0	not played

	Sao Paulo FC	6	4	2	0	14-5	10
	Palmeiras	6	3	0	3	7-5	6
	Jorge Wilsterman	5	2	0	3	2-8	4
	Municipal La Paz	5	0	2	3	4-9	2

Group 3

Portuguesa Acarigua, Venezuela	v Valencia FC Acarigua, Venezuela	0-0	1-0
Millonarios Bogota, Colombia	v Nacional Medellin, Colombia	3-0	2-1
Nacional Medellin, Colombia	v Valencia FC Acarigua, Venezuela	2-1	2-1
Portuguesa Acarigua, Venezuela	v Millonarios Bogota, Colombia	2-0	1-2
Portuguesa Acarigua, Venezuela	v Nacional Medellin, Colombia	0-0	0-3
Valencia FC Acarigua, Venezuela	v Millonarios Bogota, Colombia	1-1	1-2

	Millonarios	6	4	1	1	10-6	9
	Nacional Medellin	6	3	1	2	8-7	7
	Portuguesa Acarigua	6	2	2	2	4-5	6
	Valencia FC	6	0	2	4	4-8	2

Group 2

Nacional Quito, Ecuador	v Universidad Catolica Quito, Ecuador	2-0	0-0
Defensor Lima, Peru	v Sporting Cristal, Peru	2-0	2-0
Universidad Catolica Quito, Ecuador	v Defensor Lima, Peru	1-0	1-0
Nacional Quito, Ecuador	v Defensor Lima, Peru	0-0	1-2
Universidad Catolica Quito, Ecuador	v Sporting Cristal, Peru	0-0	1-2
Nacional Quito, Ecuador	v Sporting Cristal, Peru	3-0	3-1

	Defensor Lima	6	4	1	1	7-2	9
	Nacional Quito	6	3	2	1	9-3	8
	Univ Catolica Quito	6	1	2	3	2-5	4
	Sporting Cristal	6	1	1	4	3-11	3

LIBERTADORES RESULTS

Group 5											
Penarol, Uruguay	v Nacional, Uruguay						1-0		0-2		
Cerro Porteno, Paraguay	v Olimpia, Paraguay						1-0		1-1		
Nacional, Uruguay	v Olimpia, Paraguay						1-1		0-2		
Penarol, Uruguay	v Olimpia, Paraguay						0-0		2-0		
Cerro Porteno, Paraguay	v Nacional, Uruguay						2-1		2-2		
Penarol, Uruguay	v Cerro Porteno, Paraguay						1-0		1-1		

Penarol	6	3	2	1	5-3	8
Cerro Porteno	6	2	3	1	7-6	7
Olimpia	6	1	3	2	4-5	5
Nacional	6	1	2	3	6-8	4

Semi-finals

Group 1				
Huracan, Argentina	v Independiente, Argentina	1-1	0-3
Penarol, Uruguay	v Huracan, Argentina	1-1	3-0
Independiente, Argentina	v Penarol, Uruguay	3-2	1-1

Independiente	4	2	2	0	8-4	6
Penarol	4	1	2	1	7-5	4
Huracan	4	0	2	2	2-8	2

Group 2				
Millonarios Bogota, Colombia	v Sao Paulo FC, Brazil	0-0	0-4
Sao Paulo FC, Brazil	v Defensor Lima, Peru	4-0	1-0
Millonarios Bogota, Colombia	v Defensor Lima, Peru	1-0	4-1

Sao Paulo FC	4	3	1	0	9-0	7
Millonarios	4	2	1	1	5-5	5
Defensor Lima	4	0	0	4	1-10	0

Independiente, Argentina	v Sao Paulo FC, Brazil	2-0	1-0*	1-2	Final
					* in Santiago

1975 XVI

		Home	**Playoff**	**Away**
Group 1 Rosario Central, Argentina	v Newell's Old Boys Rosario, Argentina	1-1	1-0*	1-1
				* play off for semi final place
Cerro Porteno, Paraguay	v Olimpia, Paraguay	0-0		1-2
Olimpia, Paraguay	v Newell's Old Boys Rosario, Argentina	2-0		2-3
Rosario Central, Argentina	v Cerro Porteno, Paraguay	2-1		3-1
Rosario Central, Argentina	v Olimpia, Paraguay	1-1		0-0
Newell's Old Boys Rosario, Argentina	v Cerro Porteno, Paraguay	1-0		3-2

Rosario Central	6	2	4	0	8-5	8
Newell's Old Boys	6	3	2	1	9-8	8
Olimpia	6	2	3	1	7-5	7
Cerro Porteno	6	0	1	5	5-11	1

Group 2				
The Strongest, Bolivia	v Jorge Wilsterman Cochabamba, Bolivia	3-1	1-1
Huachipato Talcahuano, Chile	v Union Espanola, Chile	0-0	2-7
Jorge Wilsterman Cochabamba, Bolivia	v Huachipato Talcahuano, Chile	0-0	0-4
The Strongest, Bolivia	v Huachipato Talcahuano, Chile	1-0	2-4
Jorge Wilsterman Cochabamba Bolivia	v Union Espanola, Chile	1-1	1-4
The Strongest, Bolivia	v Union Espanola, Chile	1-1	0-4

Union Espanola	6	3	3	0	17-5	9
Huachipato	6	2	2	2	10-10	6
The Strongest	6	2	2	2	8-11	6
Jorge Wilsterman	6	0	3	3	4-13	3

Group 3				
Cruzeiro Belo Horizonte, Brazil	v Vasco de Gama Rio de Jan, Brazil	3-2	1-1
Deportivo Cali, Colombia	v Nacional Medellin, Colombia	0-0	1-2
Nacional Medellin, Colombia	v Vasco de Gama Rio de Jan, Brazil	1-1	0-2
Deportivo Cali, Colombia	v Cruzeiro Belo Horizonte Brazil, 1-0		1-2
Deportivo Cali, Colombia	v Vasco de Gama Rio de Jan, Brazil	2-1	0-0
Nacional Medellin, Colombia	v Cruzeiro Belo Horizonte, Brazil	1-2	3-2

Cruzeiro	6	3	1	2	11-10	7
Deportivo Cali	6	2	2	2	6-6	6

Nacional Medellin	6	2	2	2	7-8	6
Vasco de Gama	6	1	3	2	7-7	5

Group 4

		Home	Away
Galicia Caracas, Venezuela	v Portuguesa Acarigua, Venezuela	0-0	1-1
Liga Dep Universitaria, Ecuador	v Nacional Quito, Ecuador	3-1	1-1
Liga Dep Universitaria, Ecuador	v Galicia Caracas, Venezuela	4-2	1-0
Nacional Quito, Ecuador	v Galicia Caracas, Venezuela	0-0	0-4
Nacional Quito, Ecuador	v Portuguesa Acarigua, Venezuela	5-1	0-1
Liga Dep Universitaria, Ecuador	v Portuguesa Acarigua, Venezuela	1-1	1-1

LD Universitaria	6	3	3	0	11-6	9
Portuguesa Acarigua	6	1	4	1	5-8	6
Galicia Caracas	6	1	3	2	7-6	5
Nacional Quito	6	1	2	3	7-10	4

Group 5

		Home	Away
Penarol, Uruguay	v Wanderers, Uruguay	1-0	2-1
Universitario Lima, Peru	v Union Huaral, Peru	1-1	2-2
Penarol, Uruguay	v Union Huaral, Peru	5-2	3-0
Wanderers, Uruguay	v Union Huaral, Peru	4-0	2-2
Wanderers, Uruguay	v Universitario Lima, Peru	0-2	1-3
Penarol, Uruguay	v Universitario Lima, Peru	0-1	2-3

Universitario Lima	6	4	2	0	12-7	10
Penarol	6	4	0	2	13-7	8
Wanderers	6	1	1	4	8-10	3
Union Huaral	6	0	3	3	7-17	3

Semi-finals
Group 1 (Atlantic Group)

		Home	Away
Rosario Central, Argentina	v Independiente, Argentina	2-0	0-2
Cruzeiro Belo Horizonte, Brazil	v Rosario Central, Argentina	2-0	1-3
Cruzeiro Belo Horizonte, Brazil	v Independiente, Argentina	2-0	0-3

Independiente	4	2	0	2	5-4*	4
				* qualified on goal difference		
Rosario Central	4	2	0	2	5-5	4
Cruzeiro	4	2	0	2	5-6	4

Group 2 (Pacific Group)

		Home	Away
Liga Dep Universitaria, Ecuador	v Universitario Lima, Peru	0-0	1-2
Liga Dep Universitaria, Ecuador	v Union Espanola, Chile	4-2	0-2
Union Espanola, Chile	v Universitario Lima, Peru	2-1	1-1

Union Espanola	4	2	1	1	7-6	5
Universitario Lima	4	1	2	1	4-4	4
LD Universitaria	4	1	1	2	5-6	3

		Home	Playoff	Away
Final Independiente, Argentina	v Union Espanola, Chile	3-1	2-0*	0-1
				* in Asuncion

1976 XVII

Group 1

		Home	Playoff	Away
River Plate, Argentina	v Estudiantes La Plata, Argentina	1-0		0-1
Galicia Caracas, Venezuela	v Portuguesa Acarigua, Venezuela	1-2		1-3
Galicia Caracas, Venezuela	v River Plate, Argentina	0-1		1-4
Portuguesa Acarigua, Venezuela	v Estudiantes La Plata, Argentina	2-2		0-3
Portuguesa Acarigua, Venezuela	v River Plate, Argentina	0-2		1-2
Galicia Caracas, Venezuela	v Estudiantes La Plata, Argentina	0-1		0-4

River Plate	6	5	0	1	10-3	10
Estudiantes	6	4	1	1	11-3	9
Portuguesa Acarigua	6	2	1	3	8-11	5
Galicia Caracas	6	0	0	6	3-15	0

35

LIBERTADORES RESULTS

Group 2	Liga Dep Universitaria, Ecuador	v Deportivo Cuenca, Ecuador			1-1	2-1*	0-0

* play off for semi final place

Guabira Santa Cruz, Bolivia	v Bolivar La Paz, Bolivia	1-0		1-7
Liga Dep Universitaria, Ecuador	v Guabira Santa Cruz, Bolivia	4-0		1-0
Deportivo Cuenca, Ecuador	v Bolivar La Paz, Bolivia	3-1		2-4
Deportivo Cuenca, Ecuador	v Guabira Santa Cruz, Bolivia	1-0		2-0
Liga Dep Universitaria, Ecuador	v Bolivar La Paz, Bolivia	2-1		2-3

LD Universitaria	6	3	2	1	10-5	8
Deportivo Cuenca	6	3	2	1	9-6	8
Bolivar	6	3	0	3	16-11	6
Guabira	6	1	0	5	2-15	2

Group 3	Cruzeiro Belo Horizonte, Brazil	v Internacional Porto Alegre, Brazil	5-4		2-0
	Olimpia, Paraguay	v Sportivo Lugueno Luque, Paraguay	2-3		1-0
	Internacional Porto Alegre, Brazil	v Olimpia, Paraguay	1-0		1-1
	Sportivo Luqueno Luque, Paraguay	v Cruzeiro Belo Horizonte, Brazil	1-3		1-4
	Olimpia, Paraguay	v Cruzeiro Belo Horizonte, Brazil	2-2		1-4
	Internacional Porto Alegre, Brazil	v Sportivo Lugueno Luque, Paraguay	3-0		1-0

Cruzeiro	6	5	1	0	20-9	11
Internacional	6	3	1	2	10-8	7
Olimpia	6	1	2	3	7-11	4
Sportivo Luqueno	6	1	0	5	5-14	2

Group 4	Independiente Santa Fe, Colombia	v Millonarios Bogota, Colombia	1-1		1-0
	Alianza Lima, Peru	v Alfonso Ufarte, Peru	0-0		0-0
	Independiente Santa Fe, Colombia	v Alfonso Peru	2-3		0-3

Alianza	6	3	2	1	8-4	8
Millonarios	6	2	2	2	8-5	6
Alfonso Ufarte	6	1	4	1	5-8	6
Independiente Santa Fe	6	1	2	3	7-11	4

Group 5	Penarol, Uruguay	v Nacional, Uruguay	1-1		2-1
	Union Espanola, Chile	v Palestino, Chile	1-0		1-0
	Union Espanola, Chile	v Penarol, Uruguay	0-0		0-2
	Palestino, Chile	v Nacional, Uruguay	2-1		1-1
	Palestino, Chile	v Penarol, Uruguay	1-0		1-2
	Union Espanola, Chile	v Nacional, Uruguay	2-0		1-1

Penarol	6	3	2	1	7-4*	8

* qualified on goal difference

Union Espanol	6	3	2	1	5-3	8
Palestino	6	2	1	3	5-6	5
Nacional	6	0	3	3	5-9	3

Semi-finals

Group 1	Liga Dep Universitaria, Ecuador	v Alianza Lima, Peru	2-1		0-2
	Liga Dep Universitaria, Ecuador	v Cruzeiro Belo Horizonte, Brazil	1-3		1-4
	Alianza Lima, Peru	v Cruzeiro Belo Horizonte, Brazil	0-4		1-7

Cruzeiro	4	4	0	0	18-3	8
LD Universitaria	4	1	0	3	4-10	2
Alianza	4	1	0	3	4-13	2

Group 2	River Plate, Argentina	v Independiente, Argentina		0-0	1-0*	1-0
	Independiente, Argentina	v Penarol, Uruguay		1-0		1-0
	River Plate, Argentina	v Penarol, Uruguay		3-0		0-1

River Plate	4	2	1	1	4-1	7

* play off for Final place

Independiente	4	2	1	1	1-2	5
Penarol	4	1	0	3	1-5	2

Final	Cruzeiro Belo Horizonte, Brazil	v River Plate, Argentina	4-1	3-2*	1-2

* in Santiago

1977 XVIII

				Home	Playoff	Away
Group 1	Penarol, Uruguay	v Defensor, Uruguay		0-2		4-2
	River Plate, Argentina	v Penarol, Uruguay		2-1		2-2
	Defensor, Uruguay	v Boca Juniors, Argentina		0-0		0-2
	Penarol, Uruguay	v Boca Juniors, Argentina		0-1		0-1
	River Plate, Argentina	v Defensor, Uruguay		1-1		0-0
	Boca Juniors, Argentina	v River Plate, Argentina		1-0		0-0

Boca Juniors	6	4	2	0	5-0	10
River Plate	6	1	4	1	5-5	6
Defensor	6	1	3	2	5-7	5
Penarol	6	1	1	4	7-10	3

			Home		Away
Group 2	Bolivar La Paz, Bolivia	v Oriente Petrolero Santa Cr, Bolivia	1-0		0-0
	Oriente Petrolero Santa Cr, Bolivia	v Nacional Medellin, Colombia	4-0		1-3
	Bolivar La Paz, Bolivia	v Deportivo Cali, Colombia	3-0		0-3
	Bolivar La Paz, Bolivia	v Nacional Medellin, Colombia	3-0		0-1
	Oriente Petrolero Santa Cr, Bolivia	v Deportivo Cali, Colombia	1-0		0-3
	Deportivo Cali, Colombia	v Nacional Medellin, Colombia	3-1		3-0

Deportivo Cali	6	4	0	2	12-5	8
Bolivar	6	3	1	2	7-4	7
Oriente Petrolero	6	2	1	3	5-7	5
Nacinal Medellin	6	2	0	4	6-14	4

			Home		Away
Group 3	Nacional Quito, Ecuador	v Deportivo Cuenca, Ecuador	0-0		2-0
	Nacional Quito, Ecuador	v Internacional Porto Alegre, Brazil	2-0		0-2
	Corinthians Sao Paulo, Brazil	v Internacional Porto Alegre, Brazil	1-1		0-1
	Deportivo Cuenca, Ecuador	v Internacional Porto Alegre, Brazil	0-2		1-3
	Nacional Quito, Ecuador	v Corinthians Sao Paulo, Brazil	2-1		0-3
	Deportivo Cuenca, Ecuador	v Corinthians Sao Paulo, Brazil	2-1		0-4

Internacional	6	4	1	1	9-4	9
Nacional Quito	6	3	1	2	6-6	7
Corinthians	6	2	1	3	10-6	5
Deportivo Cuenca	6	1	1	4	3-12	3

			Home		Away
Group 4	Everton Vina del Mar, Chile	v Universidad de Chile, Chile	0-0		0-1
	Libertad, Paraguay	v Olimpia, Paraguay	2-2		0-0
	Universidad de Chile, Chile	v Libertad, Paraguay	1-0		0-3
	Universidad de Chile, Chile	v Olimpia, Paraguay	1-0		0-1
	Everton Vina del Mar, Chile	v Libertad, Paraguay	1-3		1-2
	Everton Vina del Mar, Chile	v Olimpia, Paraguay	1-0		2-2

Libertad	6	3	2	1	10-5	8
Univ de Chile	6	3	0	3	3-6	6
Everton	6	2	1	3	7-8	5
Olimpia	6	1	3	2	5-6	5

			Home		Away
Group 5	Union Huaral, Peru	v Sport Boys Callao, Peru	1-0		0-0
	Estudiantes de Merida, Venezuela	v Portuguesa Acarigua, Venezuela	0-2		0-3
	Union Huaral, Peru	v Portuguesa Acarigua, Venezuela	1-1		0-2
	Sport Boys Callao, Peru	v Portuguesa Acarigua, Venezuela	1-2		0-0
	Estudiantes de Merida, Venezuela	v Union Huaral, Peru	1-0		1-2
	Sport Boys Callao, Peru	v Estudiantes de Merida, Venezuela	1-3		0-1

Portuguesa Acarigua	6	4	2	0	10-2	10
Union Huaral	6	2	2	2	4-5	6
Estudiantes	6	3	0	3	6-8	6
Sport Boys Callao	6	0	2	4	2-7	2

Semi finals

			Home		Away
Group 1	Boca Juniors, Argentina	v Libertad, Paraguay	1-0		1-0
	Deportivo Cali, Colombia	v Libertad, Paraguay	0-0		1-2
	Deportivo Cali, Colombia	v Boca Juniors, Argentina	1-1		1-1

37

	Boca Juniors	4	2	2	0	4-2	6	
	Deportivo Cali	4	0	3	1	3-4	3	
	Libertad	4	1	1	2	2-3	3	

			Home		Away
Group 2	Internacional Porto Alegre, Brazil	v Cruzeiro Belo Horizonte, Brazil	0-1		0-0
	Portuguesa Acarigua, Venezuela	v Internacional Porto Alegre, Brazil	3-0		1-2
	Portuguesa Acarigua, Venezuela	v Cruzeiro Belo Horizonte, Brazil	0-4		1-2

	Cruzeiro	4	3	1	0	7-1	7	
	Internacional	4	1	1	2	2-5	3	
	Portuguesa Acarigua	4	1	0	3	5-8	2	

			Home	Playoff	Away
Final	Boca Juniors, Argentina	v Cruzeiro Belo Horizonte, Brazil	1-0	0-0*	0-1
					* in Montevideo 5-4 penalties

1978 XIX

			Home	Playoff	Away
Group 1	Independiente, Argentina	v Liga Dep Universitaria, Ecuador	2-0		0-1
	Independiente, Argentina	v Nacional Quito, Ecuador	2-0		2-1
	Independiente, Argentina	v River Plate, Argentina	0-0	1-4*	0-0
					* play off for semi final place
	River Plate, Argentina	v Nacional Quito, Ecuador	2-0		1-1
	River Plate, Argentina	v Liga Dep Universitaria, Ecuador	4-0		0-0
	Nacional Quito, Ecuador	v Liga Dep Universitaria, Ecuador	2-0		2-3

	River Plate	6	2	4	0	7-1	8	
	Independiente	6	3	2	1	6-2	8	
	LD Universitaria	6	2	1	3	4-10	5	
	Nacional Quito	6	1	1	4	6-10	3	

			Home		Away
Group 2	Alianza Lima, Peru	v Sporting Cristal, Peru	4-1		2-2
	Alianza Lima, Peru	v Oriente Petrolero Santa Cr, Bolivia	5-1		4-0
	Alianza Lima, Peru	v The Strongest, Bolivia	2-0		2-0
	Sporting Cristal, Peru	v Oriente Petrolero Santa Cr, Bolivia	1-0		1-0
	Sporting Cristal, Peru	v The Strongest, Bolivia	1-3		3-0
	Oriente Petrolero Santa Cr, Bolivia	v The Strongest, Bolivia	4-1		0-2

	Alianza	6	5	1	0	19-4	11	
	Sporting Cristal	6	3	1	2	9-9	7	
	The Strongest	6	2	0	4	6-12	4	
	Oriente Petrolero	6	1	0	5	5-14	2	

			Home		Away
Group 3	Union Espanola, Chile	v Palestino, Chile	0-0		2-3
	Union Espanola, Chile	v Sao Paulo FC, Brazil	1-1		1-1
	Union Espanola, Chile	v Atletico Mineiro Belo Horizonte, Brazil	1-5		1-1
	Palestino, Chile	v Atletico Mineiro Belo Horizonte, Brazil	4-5		0-2
	Palestino, Chile	v Sao Paulo FC, Brazil	2-1		0-1
	Atletico Mineiro Belo Horizonte, Brazil	v Sao Paulo FC, Brazil	1-1		2-1

	Atletico Mineiro	6	3	3	0	15-9	9	
	Palestino	6	2	2	2	10-10	6	
	Sao Paulo FC	6	1	3	2	6-7	5	
	Union Espanola	6	0	4	2	6-11	4	

			Home		Away
Group 4	Penarol, Uruguay	v Danubio, Uruguay	4-2		2-1
	Penarol, Uruguay	v Deportivo Cali, Colombia	0-1		0-2
	Penarol, Uruguay	v Junior Barranquilla, Colombia	0-1		1-0
	Danubio, Uruguay	v Deportivo Cali, Colombia	3-0		0-2
	Danubio, Uruguay	v Junior Barranquilla, Colombia	0-0		0-0
	Junior Barranquilla, Colombia	v Deportivo Cali, Colombia	0-0		0-0

	Deportivo Cali	6	3	2	1	5-3	8	
	Penarol	6	3	0	3	7-7	6	
	Junior Barranquilla	6	1	4	1	1-1	6	
	Danubio	6	1	2	3	6-8	4	

Group 5
			Home	Away
Cerro Porteno, Paraguay	v Libertad, Paraguay		1-0	0-0
Cerro Porteno, Paraguay	v Portuguesa Acarigua, Venezuela		1-0	1-1
Cerro Porteno, Paraguay	v Estudiantes de Merida, Venezuela		2-3	1-1
Libertad, Paraguay	v Estudiantes de Merida, Venezuela		1-1	2-1
Libertad, Paraguay	v Portuguesa Acarigua, Venezuela		0-1	1-2
Estudiantes de Merida, Venezuela	v Portuguesa Acarigua, Venezuela		0-0	0-0

Cerro Porteno	6	2	3	1	6-5	7
Portuguesa Acarigua	6	2	2	2	4-3	6
Estudiantes	6	1	4	1	6-6	6
Libertad	6	1	2	3	4-6	4

Semi-finals
Group 1
			Home	Away
Boca Juniors, Argentina	v River Plate, Argentina		0-0	2-0
Boca Juniors, Argentina	v Atletico Mineiro Belo Hor, Brazil		3-1	2-1
River Plate, Argentina	v Atletico Mineiro Belo Hor Brazil		1-0	0-1

Boca Juniors	4	3	1	0	7-2	7
River Plate	4	1	1	2	1-3	3
Atletico Mineiro	4	1	0	3	3-6	2

Group 2
			Home	Away
Alianza Lima, Peru	v Cerro Porteno, Paraguay		3-0	1-3
Alianza Lima, Peru	v Deportivo Cali, Colombia		1-4	2-3
Deportivo Cali, Colombia	v Cerro Porteno, Paraguay		1-1	4-0

Deportivo Cali	4	3	1	0	12-4	7
Cerro Porteno	4	1	1	2	4-9	3
Alianza	4	1	0	3	7-10	2

Final
			Home	Away
Boca Juniors, Argentina	v Deportivo Cali, Colombia		4-0	0-0

1979 XX
Group 1
			Home	Playoff	Away
Millonarios Bogota, Colombia	v Deportivo Cali, Colombia		1-1		0-2
Millonarios Bogota, Colombia	v Independiente, Argentina		3-3		1-4
Millonarios Bogota, Colombia	v Quilmes, Argentina		1-0		2-1
Deportivo Cali, Colombia	v Quilmes, Argentina		3-2		1-3
Deportivo Cali, Colombia	v Independiente, Argentina		1-0		0-1
Quilmes, Argentina	v Independiente, Argentina		1-2		0-2

Independiente	6	4	1	1	12-6	9
Deportivo Cali	6	3	1	2	8-7	7
Millonarios	6	2	2	2	8-11	6
Quilmes	6	1	0	5	7-11	2

Group 2
			Home	Away
Olimpia, Paraguay	v Sol de America, Paraguay		1-0	1-0
Olimpia, Paraguay	v Jorge Wilsterman Cochabamba, Bolivia	4-2	2-0
Olimpia, Paraguay	v **Bolivar La Paz, Bolivia**		3-0	1-2
Bolivar La Paz, Bolivia	v Jorge Wilsterman Cochabamba, Bolivia	4-0	6-0
Bolivar La Paz, Bolivia	v Sol de America, Paraguay		4-1	2-2
Jorge Wilsterman Cochabamba, Bolivia	v Sol de America, Paraguay	2-3	1-2

Olimpia	6	5	0	1	12-4	10
Bolivar	6	4	1	1	18-7	9
Sol de America	6	2	1	3	8-11	5
Jorge Wilsterman	6	0	0	6	5-21	0

Group 3
			Home	Away
Alianza Lima, Peru	v Universitario Lima, Peru		3-6	0-1
Alianza Lima, Peru	v Guarani FC Campinas, Brazil		0-3	1-2
Alianza Lima, Peru	v **Palmeiras Sao Paulo, Brazil**		2-4	0-4
Universitario Lima, Peru	v Guarani FC Campinas, Brazil		3-0	1-6
Universitario Lima, Peru	v Palmeiras Sao Paulo, Brazil		2-5	2-1
Palmeiras Sao Paulo, Brazil	v Guarani FC Campinas, Brazil		1-4	0-1

Guarani Campinas	6	5	0	1	16-6	10
Universitario Lima	6	4	0	2	15-15	8
Palmeiras	6	3	0	3	15-11	6
Alianza	6	0	0	6	6-20	0

LIBERTADORES RESULTS

Group 4									
Galicia Caracas, Venezuela	v Portuguesa Acarigua, Venezuela					1-1			1-1
Galicia Caracas, Venezuela	v Palestino, Chile					1-1			0-5
Galicia Caracas, Venezuela	v O'Higgins Rancagua, Chile					0-1			0-6
Portuguesa Acarigua, Venezuela	v O'Higgins Rancagua, Chile					1-1			1-1
Portuguesa Acarigua, Venezuela	v Palestino, Chile					0-2			0-6
O'Higgins Rancagua, Chile	v Palestino, Chile					1-1			0-1

Palestino	6	4	2	0	16-2	10
O'Higgins	6	2	3	1	10-4	7
Portuguesa Acarigua	6	0	4	2	4-12	4
Galicia Caracas	6	0	3	3	3-15	3

Group 5			
Nacional Quito, Ecuador	v Tecnico Universitario Ambato, Ecuador	2-1	2-2
Nacional Quito, Ecuador	v Penarol, Uruguay	0-2	1-2
Nacional Quito, Ecuador	v Nacional, Uruguay	1-0	0-3
Penarol, Uruguay	v Tecnico Universitario Ambato, Ecuador	4-0	1-0
Penarol, Uruguay	v Nacional, Uruguay	1-1	0-0
Nacional, Uruguay	v Tecnico Universitario Ambato, Ecuador	2-0	1-1

Penarol	6	4	2	0	10-2	10
Nacional	6	2	3	1	7-3	7
Nacional Quito	6	2	1	3	6-10	5
Tecnico Univ	6	0	2	4	4-12	2

Semi-finals

Group 1			
Palestino, Chile	v Guarani FC Campinas, Brazil	0-0	2-2
Olimpia, Paraguay	v Guarani FC Campinas, Brazil	2-1	1-1
Palestino, Chile	v Olimpia, Paraguay	0-2	0-3

Olimpia	4	3	1	0	8-2	7
Guarani Campinas	4	0	3	1	4-5	3
Palestino	4	0	2	2	2-7	2

Group 2				
Penarol, Uruguay	v Independiente, Argentina	0-0		0-1
Boca Juniors, Argentina	v Penarol, Uruguay	1-0		0-0
Boca Juniors, Argentina	v Independiente, Argentina	2-0	1-0*	0-1
	* play off for Final place			

Boca Juniors	4	2	1	1	3-1	5
Independiente	4	2	1	1	2-2	5
Penarol	4	0	2	2	0-2	2

Final			
Olimpia, Paraguay	v Boca Juniors, Argentina	2-0	0-0

1980 XXI

Group 1		Home	Playoff	Away
Sporting Cristal, Peru	v Atletico Chalaco Callao, Peru	0-0		2-0
Sporting Cristal, Peru	v Velez Sarsfield, Argentina	0-1		0-2
Sporting Cristal, Peru	v River Plate, Argentina	1-2		2-3
Atletico Chalaco Callao, Peru	v Velez Sarsfield, Argentina	0-2		2-5
Atletico Chalaco Callao, Peru	v River Plate, Argentina	0-2		0-3
Velez Sarsfirld, Argentina	v River Plate, Argentina	0-0		0-0

Velez Sarsfield	6	4	2	0	10-2*	10
River Plate	6	4	2	0	10-4	10
Sporting Cristal	6	1	1	4	5-8	3
Atletico Chalaco	6	0	1	5	2-14	1
* qualified on goal difference						

Group 2			
Oriente Petrolero Santa Cr, Bolivia	v The Strongest, Bolivia	1-0	2-3
Oriente Petrolero Santa Cr, Bolivia	v Nacional, Uruguay	1-3	0-5
Oriente Petrolero Santa Cr, Bolivia	v Defensor, Uruguay	0-1	1-1
The Strongest, Bolivia	v Nacional, Uruguay	3-0	0-2
The Strongest, Bolivia	v Defensor, Uruguay	2-0	1-1
Nacional, Uruguay	v Defensor, Uruguay	1-0	3-0

Nacional	6	5	0	1	14-4	10	
The Strongest	6	3	1	2	9-6	7	
Defensor	6	1	2	3	3-8	4	
Oriente Petrolero	6	1	1	4	5-13	3	

Group 3

Galicia Caracas, Venezuela	v Tachira San Cristobal, Venezuela	1-0	1-0
Galicia Caracas, Venezuela	v Internacional Porto Alegre, Brazil	2-1	0-2
Galicia Caracas, Venezuela	v Vasco de Gama Rio de Jan, Brazil	0-0	0-4
Tachira San Cristobal, Venezuela	v **Internacional Porto Alegre, Brazil**	0-1	0-4
Tachira San Cristobal, Venezuela	v Vasco de Gama Rio de Jan, Brazil	0-1	0-1
Internacional Porto Alegre, Brazil	v Vasco de Gama Rio de Jan, Brazil	2-1	0-0

Internacional	6	4	1	1	10-3	9
Vasco de Gama	6	3	2	1	7-2	8
Galicia Caracas	6	3	1	2	4-7	7
Tachira	6	0	0	6	0-9	0

Group 4

Independiente Santa Fe, Colombia	v America de Cali, Colombia	1-1	0-1
Independiente Santa Fe, Colombia	v Universidad Catolica Quito, Ecuador	1-0	0-1
Independiente Santa Fe, Colombia	v Emelec Guayaquil, Ecuador	1-2	2-0
America de Cali, Colombia	v **Universidad Catolica Quito, Ecuador**	1-0	2-4
America de Cali, Colombia	v Emelec Guayaquil, Ecuador	4-1	2-1
Universidad Catolica Quito, Ecuador	v Emelec Guayaquil, Ecuador	5-0	0-1

America de Cali	6	4	1	1	11-7	9
Univ Catolica	6	3	0	3	10-5	6
Independiente	6	2	1	3	5-5	5
Emelec	6	2	0	4	5-14	4

Group 5

Colo Colo, Chile	v O'Higgins Rancagua, Chile	1-1	1-3
Colo Colo, Chile	v Sol de America, Paraguay	1-1	1-2
Colo Colo, Chile	v Cerro Porteno, Paraguay	2-1	3-5
O'Higgins Rancagua, Chile	v **Sol de America, Paraguay**	2-0	4-1
O'Higgins Rancagua, Chile	v Cerro Porteno, Paraguay	0-0	0-1
Sol de America, Paraguay	v Cerro Porteno, Paraguay	2-1	0-0

O'Higgins	6	2	2	2	8-6*	6
Cerro Porteno	6	2	2	2	9-7	6
Colo Colo	6	2	2	2	11-11	6
Sol de America	6	2	2	2	6-9	6

* qualified on goal difference

Semi-finals

Group 1

Velez Sarsfield, Argentina	v Internacional Porto Alegre, Brazil	0-1	1-3
America de Cali, Colombia	v **Velez Sarsfield, Argentina**	0-0	0-0
America de Cali, Colombia	v Internacional Porto Alegre, Brazil	0-0	0-0

Internacional	4	2	2	0	4-1	6
America de Cali	4	0	4	0	0-0	4
Velez Sarsfield	4	0	2	2	1-4	2

Group 2

Nacional, Uruguay	v O'Higgins Rancagua, Chile	2-0	1-0
O'Higgins Rancagua, Chile	v Olimpia, Paraguay	0-1	0-2
Olimpia, Paraguay	v Nacional, Uruguay	0-1	1-1

Nacional	4	3	1	0	5-1	7
Olimpia	4	2	1	1	4-2	5
O'Higgins	4	0	0	4	0-6	0

Final

Nacional, Uruguay	v Internacional Porto Alegre, Brazil	1-0	0-0

LIBERTADORES RESULTS

1981 XXII			Home	Playoff	Away
Group 1	River Plate, Argentina	v Rosario Central, Argentina	3-2		1-0
	River Plate, Argentina	v Junior Barranquilla, Colombia	3-0		0-0
	River Plate, Argentina	v Deportivo Cali, Colombia	1-2		1-2
	Rosario Central, Argentina	v Deportivo Cali, Colombia	2-1		0-1
	Rosario Central, Argentina	v Junior Barranquilla, Colombia	5-0		2-1
	Junior Barranquilla, Colombia	v Deportivo Cali, Colombia	1-0		1-4

Deportivo Cali	6	4	0	2	10-6	8
River Plate	6	3	1	2	9-6	7
Rosario central	6	3	0	3	11-7	6
Junior Barranquilla	6	2	1	3	3-14	5

Group 2	Sporting Cristal, Peru	v Atletico Torino Talara, Peru	2-1		2-0
	Sporting Cristal, Peru	v Cobreloa Calama, Chile	0-0		1-6
	Sporting Cristal, Peru	v Universidad de Chile, Chile	2-2		1-1
	Atletico Torino Talara, Peru	v Cobreloa Calama, Chile	1-1		1-6
	Atletico Torino Talara, Peru	v Universidad de Chile, Chile	1-2		0-3
	Cobreloa Calama, Chile	v Universidad de Chile, Chile	1-0		0-0

Cobreloa	6	3	3	0	14-3	9
Sporting Cristal	6	3	2	1	9-10	8
Univ de Chile	6	2	2	2	8-6	6
Atletico Torino	6	0	1	5	4-16	1

Group 3	Cerro Porteno, Paraguay	v Olimpia, Paraguay	0-0		0-3
	Cerro Porteno, Paraguay	v Flamengo Rio de Janeiro, Brazil	2-4		2-5
	Cerro Porteno, Paraguay	v Atletico Mineiro Belo Hor, Brazil	2-2		2-2
	Olimpia, Paraguay	v Flamengo Rio de Janeiro, Brazil	0-0		1-1
	Olimpia, Paraguay	v Atletico Mineiro Belo Hor, Brazil	0-0		0-1
	Flamengo Rio de Janeiro, Brazil	v Atletico Mineiro Belo Hor, Brazil	2-2	0-0*	2-2

* abandoned after 35 minutes, Mineiro having 5 players sent off

Flamengo	6	2	4	0	14-9	8
Atletico Mineiro	6	2	4	0	8-6	8
Cerro Porteno	6	1	2	3	9-12	4
Olimpia	6	0	4	2	1-5	4

Group 4	Barcelona Sporting Guayaquil, Ecuador	v Tecnico Universitario Ambato, Ecuador	2-1		1-4
	Barcelona Sporting Guayaquil, Ecuador	v Jorge Wilsterman Cochabamba Bolivia	3-0		0-1
	Barcelona Sporting Guayaquil, Ecuador	v The Strongest, Bolivia	2-1		0-1
	Tecnico Universitario Ambato, Ecuador	v Jorge Wilsterman Cochabamba, Bolivia	1-2		1-3
	Tecnico Universitario Ambato, Ecuador	v The Strongest, Bolivia	2-3		2-4
	Jorge Wilsterman Cochabamba, Bolivia	v The Strongest, Bolivia	3-2	4-1*	0-2

* play off for semi-final place

Jorge Wilsterman	6	4	0	2	9-9	8
The Strongest	6	4	0	2	13-9	8
Barcelona	6	3	0	3	8-8	6
Tecnico Univ	6	1	0	5	11-15	2

Group 5	Estudiantes de Merida, Venezuela	v Portuguesa Acarigua, Venezuela	1-1		0-0
	Estudiantes de Merida, Venezuela	v Bella Vista, Uruguay	1-4		1-3
	Estudiantes de Merida, Venezuela	v Penarol, Uruguay	0-2		2-4
	Portuguesa Acarigua, Venezuela	v Penarol, Uruguay	0-1		0-3
	Portuguesa Acarigua, Venezuela	v Bella Vista, Uruguay	0-4		0-4
	Penarol, Uruguay	v Bella Vista, Uruguay	3-1		0-0

Penarol	6	5	1	0	13-3	11
Bella Vista	6	4	1	1	16-5	9
Estudiantes	6	0	2	4	5-14	2
Portuguesa Acarigua	6	0	2	4	1-13	2

Semi-finals					
Group 1	Penarol, Uruguay	v Nacional, Uruguay	1-1		1-1
	Nacional, Uruguay	v Cobreloa Calama, Chile	1-2		1-2
	Penarol, Uruguay	v Cobreloa Calama, Chile	0-1		2-4

Cobreloa	4	3	1	0	9-5	7
Nacional	4	0	3	1	5-6	3
Penarol	4	0	2	2	4-7	2

			Home	Playoff	Away
Group 2	Deportivo Cali, Colombia	v Flamengo Rio de Janeiro, Brazil	0-1		0-3
	Jorge Wilsterman Cochabamba, Bolivia	v Flamengo Rio de Janeiro, Brazil	1-2		1-4
	Deportivo Cali, Colombia	v Jorge Wilsterman Cochabamb, Bolivia	1-0		1-1

Flamengo	4	4	0	0	10-2	8
Deportivo Cali	4	1	1	2	2-5	3
Jorge Wilsterman	4	0	1	3	3-8	1

Final	Flamengo Rio de Janeiro, Brazil	v Cobreloa Calama, Chile	2-1	2-0*	0-1
					* in Montevideo

1982 XXIII

			Home	Playoff	Away
Group 1	River Plate, Argentina	v Boca Juniors, Argentina	1-0		0-0
	River Plate, Argentina	v The Strongest, Bolivia	4-1		0-1
	The Strongest, Bolivia	v Jorge Wilsterman Cochabamb, Bolivia	1-1		2-1
	Jorge Wilsterman Cochabamb, Bolivia	v Boca Juniors, Argentina	1-0		2-2
	The Strongest, Bolivia	v Boca Juniors, Argentina	1-0		0-1
	Jorge Wilsterman Cochabamb, Bolivia	v River Plate, Argentina	0-1		0-3

River Plate	6	5	1	0	9-2	11
The Strongest	6	2	1	3	6-7	5
Boca Juniors	6	1	2	3	3-5	4
Jorge Wilsterman	6	1	2	3	5-9	4

			Home		Away
Group 2	Penarol, Uruguay	v Defensor, Uruguay	0-0		3-0
	Sao Paulo FC, Brazil	v Gremio Porto Alegre, Brazil	2-2		0-0
	Defensor, Uruguay	v Sao Paulo FC, Brazil	1-3		1-2
	Penarol, Uruguay	v Sao Paulo FC, Brazil	1-0		1-0
	Defensor, Uruguay	v Gremio Porto Alegre, Brazil	0-0		np
	Penarol, Uruguay	v Gremio Porto Alegre, Brazil	1-0		1-3

Penarol	6	4	1	1	7-3	9
Sao Paulo FC	6	2	2	2	7-6	6
Gremio Porto Alegre	6	1	3	1	5-4	5
Defensor	6	0	2	3	2-8	2

			Home		Away
Group 3	Tachira San Cristobal, Venezuela	v Estudiantes de Merida, Venezuela	0-0		0-1
	Nacional Medellin, Colombia	v Tolima Ibague, Colombia	0-3		0-0
	Estudiantes de Merida, Venezuela	v Nacional Medellin, Colombia	1-3		0-2
	Tachira San Cristobal, Venezuela	v Tolima Ibague, Colombia	0-2		2-2
	Tachira San Cristobal, Venezuela	v Nacional Medellin, Colombia	0-0		0-1
	Estudiantes de Merida, Venezuela	v Tolima Ibague, Colombia	1-1		0-1

Tolima	6	3	3	0	9-3	9
Nacional Medellin	6	3	2	1	6-4	8
Estudiantes	6	1	2	3	3-7	4
Tachira	6	0	3	3	3-7	3

			Home		Away
Group 4	Barcelona Sporting Guayaquil, Ecuador	v Liga Dep Universitaria, Ecuador	4-1		2-4
	Colo Colo, Chile	v Cobreloa Calama, Chile	0-0		0-2
	Barcelona Sporting Guayaquil, Ecuador	v Cobreloa Calama, Chile	1-1		0-3
	Liga Dep Universitaria, Ecuador	v Colo Colo, Chile	2-2		0-1
	Liga Dep Universitaria, Ecuador	v Cobreloa Calama, Chile	0-0		1-3
	Barcelona Sporting Guayaquil, Ecuador	v Colo Colo, Chile	1-3		0-2

Cobreloa	6	3	3	0	9-2	9
Colo Colo	6	3	2	1	8-5	8
LD Universitaria	6	1	2	3	8-12	4
Barcelona	6	1	1	4	8-14	3

LIBERTADORES RESULTS

Group 5	Mariano Melgar FC Arequipa, Peru	v Deportivo Municipal Lima, Peru	2-1	2-0
	Olimpia, Paraguay	v Sol de America, Paraguay	1-1	1-1
	Deportivo Municipal Lima, Peru	v Olimpia, Paraguay	1-2	0-1
	Mariano Melgar FC Arequipa, Peru	v Olimpia, Paraguay	0-3	0-4
	Deportivo Municipal Lima, Peru	v Sol de America, Paraguay	0-3	1-2
	Mariano Melgar FC Arequipa, Peru	v Sol de America, Paraguay	3-2	2-0

Olimpia	6	4	2	0	12-3	10
Mariano Melgar FC	6	4	0	2	9-10	8
Sol de America	6	2	2	2	9-8	6
Municipal Lima	6	0	0	6	3-12	0

Semi-finals

Group 1	Flamengo Rio de Janeiro, Brazil	v River Plate, Argentina	4-2	3-0
	Penarol, Uruguay	v Flamengo Rio de Janeiro, Brazil	1-0	1-0
	River Plate, Argentina	v Penarol, Uruguay	2-4	1-2

Penarol	4	4	0	0	8-3	8
Flamengo	4	2	0	2	7-4	4
River Plate	4	0	0	4	5-13	0

Group 2	Tolima Ibague, Colombia	v Cobreloa Calama, Chile	1-0	0-3
	Tolima Ibague, Colombia	v Olimpia, Paraguay	1-1	0-2
	Olimpia, Paraguay	v Cobreloa Calama, Chile	1-1	0-1

Cobreloa	4	2	1	1	5-2	5
Olimpia	4	1	2	1	4-3	4
Tolima	4	1	1	2	2-6	3

Final	Penarol, Uruguay	v Cobreloa Calama, Chile	0-0	1-0

1983 XXIV			**Home**	**Playoff**	**Away**
Group 1	Colo Colo, Chile	v Cobreloa Calama, Chile	2-1		0-2
	Colo Colo, Chile	v FC Oeste, Argentina	1-0		0-1
	Cobreloa Calama, Chile	v **Estudiantes La Plata, Argentina**	3-0		0-2
	Cobreloa Calama, Chile	v FC Oeste, Argentina	2-1		0-1
	Colo Colo, Chile	v Estudiantes La Plata, Argentina	1-0		1-4
	Estudiantes La Plata, Argentina	v FC Oeste, Argentina	0-0		2-1

Estudiantes	6	3	1	2	8-6	7
Cobreloa	6	3	0	3	8-6	6
Colo Colo	6	3	0	3	5-8	6
FC Oeste	6	2	1	3	4-5	5

Group 2	Blooming Santa Cruz, Bolivia	v Gremio Porto Alegre, Brazil	0-2	0-2
	Bolivar La Paz, Bolivia	v Gremio Porto Alegre, Brazil	1-2	1-3
	Blooming Santa Cruz, Bolivia	v **Flamengo Rio de Janeiro, Brazil**	0-0	1-7
	Bolivar La Paz, Bolivia	v Flamengo Rio de Janeiro, Brazil	3-1	2-5
	Blooming Santa Cruz, Bolivia	v Bolivar La Paz, Bolivia	3-0	0-6
	Gremio Porto Alegre, Brazil	v Flamengo Rio de Janeiro, Brazil	1-1	3-1

Gremio Porto Alegre	6	5	1	0	18-4	11
Flamengo	6	2	2	2	15-10	6
Bolivar	6	2	0	4	13-14	4
Blooming	6	1	1	4	4-17	3

Group 3	America de Cali, Colombia	v Tolima Ibague, Colombia	1-1	2-0
	Alianza Lima, Peru	v Universitario Lima, Peru	2-1	0-0
	Universitario Lima, Peru	v **Tolima Ibague, Colombia**	2-2	1-1
	Alianza Lima, Peru	v Tolima Ibague, Colombia	0-1	0-0
	Alianza Lima, Peru	v America de Cali, Colombia	1-2	0-2
	Universitario Lima, Peru	v America de Cali, Colombia	1-1	0-2

America de Cali	6	4	2	0	10-3	10
Tolima	6	1	4	1	5-6	6
Universitario Lima	6	0	4	2	5-8	4
Alianza	6	1	2	3	3-6	4

Group 4									
San Cristobal, Venezuela	v Tachira San Cristobal, Venezuela				2-0				0-0
Nacional Quito, Ecuador	v Barcelona Sporting Guayaquil, Ecuador				3-1				0-2
San Cristobal, Venezuela	v **Barcelona Sporting Guayaquil, Ecuador**				2-0				3-3
Tachira San Cristobal, Venezuela	v Barcelona Sporting Guayaquil, Ecuador				1-1				np
San Cristobal, Venezuela	v Nacional Quito, Ecuador				1-0				0-1
Tachira San Cristobal, Venezuela	v Nacional Quito, Ecuador				0-0				0-3

San Cristobal	6	3	2	1	8-4	8
Nacional Quito	6	3	1	2	7-4	7
Barcelona	5	1	2	2	7-9	4
Tachira	5	0	3	2	1-6	3

Group 5					
Nacional Asuncion, Paraguay	v Nacional, Uruguay	0-3			2-4
Wanderers, Uruguay	v Nacional, Uruguay	1-1	0-2*		1-0
				* play off for semi-final place	
Nacional Asuncion, Paraguay	v Olimpia, Paraguay	2-1			0-0
Wanderers, Uruguay	v Nacional Asuncion, Paraguay	3-1			1-1
Olimpia, Paraguay	v Nacional, Uruguay	0-1			0-3
Wanderers, Uruguay	v Olimpia, Paraguay	0-0			3-2

Nacional	6	4	1	1	12-5	9
Wanderers	6	3	3	0	10-5	9
Nacional Asuncion	6	1	2	3	6-12	4
Olimpia	6	0	2	4	3-9	2

Semi-finals

Group 1			
San Cristobal, Venezuela	v Penarol, Uruguay	0-0	0-1
San Cristobal, Venezuela	v Nacional, Uruguay	1-2	1-5
Penarol, Uruguay	v Nacional, Uruguay	2-0	2-1

Penarol	4	3	1	0	5-1	7
Nacional	4	2	0	2	8-6	4
San Cristobal	4	0	1	3	2-8	1

Group 2			
Estudiantes La Plata, Argentina	v America de Cali, Colombia	2-0	0-0
Estudiantes La Plata, Argentina	v **Gremio Porto Alegre, Brazil**	3-3	1-2
Gremio Porto Alegre, Brazil	v America de Cali, Colombia	2-1	0-1

Gremio Porto Alegre	4	2	1	1	7-6	5
Estudiantes	4	1	2	1	6-5	4
America de Cali	4	1	1	2	2-4	3

Final			
Gremio Porto Alegre, Brazil	v Penarol, Uruguay	2-1	1-1

1984 XXV

Group 1		Home	Playoff	Away
Independiente, Argentina	v Estudiantes La Plata, Argentina	4-1		1-1
Independiente, Argentina	v Olimpia, Paraguay	3-2		0-1
Independiente, Argentina	v **Sportivo Luqueno Luque, Paraguay**	2-0		1-0
Estudiantes La Plata, Argentina	v Olimpia, Paraguay	0-1		1-2
Estudiantes La Plata, Argentina	v Sportivo Luqueno Luque, Paraguay	1-1		0-0
Olimpia, Paraguay	v Sportivo Luqueno Luque, Paraguay	0-0		2-1

Independiente	6	4	1	1	11-5	9
Olimpia	6	4	1	1	8-5	9
Sportivo Luqueno	6	0	3	3	2-6	3
Estudiantes	6	0	3	3	4-9	3

Group 2			
Universidad Catolica, Chile	v O'Higgins Rancagua, Chile	2-0	2-0
Universidad de Chile, Chile	v Bolivar La Paz, Bolivia	3-1	2-3
Universidad de Chile, Chile	v **Blooming Santa Cruz, Bolivia**	0-0	2-1
O'Higgins Rancagua, Chile	v Bolivar La Paz, Bolivia	0-0	1-5
Bolivar La Paz, Bolivia	v Blooming Santa Cruz, Bolivia	0-0	1-2
O'Higgins Rancagua, Chile	v Blooming Santa Cruz, Bolivia	3-4	0-3

Univ Catolica	6	4	1	1	11-5	9
Blooming	6	3	2	1	10-6	8
Bolivar	6	2	2	2	10-8	6
O'Higgins	6	0	1	5	4-16	1

LIBERTADORES RESULTS

Group 3					
Flamengo Rio de Janeiro, Brazil	v	Santos FC Sao Paulo, Brazil		4-1	5-0
Flamengo Rio de Janeiro, Brazil	v	America de Cali, Colombia		4-2	1-1
Flamengo Rio de Janeiro, Brazil	v	Junior Barranquilla, Colombia		3-1	2-1
Santos FC Sao Paulo, Brazil	v	America de Cali, Colombia		0-1	0-1
Santos FC Sao Paulo, Brazil	v	Junior Barranquilla, Colombia		1-3	3-0
America de Cali, Colombia	v	Junior Barranquilla, Colombia		2-0	1-4

Flamengo	6	5	1	0	19-6	11
America de Cali	6	3	1	2	8-9	7
Junior Barranquilla	6	2	0	4	9-12	4
Santos FC	6	1	0	5	5-15	2

Group 4					
Danubio, Uruguay	v	Nacional, Uruguay		0-1	0-1
Nacional Quito, Ecuador	v	Nueve de Octubre Guayaquil, Ecuador		3-1	2-2
Nueve de Octubre, Ecuador	v	Danubio, Uruguay		2-2	1-5
Nacional Quito, Ecuador	v	Nacional, Uruguay		3-1	1-1
Nacional Quito, Ecuador	v	Danubio, Uruguay		3-0	0-1
Nueve de Octubre, Ecuador	v	Nacional, Uruguay		1-3	0-6

Nacional	6	4	1	1	13-5	9
Nacional Quito	6	3	2	1	12-6	8
Danubio	6	2	1	3	8-8	5
Nueve de Octubre	6	0	2	4	7-21	2

Group 5						
Sporting Cristal, Peru	v	Mariano Melgar FC Arequipa Peru		3-2		0-2
Sporting Cristal, Peru	v	Universidad Los Andes (ULA), Venezuela	2-0	1-2*	1-0
					* play off for semi-final place
Sporting Cristal, Peru	v	Portuguesa Acarigua, Venezuela		2-1		0-1
Mariano Melgar FC Arequipa Peru	v	Universidad Los Andes (ULA), Venezuela	0-1		0-1
Mariano Melgar FC Arequipa, Peru	v	Portuguesa Acarigua, Venezuela		1-2		0-4
Universidad Los Andes (ULA), Venezuela	v	Portuguesa Acarigua, Venezuela	2-0		2-1

Univ Los Andes	6	4	0	2	6-4	8
Sporting Cristal	6	4	0	2	8-6	8
Portuguesa Acarigua	6	3	0	3	9-7	6
Mariano Melgar FC	6	1	0	5	5-11	2

Semi-finals

Group 1					
Nacional, Uruguay	v	Independiente, Argentina		1-1	0-1
Universidad Catolica, Chile	v	Independiente, Argentina		0-0	1-2
Nacional, Uruguay	v	Universidad Catolica, Chile		2-0	np

Independiente	4	2	2	0	4-2	6
Nacional	3	1	1	1	3-2	3
Univ Catolica	3	0	1	2	1-4	1

Group 2						
Flamengo Rio de Janeiro, Brazil	v	Universidad Los Andes (ULA), Venezuela	2-1		3-0
Flamengo Rio de Janeiro, Brazil	v	Gremio Porto Alegre, Brazil	3-1	0-0*	1-5
					* play off for Final goal difference
Universidad Los Andes (ULA), Venezuela	v	Gremio Porto Alegre, Brazil	0-2		1-6

Gremio Porto Alegre	4	3	0	1	14-5	7
Flamengo	4	3	0	1	9-7	7
Univ Los Andes	4	0	0	4	2-13	0

Final					
Independiente, Argentina	v	Gremio Porto Alegre, Brazil		0-0	1-0

1985 XXVI

			Home	Playoff	Away
Group 1					
Vasco de Gama, Brazil	v	Fluminense Rio de Janeiro, Brazil	3-3		0-0
Argentinos Juniors, Argentina	v	Vasco de Gama Rio de Jan, Brazil	2-2		2-1
FC Oeste, Argentina	v	Fluminense Rio de Janeiro, Brazil	1-0		0-0
Argentinos Juniors, Argentina	v	Fluminense Rio de Janeiro, Brazil	1-0		1-0
Vasco de Gama, Brazil	v	FC Oeste, Argentina	0-2		0-2
Argentinos Juniors, Argentina	v	FC Oeste, Argentina	0-1	3-1*	3-1
					* play off for semi-final place

Argentinos Juniors	6	4	1	1	12-6	9
FC Oeste	6	4	1	1	7-3	9

Vasco de Gama	6	0	3	3	6-11	3
Fluminense	6	0	3	3	3-6	3

Group 2

Tachira San Cristobal, Venezuela	v Italia Caracas, Venezuela	0-0	3-1
Blooming Santa Cruz, Bolivia	v Oriente Petrolero Santa Cruz, Bolivia	1-1	1-0
Italia Caracas, Venezuela	v Blooming Santa Cruz, Bolivia	0-3	0-8
Tachira San Cristobal, Venezuela	v Oriente Petrolero Santa Cruz, Bolivia	1-1	2-3
Italia Caracas, Venezuela	v Oriente Petrolero Santa Cruz, Bolivia	0-3	1-3
Tachira San Cristobal, Venezuela	v Blooming Santa Cruz, Bolivia	0-1	1-6

Blooming	6	5	1	0	20-4	11
Oriente Petrolero	6	3	2	1	11-6	8
Tachira	6	1	2	3	9-12	4
Italia Caracas	6	0	1	5	2-20	1

Group 3

Penarol, Uruguay	v Bella Vista, Uruguay	1-0	2-0
Colo Colo, Chile	v Magallanes San Bernado, Chile	2-0	3-1
Magallanes San Bernado, Chile	v Penarol, Uruguay	1-1	0-1
Colo Colo, Chile	v Bella Vista, Argentina	2-0	1-2
Magallanes San Bernado, Chile	v Bella Vista, Argentina	2-1	1-0
Colo Colo, Chile	v Penarol, Uruguay	1-2	1-3

Penarol	6	5	1	0	10-3	11
Colo Colo	6	3	0	3	10-8	6
Magallanes	6	2	1	3	5-8	5
Bella Vista	6	1	0	5	3-9	2

Group 4

Guarani, Paraguay	v Cerro Porteno, Paraguay	0-0	1-3
America de Cali, Colombia	v Millonarios Bogota, Colombia	0-0	0-0
Guarani, Paraguay	v Millonarios Bogota, Colombia	2-0	1-5
Cerro Porteno, Paraguay	v Millonarios Bogota, Colombia	0-0	2-0
Cerro Porteno, Paraguay	v America de Cali, Colombia	0-0	0-2
Guarani, Paraguay	v America de Cali, Colombia	1-1	1-2

America de Cali	6	2	4	0	5-2	8
Cerro Porteno	6	2	3	1	5-3	7
Millonarios	6	1	3	2	5-5	5
Guarani	6	1	2	3	6-11	4

Group 5

Sport Boys Callao, Peru	v Universitario Lima, Peru	0-2	0-4
Nacional Quito, Ecuador	v Nueve de Octubre Guayaquil, Ecuador	3-1	1-0
Nueve de Octubre, Ecuador	v Universitario Lima, Peru	1-0	np
Nacional Quito, Ecuador	v Sport Boys Callao, Peru	2-0	2-1
Nueve de Octubre, Ecuador	v Sport Boys Callao, Peru	4-0	np
Nacional Quito, Ecuador	v Universitario Lima, Peru	4-1	np

Nacional Quito	5	5	0	0	12-3	10
Nueve de Octubre	4	2	0	2	6-4	4
Universitario Lima	4	2	0	2	7-5	4
Sport Boys Callao	5	0	0	5	1-14	0

Semi-finals

Group 1

Argentinos Juniors, Argentina	v Independiente, Argentina	2-2	2-1
Blooming Santa Cruz, Bolivia	v Argentinos Juniors, Argentina	1-1	0-1
Independiente, Argentina	v Blooming Santa Cruz, Bolivia	2-0	1-1

Argentinos Juniors	4	2	2	0	6-4	6
Independiente	4	1	2	1	6-5	4
Blooming	4	0	2	2	2-5	2

Group 2

Penarol, Uruguay	v America de Cali, Colombia	1-1	0-4
Nacional Quito, Ecuador	v America de Cali, Colombia	2-0	0-5
Penarol, Uruguay	v Nacional Quito, Ecuador	2-0	0-2

America de Cali	4	2	1	1	10-3	5
Nacional Quito	4	2	0	2	4-7	4
Penarol	4	1	1	2	3-7	3

Final

Argentinos Juniors, Argentina	v America de Cali, Colombia	1-0	1-1 5-4p 0-1

LIBERTADORES RESULTS

1986 XXVII

				Home	Playoff	Away
Group 1	Boca Juniors, Argentina	v River Plate, Argentina		1-1		0-1
	Boca Juniors, Argentina	v Wanderers, Uruguay		3-2		0-2
	Boca Juniors, Argentina	v Penarol, Uruguay		3-1		2-0
	River Plate, Argentiana	v Wanderers, Uruguay		4-2		2-0
	River Plate, Argentiana	v Penarol, Uruguay		3-1		2-0
	Wanderers, Uruguay	v Penarol, Uruguay		1-0		3-1

River Plate	6	5	1	0	13-4	11
Wanderers	6	3	0	3	10-10	6
Boca Juniors	6	2	2	2	7-8	6
Penarol	6	0	1	5	4-12	1

				Home		Away
Group 2	America de Cali, Colombia	v Deportivo Cali, Colombia		0-0		1-0
	America de Cali, Colombia	v Cobresal El Salvador, Chile		0-0		2-2
	Deportivo Cali, Colombia	v Cobresal El Salvador, Chile		1-1		1-1
	Universidad Catolica, Chile	v America de Cali, Colombia		1-3		1-2
	Cobresal El Salvador, Chile	v Universidad Catolica, Chile		1-1		1-0
	Deportivo Cali, Colombia	v Universidad Catolica, Chile		3-1		3-1

America de Cali	6	3	3	0	8-4	9
Deportivo Cali	6	2	3	1	8-5	7
Cobresal	6	1	5	0	6-5	7
Univ Catolica	6	0	1	5	5-13	1

				Home		Away
Group 3	Universitario Lima, Peru	v Univ Tecnica Cajarmarca, Peru		2-0		3-1
	Bolivar La Paz, Bolivia	v Jorge Wilsterman Cochabamb, Bolivia		2-0		2-1
	Bolivar La Paz, Bolivia	v Universitario Lima, Peru		4-0		0-3
	Bolivar La Paz, Bolivia	v Univ Tecnica Cajarmarca Peru		2-1		2-2
	Universitario Lima, Peru	v Jorge Wilsterman Cochabamb, Bolivia		1-2		0-4
	Univ Tecnica Cajarmarca, Peru	v Jorge Wilsterman Cochabamb, Bolivia		3-2		0-2

Bolivar	6	4	1	1	12-7	9
Jorge Wilsterman	6	3	0	3	11-8	6
Universitario Lima	6	3	0	3	9-11	6
Univ Tecnica	6	1	1	4	7-13	3

				Home		Away
Group 4	Barcelona Sporting Guayaquil, Ecuador	v Deportivo Quito, Ecuador		3-3		0-0
	Barcelona Sporting Guayaquil, Ecuador	v Coritiba FC Curitiba, Brazil		1-1		0-0
	Barcelona Sporting Guayaquil, Ecuador	v Bangu Rio de Janeiro, Brazil		1-0		2-1
	Deportivo Quito, Ecuador	v Coritiba FC Curitiba, Brazil		2-1		1-3
	Deportivo Quito, Ecuador	v Bangu Rio de Janeiro, Brazil		3-1		3-3
	Coritiba FC Curitiba, Brazil	v Bangu Rio de Janeiro, Brazil		np		1-1

Barcelona	6	2	4	0	7-5	8
Deportivo Quito	6	2	3	1	12-11	7
Coritiba FC	6	1	3	1	6-5	5
Bangu	6	0	2	3	6-10	2

				Home		Away
Group 5	Nacional Asuncion, Paraguay	v Olimpia, Paraguay		1-2		1-3

Semi-final

				Home	Playoff	Away
Group 1	River Plate, Argentina	v Argentinos Juniors, Argentina		0-2	0-0*	0-0
						* play off for Final place
	River Plate, Argentina	v Barcelona Sporting Guayaqu, Ecuador		4-1		3-0
	Argentinos Juniors, Argentina	v Barcelona Sporting Guayaqu, Ecuador		1-0		0-1

River Plate	4	2	1	1	7-3	5
Argentinos Juniors	4	2	1	1	3-1	5
Barcelona	4	1	0	3	2-8	2

				Home		Away
Group 2	Olimpia, Paraguay	v America de Cali, Colombia		1-1		0-1
	Olimpia, Paraguay	v Bolivar La Paz, Bolivia		3-1		1-1
	America de Cali, Colombia	v Bolivar La Paz, Bolivia		2-1		0-2

America de Cali	4	2	1	1	4-4	5
Olimpia	4	1	2	1	5-4	4
Bolivar	4	1	1	2	5-6	3

LIBERTADORES RESULTS

				Home	Playoff	Away
Final	River Plate, Argentina	v	America de Cali, Colombia	1-0		2-1

1987 XXVIII

Group 1

				Home	Playoff	Away
	Tachira San Cristobal, Venezuela	v	Estudiantes de Merida, Venezuela	3-2		3-0
	Independiente, Argentina	v	Rosario Central, Argentina	3-1		0-0
	Estudiantes de Merida, Venezuela	v	Rosario Central, Argentina	0-3		2-5
	Tachira San Cristobal, Venezuela	v	Independiente, Argentina	3-2		0-5
	Tachira San Cristobal, Venezuela	v	Rosario Central, Argentina	0-0		2-3
	Estudiantes de Merida, Venezuela	v	Independiente, Argentina	0-1		0-2

Independiente	6	4	1	1	13-4	9
Rosario Central	6	3	2	1	12-7	8
Tachira	6	3	1	2	11-12	7
Estudiantes Merida	6	0	0	6	4-17	0

Group 2

			Home	Playoff	Away
America de Cali, Colombia	v	Deportivo Cali, Colombia	1-0	0-0 4-2p*	1-2

* play off for semi-final place

			Home	Playoff	Away
The Strongest, Bolivia	v	Oriente Petrolero Santa Cruz, Bolivia		3-2	1-2
The Strongest, Bolivia	v	Deportivo Cali, Colombia	2-1		0-4
Oriente Petrolero Santa Cruz, Bolivia	v	Deportivo Cali, Colombia	0-1		1-5
The Strongest, Bolivia	v	America de Cali, Colombia	1-1		0-6
Oriente Petrolero Santa Cruz, Bolivia	v	America de Cali, Colombia	1-1		1-3

America de Cali	6	3	2	1	13-5	8
Deportivo Cali	6	4	0	2	13-5	8
The Strongest	6	2	1	3	7-16	5
Oriente Petrolero	6	1	1	4	7-14	3

Group 3

			Home	Away
Sao Paulo FC, Brazil	v	Guarani FC Campinas, Brazil	2-2	1-3
Colo Colo, Chile	v	Cobreloa Calama, Chile	0-0	0-1
Guarani FC Campinas, Brazil	v	Cobreloa Calama, Chile	0-0	1-3
Sao Paulo FC, Brazil	v	Cobreloa Calama, Chile	2-1	1-3
Guarani FC Campinas, Brazil	v	Colo Colo, Chile	0-0	0-2
Sao Paulo FC, Brazil	v	Colo Colo, Chile	1-2	2-2

Cobreloa	6	3	2	1	8-4	8
Colo Colo	6	2	3	1	6-4	7
Guarani FC Campinas	6	1	3	2	6-8	5
Sao Paulo FC	6	1	1	2	3	9-13	4

Group 4

			Home	Away
Sol de America, Paraguay	v	Olimpia, Paraguay	1-2	2-2
Nacional Quito, Ecuador	v	Barcelona Sporting Guayaquil, Ecuador	2-0	1-2
Sol de America, Paraguay	v	Nacional Quito, Ecuador	2-1	1-4
Olimpia, Paraguay	v	Barcelona Sporting Guayaquil, Ecuador	1-0	2-3
Olimpia, Paraguay	v	Nacional Quito, Ecuador	2-0	0-4
Sol de America, Paraguay	v	Barcelona Sporting Guayaquil, Ecuador	1-2	0-1

Barcelona	6	4	0	2	8-7	8
Olimpia	6	3	1	2	9-10	7
Nacional Quito	6	3	0	3	12-7	6
Sol de America	6	1	1	4	7-12	3

Group 5

			Home	Away
Penarol, Uruguay	v	Progreso, Uruguay	3-2	1-1
Colegio San Agustin Lima, Peru	v	Alianza Lima, Peru	1-2	0-0
Colegio San Agustin Lima, Peru	v	Progreso, Uruguay	3-1	0-3
Alianza Lima, Peru	v	Progreso, Uruguay	0-0	0-0
Colegio San Agustin Lima, Peru	v	Penarol, Uruguay	1-1	0-2
Alianza Lima, Peru	v	Penarol, Uruguay	0-1	0-2

Penarol	6	4	2	0	10-4	10
Progreso	6	1	3	2	7-7	5
Alianza	6	1	3	2	2-5	5
Colegio	6	1	2	3	5-9	4

Semi-finals

Group 1

			Home	Away
Penarol, Uruguay	v	Independiente, Argentina	3-0	4-2
Penarol, Uruguay	v	River Plate, Argentina	0-0	0-1
Independiente, Argentina	v	River Plate, Argentina	2-1	0-0

49

LIBERTADORES RESULTS

Penarol	4	2	1	1	7-3	5			
River Plate	4	1	2	1	2-2	4			
Independiente	4	1	1	2	4-8	3			

Group 2	Cobreloa Calama, Chile	v America de Cali, Colombia	2-2	1-1
	Cobreloa Calama, Chile	v Barcelona Sporting Guayaquil, Ecuador 3-0	2-0
	America de Cali, Colombia	v Barcelona Sporting Guayaquil, Ecuador 4-0	2-0

America de Cali	4	2	2	0	9-3	6
Cobreloa	4	2	2	0	8-3	6
Barcelona	4	0	0	4	0-11	0

Final	Penarol, Uruguay	v America de Cali, Colombia	2-1	1-0*	0-2

* Santiago

1988 XXIX

Group 1			Home	Playoff	Away
Tachira San Cristobal, Venezuela	v Sport Maritimo, Venezuela	0-0		1-1
Universidad Catolica, Chile	v Colo Colo, Chile	1-0		2-2
Sport Maritimo, Venezuela	v Universidad Catolica, Chile	0-0		1-2
Sport Maritimo, Venezuela	v Colo Colo, Chile	0-1		0-1
Tachira San Cristobal, Venezuela	v Colo Colo, Chile	0-1		0-2
Tachira San Cristobal, Venezuela	v Universidad Catolica, Chile	0-1		1-3

Univ Catolica	6	4	2	0	9-4	10
Colo Colo	6	4	1	1	7-3	9
Sport Maritimo	6	0	3	3	2-5	3
Tachira	6	0	2	4	2-8	2

Group 2	Newell's Old Boys Rosario, Argentina	v San Lorenzo, Argentina	0-0	1-0*	0-0

* play off for semi final place

Newell's Old Boys Rosario, Argentina	v Barcelona Sporting Guayaquil, Ecuador 3-0	0-0
Newell's Old Boys Rosario, Argentina	v Filanbanco Guayaquil, Ecuador	1-0	1-1
San Lorenzo, Argentina	v Barcelona Sporting Guayaquil, Ecuador 2-1	0-2
San Lorenzo, Argentina	v Filanbanco Guayaquil, Ecuador	2-0	2-1
Barcelona Sporting Guayaquil, Ecuador v Filanbanco Guayaquil, Ecuador	4-2	2-1

Newell's Old Boys	6	2	4	0	6-1	8
San Lorenzo	6	3	2	1	6-4	8
Barcelona	6	3	1	2	9-8	7
Filanbanco	6	0	1	5	5-12	1

Group 3	Nacional, Uruguay	v Wanderers, Uruguay	1-0	0-0
	Nacional, Uruguay	v America de Cali, Colombia	2-0	0-0
	Nacional, Uruguay	v Millonarios Bogota, Colombia	4-1	1-6
	Wanderers, Uruguay	v America de Cali, Colombia	1-2	0-1
	Wanderers, Uruguay	v Millonarios Bogota, Colombia	2-1	0-3
	America de Cali, Colombia	v Millonarios Bogota, Colombia	2-1	3-2

America de Cali	6	4	1	1	8-6	9
Nacional	6	3	2	1	8-7	8
Millonarios	6	2	0	4	14-12	4
Wanderers	6	1	1	4	3-8	3

Group 4	Oriente Petrolero Santa Cruz, Bolivia	v Bolivar La Paz, Bolivia	2-1	1-3
	Oriente Petrolero Santa Cruz, Bolivia	v Olimpia, Paraguay	1-0	2-1
	Oriente Petrolero Santa Cruz, Bolivia	v Cerro Porteno, Paraguay	2-2	0-1
	Bolivar La Paz, Bolivia	v Olimpia, Paraguay	2-0	2-4
	Bolivar La Paz, Bolivia	v Cerro Porteno, Paraguay	2-0	2-3
	Olimpia, Paraguay	v Cerro Porteno, Paraguay	1-0	0-0

Oriente Petrolero	6	4	1	1	8-6	9
Cerro Porteno	6	2	2	2	6-7	6
Olimpia	6	2	1	3	6-7	5
Bolivar	6	2	0	4	12-10	4

LIBERTADORES RESULTS

Group 5									
Universitario Lima, Peru	v Alianza Lima, Peru					2-0		0-0
Sport Recife, Brazil	v Guarani FC Campinas, Brazil					0-1		1-4
Alianza Lima, Peru	v Guarani FC Campinas, Brazil					2-1		0-1
Universitario Lima, Peru	v Guarani FC Campinas, Brazil					1-1		1-1
Universitario Lima, Peru	v Sport Recife, Brazil					1-0		0-0
Alianza Lima, Peru	v Sport Recife, Brazil					0-1		0-5

Guarani FC Campinas	6	3	2	1	9-5	8
Universitario Lima	6	2	4	0	5-2	8
Sport Recife	6	2	1	3	7-6	5
Alianza	6	1	1	4	2-10	3

2nd Round

Universidad Catolica, Chile	v Nacional, Uruguay	1-1		0-0
San Lorenzo, Argentina	v Guarani FC Campinas, Brazil	1-1		1-0
Bolivar La Paz, Bolivia	v Newell's Old Boys Rosario, Argentina	1-0	2-3p	0-1
America de Cali, Colombia	v Universitario Lima, Peru	1-0		2-2
Oriente Petrolero Santa Cr, Bolivia	v Colo Colo, Chile	2-1		0-0

Quarter finals

Newell's Old Boys Rosario, Argentina	v Nacional, Uruguay	1-1		1-2
San Lorenzo, Argentina	v Penarol, Uruguay	1-0		0-0
America de Cali, Colombia	v Oriente Petrolero Santa Cruz, Bolivia	2-0		1-1

Semi-finals

Newell's Old Boys Rosario, Argentina	v San Lorenzo, Argentina	1-0		2-1
Nacional, Uruguay	v America de Cali, Colombia	1-0		1-1

Final

Nacional, Uruguay	v Newell's Old Boys Rosario, Argentina	3-0		0-1

1989 XXX

Group 1		Home	Playoff	Away
Olimpia, Paraguay	v Sol de America, Paraguay	0-0		4-5
Cobreloa Calama, Chile	v Colo Colo, Chile	2-0		2-2
Colo Colo, Chile	v Sol de America, Paraguay	3-1		0-1
Cobreloa Calama, Chile	v Sol de America, Paraguay	1-0		0-0
Olimpia, Paraguay	v Colo Colo, Chile	2-0		0-2
Cobreloa Calama, Chile	v Olimpia, Paraguay	2-0		0-2

Cobreloa	6	3	2	1	7-4	8
Sol de America	6	2	2	2	7-8	6
Olimpia	6	2	1	3	8-9	5
Colo Colo	6	2	1	3	7-8	5

Group 2				
Sport Maritimo, Venezuela	v Tachira San Cristobal, Venezuela	0-1		0-2
Esporte Clube Bahia, Brazil	v Internacional Porto Alegre, Brazil	2-1		1-0
Tachira San Cristobal, Venezuela	v Internacional Porto Alegre, Brazil	1-0		1-3
Sport Maritimo, Venezuela	v Internacional Porto Alegre, Brazil	1-1*		0-3
Sport Maritimo, Venezuela	v Esporte Clube Bahia Salvador, Brazil	0-0*		2-3
Tachira San Cristobal, Venezuela	v Esporte Clube Bahia Salvador, Brazil	1-1		1-4

Esporte Clube Bahia	6	4	2	0	11-4	10
Tachira	6	3	1	2	7-8	7
Internacional	6	2	1	3	8-5	5
Sport Maritimo	6	0	2	4	3-10	2

Group 3				
Emelec Guayaquil, Ecuador	v Deportivo Quito, Ecuador	1-0		0-1
Millonarios Bogota, Colombia	v Nacional Medellin, Colombia	1-1		2-0
Emelec Guayaquil, Ecuador	v Nacional Medellin, Colombia	1-1		1-3
Deportivo Quito, Ecuador	v Nacional Medellin, Colombia	1-1		1-2
Emelec Guayaquil, Ecuador	v Millonarios Bogota, Colombia	0-2		1-4
Deportivo Quito, Ecuador	v Millonarios Bogota, Colombia	0-0		1-3

Millonarios	6	4	2	0	12-3	10
Nacional Medellin	6	2	3	1	8-6	7
Deportivo Quito	6	1	2	3	4-7	4
Emelec	6	1	1	4	6-12	3

LIBERTADORES RESULTS

Group 4	Sporting Cristal, Peru	v Universitario Lima, Peru	1-0		0-4
	Racing Club Avellaneda, Argentina	v Boca Juniors, Argentina	0-0	1-3*	2-3

play off for 1st place

	Universitario Lima, Peru	v Boca Juniors, Argentina	1-0	0-2
	Sporting Cristal, Peru	v Boca Juniors, Argentina	1-0	3-4
	Universitario Lima, Peru	v Racing Club Avellaneda, Argentina	2-1	0-2
	Sporting Cristal, Peru	v Racing Club Avellaneda, Argentina	1-2	0-2

Boca Juniors	6	3	1	2	9-7	7
Racing Club	6	3	1	2	9-6	7
Universitario Lima	6	3	0	3	7-6	6
Sporting Cristal	6	2	0	4	6-12	4

Group 5	Danubio, Uruguay	v Penarol, Uruguay	4-1	0-2
	Bolivar La Paz, Bolivia	v The Strongest, Bolivia	0-0	0-0
	The Strongest, Bolivia	v Penarol, Uruguay	1-2	1-1
	Bolivar La Paz, Bolivia	v Penarol, Uruguay	3-0	0-5
	The Strongest, Bolivia	v Danubio, Uruguay	1-0	0-1
	Bolivar La Paz, Bolivia	v Danubio, Uruguay	3-1	0-1

Penarol	6	3	1	2	11-9	7
Danubio	6	3	0	3	7-7	6
Bolivar	6	2	2	2	6-7	6
The Strongest	6	1	3	2	3-4	5

2nd Round

	Internacional Porto Alegre, Brazil	v Penarol, Uruguay	6-2		2-1
	Sol de America, Paraguay	v Tachira San Cristobal, Venezuela	3-0	3-2p	0-3
	Deportivo Quito, Ecuador	v Cobreloa Calama, Chile	0-0		0-1
	Bolivar La Paz, Bolivia	v Millonarios Bogota, Colombia	1-0	3-4p	2-3
	Nacional Medellin, Colombia	v Racing Club Avellaneda, Argentina	2-0		1-2
	Olimpia, Paraguay	v Boca Juniors, Argentina	2-0	7-6p	3-5
	Universitario Lima, Peru	v Esporte Clube Bahia Salvador, Brazil	1-1		1-2
	Nacional, Uruguay	v Danubio, Uruguay	1-3		0-0

Quarter finals

	Cobreloa Calama, Chile	v Danubio, Uruguay	0-2	1-2
	Olimpia, Paraguay	v Sol de America, Paraguay	2-0	4-4
	Internacional Porto Alegre, Brazil	v Esporte Clube Bahia Salvador, Brazil	1-0	0-0
	Nacional Medellin, Colombia	v Millonarios Bogota, Colombia	1-0	1-1

Semi-finals

	Danubio, Uruguay	v Nacional Medellin, Colombia	0-0		0-6
	Olimpia, Paraguay	v Internacional Porto Alegre, Brazil	0-1	5-3p	3-2 aet

Final	Nacional Medellin, Colombia	v Olimpia, Paraguay	2-0	5-4p	0-2

1990 XXX			**Home**	**Playoff**	**Away**
Group 1	The Strongest, Bolivia	v Oriente Petrolero, Bolivia	2-0		0-1
	Barcelona Guayaquil, Ecuador	v Emelec, Ecuador	0-0		1-3
	The Strongest, Bolivia	v Emelec, Ecuador	4-3		0-1
	Oriente Petrolero, Bolivia	v Emelec, Ecuador	1-0		2-2
	Barcelona Guayaquil, Ecuador	v Oriente Petrolero, Bolivia	2-1		1-1
	The Strongest, Bolivia	v Barcelona Guayaquil, Ecuador	2-1		0-1

Emelec	6	2	2	2	9-8	6
The Strongest	6	3	0	3	8-7	6
Barcelona Guayaquil	6	2	2	2	6-7	6
Oriente Petrolero	6	2	2	2	6-7	6

Play-offs	Barcelona Guayaquil, Ecuador	v Oriente Petrolero, Bolivia	3-1	2-3

Barcelona qualify on away goals

Group 2	River Plate, Argentina	v Independiente, Argentina	0-0	0-1

Independiente	2	1	1	0	1-0	3
River Plate	2	0	1	1	0-1	1

LIBERTADORES RESULTS

Group 3	Universidad Catolica, Chile	v Colo Colo, Chile	0-0		1-2
	Sporting Cristal, Peru	v Union Huaral, Peru	0-0		3-0
1990	**Sporting Cristal, Peru**	v **Universidad Catolica, Chile**	0-0		0-2
	Union Huaral, Peru	v Universidad Catolica, Chile	1-0		2-2
	Sporting Cristal, Peru	v Colo Colo, Chile	1-2		0-2
	Union Huaral, Peru	v Colo Colo, Chile	1-1		1-3

Colo Colo	6	3	2	1	9-5	8
Universidad Catolica	6	2	3	1	6-4	7
Union Huaral	6	1	3	2	5-9	5
Sporting Cristal	6	1	2	3	4-6	4

Group 4	Defensor Sporting, Uruguay	v Progreso, Uruguay	0-0	4-0	1-1
	Mineros De Guyana, Venezuela	v Pepeganga Margarita, Venezuela	1-0		1-2
	Mineros De Guyana, Venezuela	v **Progreso, Uruguay**	1-3		1-1
	Mineros De Guyana, Venezuela	v Defensor Sporting, Uruguay	0-0		1-3
	Pepeganga Margarita, Venezuela	Progreso, Uruguay	1-0		0-2
	Pepeganga Margarita, Venezuela	Defensor Sporting, Uruguay	1-0		0-1

Progreso	6	2	3	1	7-4	7
Defensor Sporting	6	2	3	1	5-3	7
Pepeganga Margarita	6	3	0	3	4-5	6
Mineros De Guyana	6	1	2	3	5-9	4

Group 5	Olimpia, Paraguay	v Cerro Porteno, Paraguay	2-1		2-3
	Gremio Porto Alegre, Brazil	v Vasco Da Gama Rio, Brazil	2-0		0-0
	Olimpia, Paraguay	v **Gremio Porto Alegre, Brazil**	1-0		2-2
	Cerro Porteno, Paraguay	v Gremio Porto Alegre, Brazil	3-1		0-0
	Cerro Porteno	v Paraguay, Vasco Da Gama Rio, Brazil	1-1		0-2
	Olimpia, Paraguay	v Vasco Da Gama Rio, Brazil	2-1		0-1

Olimpia	6	3	1	2	9-8	7
Cerro Porteno	6	2	2	2	8-8	6
Vasco Da Gama Rio	6	2	2	2	5-5	6
Gremio Porto Alegre	6	1	3	2	5-6	5

2nd Round

Union Huaral, Peru	v Emelec, Ecuador	1-0		0-2
Pepeganga Margarita, Venezuela	v **Independiente, Argentina**	0-6		0-3
Vasco Da Gama, Brazil	v Colo Colo, Chile	0-0 5-4p		3-3
Barcelona Guayaquil, Ecuador	v Progreso, Uruguay	2-0		2-2
Olimpia, Paraguay			bye	
Universidad Catolica, Chile	v The Strongest, Bolivia	3-1		1-1
Defensor Sporting, Uruguay	v River Plate, Argentina	1-2		1-2
Cerro Porteno, Paraguay	v **Nacional Medellin, Colombia**	0-0		0-1

3rd Round

Olimpia, Paraguay	v Universidad Catolica, Chile	2-0		4-4
River Plate, Argentina	v Independiente, Argentina	2-0		1-1
Emelec, Ecuador	v Barcelona Guayaquil, Ecuador	0-0		0-1
Vasco da Gama Rio, Brazil	v Nacional Medellin, Colombia	0-0	0-1	0-2*

* dispute

Semi-finals

Nacional Medellin, Colombia	v Olimpia, Paraguay	1-2*	1-2p	3-2et

* Santiago

River Plate, Argentina	v **Barcelona Guayaquil, Ecuador**	1-0 3-4p		0-1

Final	Olimpia, Paraguay	v Barcelona Guayaquil, Ecuador	2-0		1-1

1969 **Estudiantes** (Argentina)

1978 **Boca Juniors** (Argentina)

54

ARGENTINA

The organisation of Argentine domestic competition reflects the dominance of the big east coast clubs: River Plate and Boca Juniors from Buenos Aires as well as Independiente and Racing from nearby Avellaneda.

For nearly 50 years after Argentine football turned professional the league championship - in common with other South American countries there is no knock-out cup - was almost a private club. Participation was restricted to sides from Buenos Aires, from Avellaneda, from La Plata and from Rosario to the north, which was one of the early traditional centres of Argentine soccer.

In this way the big clubs maintained political and financial power within the federation and kept their travelling expenses to a minimum.

It was only with the arrival of Cesar Luis Menotti as national manager in 1975 that the Argentine game opened up. Menotti looked to the previously unrated, unpublicised provincial championships for national team players - of whom Osvaldo Ardiles from Instituto Cordoba was a prime example of an 'outsider'.

To answer increasing provincial pressure for a share in the cake, the federation organised a 'national championship' which was played in the spring traditionally the close-season. The big clubs were reluctant to compete, preferring lucrative foreign trips but were 'persuaded' to enter since the national champions were guaranteed a place in the all-important South American club cup (the Copa Libertadores).

As Argentine society and soccer found growing financial problems, the original 'Metropolitan' championship was also opened out to the provincial clubs - more matches meaning more income at the gate.

Now there is competitive soccer in Argentina virtually all year round with the national championship early in the year and the old, revamped league championship running the rest of the year.

However, a sign of the big clubs' continuing influence is to be found in the various relegation arrangements. One formula provided for relegation for the clubs with the lowest points-per-match ratio over the previous few seasons. This was a form of protectionism, on the basis that while Boca or River or Racing might have one bad season, two or more was extremely unlikely.

And all the big clubs need each other in the league: with attendance levels plummeting it is only the 'Clasico' derby matches which can be relied on to pull in a decent crowd.

Founded 1893
Asociacion del Futbol Argentino, Viamonte 1366, Buenos Aires ☎ 1053 010 54-1 40 4276/45 5529 Telex 22710 afa.ar
Fax (54-1) 953 3469
Language Spanish, English, French
National colours sky blue and white striped shirts, blue shorts
Season September to June

LEAGUE CHAMPIONS

1893 Lomas AC	**1902** Alumni	**1912*** Quilmes and Porteno	**1920†** Boca Juniors and
1894 Lomas AC	**1903** Alumni	**1913*** Racing Club Avellaneda	River Plate
1895 Lomas AC	**1904** Belgrano AC	and Est La Plata	**1921†** Racing Club Avellaneda
1896 Lomas Academicals	**1905** Alumni	**1914*** Racing Club Avellaneda	and Huracan
1897 Lomas AC	**1906** Alumni	and Porteno	**1922†** Huracan and
1898 Lomas AC	**1907** Alumni	**1915** Racing Club Avellaneda	Independiente
1899 Belgrano AC	**1908** Belgrano AC	**1916** Racing Club Avellaneda	**1923†** Boca Juniors and
	1909 Alumni	**1917** Racing Club Avellaneda	San Lorenzo
1900 English High School		**1918** Racing Club Avellaneda	**1924†** Boca Juniors and
1901 Alumni	**1910** Alumni	**1919†** Racing Club Avellaneda	San Lorenzo
(ex English High School)	**1911** Alumni	and Boca Juniors	

ARGENTINA

1925† Huracan and Racing Club Avellaneda	1933† San Lorenzo and S Dock Sud	1944 Boca Juniors	1957 River Plate
1926† Boca Juniors and Independiente	1934† Boca Juniors and Estudiantil	1945 River Plate	1958 Racing Club Avellaneda
1927 San Lorenzo	1935 Boca Juniors	1946 San Lorenzo	1959 San Lorenzo
1928 Huracan	1936 River Plate	1947 River Plate	
1929 Gimnasia y Esgrima La Plata	1937 River Plate	1948 Independiente	1960 Independiente
	1938 Independiente	1949 Racing Club Avellaneda	1961 Racing Club Avellaneda
	1939 Independiente		1962 Boca Juniors
1930 Boca Juniors		1950 Racing Club Avellaneda	1963 Independiente
1931† Boca Juniors and Estudiantil	1940 Boca Juniors	1951 Racing Club Avellaneda	1964 Boca Juniors
	1941 River Plate	1952 River Plate	1965 Boca Juniors
1932† River Plate and Sportivo Barracas	1942 River Plate	1953 River Plate	1966 Racing Club Avellaneda
	1943 Boca Juniors	1954 Boca Juniors	
		1955 River Plate	
		1956 River Plate	

* shared Championship
† two Leagues in operation

AMATEUR LEAGUE CHAMPIONS

1931 Estudiantil Porteno
1932 Sportivo Barracas
1933 Dock Sud
1934 Estudiantil Porteno

METROPOLITAN CHAMPIONS

1967 Estudiantes	1971 Independiente	1976 Boca Juniors	**CUARTO CENTENARIO**
1968 San Lorenzo	1972 San Lorenzo	1977 River Plate	**Anniversary championships**
1969 Chacarita Juniors	1973 Huracan	1978 Quilmes	1980 River Plate
	1974 Newell's Old Boys	1979 River Plate	
1970 Independiente	1975 River Plate		

PRIMERA

1981 Boca Juniors	1983 Independiente	1984 Argentinos Juniors	1985 Argentinos
1982 Estudiantes			

NATIONAL CHAMPIONS

1967 Independiente	1973 Rosario Central	1980 Rosario Central	1986 River Plate
1968 Velez Sarsfield	1974 San Lorenzo	1981 River Plate	1987 Rosario Central
1969 Boca Juniors	1975 River Plate	1982 Ferro Carril Oeste	1988 Newell's Old Boys
	1976 Boca Juniors	1983 Estudiantes de la Plata	1989 Independiente
1970 Boca Juniors	1977 Independiente	1984 Ferro Carril Oeste	
1971 Rosario Central	1978 Independiente	1985 Argentinos Juniors	1990 River Plate
1972 San Lorenzo	1979 River Plate		

PROVINCIAL LEAGUE'S CHAMPIONS

LIGA DE FUTBOL DE AZUL (AZUL)

1967	Estudiantes	1950	Alumni	1963	Velez Sarsfield	1976	Alumni
1939	Cemento Armado	1951	Sportivo Piazza	1964	Union Chillar	1977	Alumni
		1952	Sportivo Piazza	1965	Azul Athletic	1978	Chacharita Juniors
1940	Deportivo Azul	1953	Alumni	1966	Cemento Armado	1979	Azul Athletic
1941	Sportivo Barracas	1954	Boca Juniors	1967	Cemento Armado		
1942	Sportivo Barracas	1955	Alumni	1968	Alumni	1980	Azul Athletic
1943	Cemento Armado	1956	Alumni	1969	Alumni	1981	Alumni
1944	Boca Juniors	1957	Boca Juniors			1982	Tapalque
1945	Alumni	1958	Boca Juniors	1970	Alumni	1983	Azul Athletic
1946	Azul Athletic	1959	Alumni	1971	Alumni	1984	Azul Athletic
1947	Azul Athletic			1972	Boca Juniors	1985	Sportivo Piazza
1948	not held	1960	Cemento Armado	1973	Boca Juniors	1986	Sportivo Piazza
1949	Alumni	1961	Cemento Armado	1974	Boca Juniors	1987	
		1962	Alumni	1975	Alumni	1988	

LIGA DEL SUR (BAHIA BLANCA)

1908	Porteno	1930	Pacifico	1951	Olimpo	1970	Huracan
1909	Pacifico	1931	Puerto Comercial	1952	Olimpo		(Ingenerio White)
		1932	Puerto Comercial	1953	Olimpo	1971	Rosario PB
1910	Ferrocarril Sud	1933	Puerto Comercial	1954	Olimpo	1972	Rosario PB
1911	Olimpo	1934	Puerto Comercial	1955	Olimpo	1973	Puerto Comercial
1912	Pacifico	1935	Puerto Comercial	1956	Libertad	1974	
1913	Pacifico	1936	Puerto Comercial	1957	Bella Vista	1975	Rosario PB
1914	Pacifico	1937	Puerto Comercial	1958	Puerto Comercial	1976	Olimpo
1915	Porteno	1938		1959	Rosario PB	1977	Olimpo
1916	Liniers	1939	Rosario PB + Liniers			1978	Olimpo
1917	Pacifico			1960	Bella Vista	1979	Olimpo
1918	Pacifico	1940	Villa Mitre	1961	Bella Vista		
1919	Liniers	1941	Puerto Comercial	1962	Olimpo	1980	Olimpo
		1942	Liniers	1963		1981	Olimpo
1920	Puerto Comercial	1943	Puerto Comercial	1964		1982	Olimpo
1921	Olimpo	1944	Villa Mitre	1965	Olimpo	1983	Olimpo
1922	Pacifico	1945	Rosario PB	1966	Olimpo	1984	Olimpo
1924	Puerto Comercial	1946	Sansinena	1967	Huracan	1985	Olimpo
1925	Pacifico	1947	not held		(Ingenerio White)	1986	Olimpo
1926	Puerto Comercial	1948	Liniers	1968	Olimpo	1987	
1927	Puerto Comercial	1949	Olimpo	1969	Rosario PB	1988	
1928	Puerto Comercial						
1929	Pacifico	1950	Olimpo				

ARGENTINA

LIGA CHAQUENA DE FUTBOL (RESISTENCIA)

Year	Champion	Year	Champion	Year	Champion	Year	Champion
1925	Sarmiento	1941	Sarmiento	1958	Sarmiento	1974	Independiente
1926	Chaco For Ever	1942	Sarmiento	1959	Don Orione	1975	Sarmiento
1927	Chaco For Ever	1943	Regional			1976	Chaco For Ever
1928	Chaco For Ever	1944	Sarmiento	1960	Sarmiento	1977	Sarmiento
1929	Chaco For Ever	1945	Sarmiento	1961	Sarmiento	1978	Chaco For Ever
		1946	Regional	1962	Chaco For Ever	1979	Chaco For Ever
1930	Chaco For Ever	1947	Sarmiento	1963	Central Norte		
1931	Chaco For Ever	1948	Chaco For Ever	1964	Velez Sarsfield	1980	Don Orione
1932	Chaco For Ever	1949	Chaco For Ever	1965	Independiente Tirol	1981	Chaco For Ever
1933	Sarmiento			1966	Chaco For Ever	1982	Don Orione
1934	Sarmiento	1950	Chaco For Ever	1967	Sarmiento	1983	Chaco For Ever
1935	Chaco For Ever	1951	Chaco For Ever	1968	Chaco For Ever	1984	Chaco For Ever
1936	Sarmiento	1952	Sarmiento	1969	Fontana	1985	Chaco For Ever
1937	Regional	1953	Sarmiento			1986	Estudiantes
1938	Sarmiento	1954	Sarmiento	1970	Don Orione	1987	
1939	Regional	1955	Sarmiento	1971	Chaco For Ever	1988	
		1956	Sarmiento	1972	Sarmiento		
1940	Independiente Tirol	1957	Sarmiento	1973	Don Orione		

ASOCIACION CORDOBESA DE FUTBOL (CORDOBA)

Year	Champion	Year	Champion	Year	Champion	Year	Champion
1913	Atletico Belgrano	1932	Atletico Belgrano	1951	Talleres	1970	Atletico Belgrano
1914	Atletico Belgrano	1933	Atletico Belgrano	1952	Atletico Belgrano	1971	Atletico Belgrano
1915	Central Cordoba	1934	Talleres	1953	Talleres	1972	Instituto
1916	Central Cordoba	1935	Atletico Belgrano	1954	Atletico Belgrano	1973	Atletico Belgrano
1917	Atletico Belgrano	1936	Atletico Belgrano	1955	Atletico Belgrano	1974	Talleres
1918	Talleres	1937	Atletico Belgrano	1956	Sportivo Belgrano	1975	Talleres
1919	Atletico Belgrano	1938	Talleres	1957	Atletico Belgrano	1976	Talleres
		1939	Talleres	1958	Talleres	1977	Talleres
1920	Atletico Belgrano			1959	Sportivo Belgrano	1978	Talleres
1921	Talleres	1940	Atletico Belgrano			1979	Talleres
1922	Talleres	1941	Talleres	1960	Talleres		
1923	Talleres	1942	Universitario	1961	Instituto	1980	Racing
1924	Talleres	1943	General Paz Juniors	1962	Racing	1981	Racing
1925	Instituto	1944	Talleres	1963	Talleres	1982	Union San Vicente
1926	Instituto	1945	Talleres	1964	General Paz Juniors	1983	Union San Vicente
1927	Instituto	1946	Atletico Belgrano	1965	Racing	1984	Atletico Belgrano
1928	Instituto	1947	Atletico Belgrano	1966		1985	Atletico Belgrano
1929	Atletico Belgrano	1948	Talleres	1967	Instituto	1986	
		1949	Talleres	1968	Sportivo Belgrano	1987	
1930	Atletico Belgrano			1969	Talleres	1988	
1931	Atletico Belgrano	1950	Atletico Belgrano				

LIGA JUJENA DE FUTBOL (JUJUY)

Year	Champion	Year	Champion	Year	Champion	Year	Champion
1975	Gimnasia y Esgrima	1979	Gimnasia y Esgrima	1982	Altos Hornos Zapla	1986	Altos Hornos Zapla
1976	Gimnasia y Esgrima			1983	Altos Hornos Zapla	1987	
1977	Gimnasia y Esgrima	1980	Gimnasia y Esgrima	1984	Altos Hornos Zapla	1988	
1978	Altos Hornos Zapla	1981	Gimnasia y Esgrima	1985	Juventud Celulosa		

LIGA SALTENA DE FUTBOL (SALTA)

1921 Correos y Telecomunicaciones	**1937** Gimnasia y Tiro	**1955** Central Norte	**1972** Juventud Antoniana
1922 Correos y Telecomunicaciones	**1938** Juventud Antoniana	**1956** Central Norte	**1973** Central Norte
	1939 Gimnasia y Tiro	**1957** Juventud Antoniana	**1974** Juventud Antoniana
1923 Central Norte		**1958** Gimnasia y Tiro	**1975** Juventud Antoniana
1924 Central Norte	**1940** Central Norte	**1959** Correos y Telecomunicaciones	**1976** Central Norte
1925 Correos y Telecomunicaciones	**1941**		**1977** Gimnasia y Tiro
	1942 Gimnasia y Tiro		**1978** Centro Policial
1926 Central Norte	**1943** Gimnasia y Tiro	**1960** Gimnasia y Tiro	**1979** Central Norte
1927 Central Norte	**1944** Central Norte	**1961** Central Norte	
1928 Juventud Antoniana	**1945** Gimnasia y Tiro	**1962** Central Norte	**1980** Juventud Antoniana
1929 Juventud Antoniana	**1946** Central Norte	**1963** Central Norte	**1981** Central Norte
	1947 Gimnasia y Tiro	**1964** Argentinos del Norte	**1982** Central Norte
1930 Juventud Antoniana	**1948** Gimnasia y Tiro	**1965** Central Norte	**1983** Central Norte
1931 Juventud Antoniana	**1949** Central Norte	**1966** Central Norte	**1984** Gimnasia y Tiro
1932 Sportivo Comercio		**1967** Juventud Antoniana	**1985** Central Norte
1933 Juventud Antoniana	**1950** Gimnasia y Tiro	**1968** Central Norte	**1986** Central Norte
1934 Juventud Antoniana	**1951** Gimnasia y Tiro	**1969** Central Norte	**1987**
1935 Juventud Antoniana	**1952** Gimnasia y Tiro		**1988**
1936 Atletico Libertad	**1953** Juventud Antoniana	**1970** Juventud Antoniana	
	1954 Central Norte	**1971** Central Norte	

TORNEO CONFRATERNIDAD (SALTA AND JUJUY)

Top 4 teams from Salta and Jujuy with nearby Cities play off for the title.

1979 Gimnasia y Esgrima	**1982** Ledesma	**1985** Gimnasia y Esgrima	**1987**
1980 Central Norte	**1983** Central Norte	**1986**	**1988**
1981 Atletico Ledesma	**1984** Juventud Antoniana		

LIGA MARPLATENSE DE FUTBOL (MAR DEL PLATA)

1909 Atletico Mar del Plata	**1930** Nacion	**1951** Quilmes	**1970** Kimberley
	1931 Independiente	**1952** Nacion	**1971** San Lorenzo
1910 Atletico Mar del Plata	**1932** Independiente	**1953** River Plate	**1972** San Lorenzo
1911 Atletico Mar del Plata	**1933** Kimberley	**1954** River Plate	**1973** Aldosivi
1912	**1934** Kimberley	**1955** River Plate	**1974** Aldosivi
1913 San Martin	**1935** Quilmes	**1956** Quilmes	**1975** Aldosivi
1914 Atletico Mar del Plata	**1936** Kimberley	**1957** Quilmes	**1976** Circulo Deportivo
1915 Nacional	**1937** Quilmes	**1958** Quilmes	**1977** Alvarardo
1916 Atletico Mar del Plata	**1938** Hurucan	**1959** Quilmes	**1978** Kimberley
1917 Atletico Mar del Plata	**1939** Quilmes		**1979** San Lorenzo
1918 Sarmiento		**1960** Circulo Deportivo (Comandante Nicanor Otamendi)	
1919 not held	**1940** Quilmes		**1980** San Lorenzo
	1941 Quilmes		**1981** San Lorenzo
1920 General Mitre	**1942** Atletico Mar del Plata	**1961** Independiente	**1982** Kimberley
1921 General Mitre	**1943** Quilmes	**1962** Kimberley	**1983** Kimberley
1922 General Mitre	**1944** General Urquiza	**1963** San Lorenzo	**1984** Circulo Deportivo
1923 Independiente	**1945** Atletico Mar del Plata	**1964** San Lorenzo	**1985** Circulo Deportivo
1924 Nacional	**1946** Union	**1965** San Lorenzo	**1986** Kimberley
1925 Nacional	**1947** Kimberley	**1966** San Lorenzo	**1987**
1926 Nacion	**1948** Quilmes	**1967** San Lorenzo	**1988**
1927 Penarol	**1949** Penarol	**1968** San Lorenzo	
1928 Nacion		**1969** Kimberley	
1929 Atletico Mar del Plata	**1950** Talleres		

ARGENTINA

LIGA MENDOCINA DE FUTBOL

1922	Gimnasia y Esgrima	1936	Independiente Rivadavia	1953	Deportivo Maipu	1970	Independiente Rivadavia
1923	Gimnasia y Esgrima			1954	Godoy Cruz	1971	Andes Talleres
1924	Independiente Rivadavia	1937	Gimnasia y Esgrima	1955	Andes Talleres	1972	Independiente Rivadavia
1925	Independiente Rivadavia	1938	Independiente Rivadavia	1956	Andes Talleres		
		1939	Gimnasia y Esgrima	1957	Boca Juniors	1973	Atletico San Martin
1926	Independiente Rivadavia			1958	Deportivo Maipu	1974	Gimnasia y Esgrima
		1940	Independiente Rivadavia	1959	Atletico Argentino	1975	Atletico San Martin
1927	Independiente Rivadavia	1941	Nacional FC	1960	Independiente Rivadavia	1976	Independiente Rivadavia
1928	Independiente Rivadavia	1942	Nacional FC	1961	Independiente Rivadavia	1977	Gimnasia y Esgrima
		1943	Nacional FC			1978	Independiente Rivadavia
1929	Independiente Rivadavia	1944	Godoy Cruz	1962	Independiente Rivadavia		
		1945	Independiente Rivadavia	1963	Atletico San Martin	1979	Atletico San Martin
1930	Palmira	1946	Andes Talleres	1964	Gimnasia y Esgrima	1980	Gimnasia y Esgrima
1931	Gimnasia y Esgrima	1947	Godoy Cruz	1965	Independiente	1981	Gimnasia y Esgrima
1932	Independiente Rivadavia	1948	Atletico Argentino		Rivadavia	1982	Gimnasia y Esgrima
		1949	Gimnasia y Esgrima	1966	Atletico San Martin	1983	Gimnasia y Esgrima
1933	Gimnasia y Esgrima			1967	Independiente Rivadavia	1984	Huracan Las Heras
1934	Nacional FC	1950	Godoy Cruz			1985	Deportivo Maipu
1935	Independiente Rivadavia	1951	Godoy Cruz	1968	Godoy Cruz	1986	Gimnasia y Esgrima
		1952	Gimnasia y Esgrima	1969	Gimnasia y Esgrima	1987	
						1988	

LIGA NECOCHEA DE FUTBOL (NECOCHEA)

1930	Huracan	1946	Rivadavia	1960	Independiente (San Cayetano)	1972	Rivadavia
1931	Huracan	1947	Rivadavia			1973	Palermo
1932	Rivadavia	1948	Huracan	1961	Independiente (San Cayetano)	1974	Estancion Quequen
1933	Rivadavia	1949	Huracan			1975	Estancion Quequen
1934	Rivadavia			1962	Independiente (San Cayetano)	1976	Estancion Quequen
1935	Huracan	1950	Independiente (San Cayetano)			1977	Estancion Quequen
1936	Rivadavia			1963	Rivadavia	1978	Estancion Quequen
1937	Ameghino	1951	Independiente (San Cayetano)	1964	Defensores (N Fernandez)	1979	Huracan
1938	Rivadavia	1952	Ameghino				
1939	Ministerio	1953	Independiente (San Cayetano)	1965	Barracas (N Fernandez)	1980	Rivadavia
				1966	Rivadavia	1981	Estancion Quequen
1940	Jorge Newbery (Loberia)	1954	Independiente (San Cayetano)	1967	Defensores (N Fernandez)	1982	Independiente (San Cayetano)
1941	Jorge Newbery (Loberia)	1955	Rivadavia	1968	Defensores (N Fernandez)	1983	Villa del Parque
1942	Rivadavia	1956	Rivadavia			1984	Villa del Parque
1943	Rivadavia	1957	Rivadavia	1969	Rivadavia	1985	Rivadavia
1944	Independiente (San Cayetano)	1958	Rivadavia			1986	Estancion Quequen
		1959	Rivadavia	1970	Estancion Quequen	1987	
1945	Huracan			1971	Rivadavia	1988	

LIGA DE FUTBOL DE OLAVARRIA (OLAVARRIA)

1926	Estudiantes	1930	Racing	1934	Estudiantes	1938	San Martin
1927	Racing	1931	Ferrocarril Sud	1935	Estudiantes	1939	Racing
1928	Ferrocarril Sud	1932	Racing	1936	San Martin		
1929	Ferrocarril Sud	1933	Estudiantes	1937	San Martin	1940	San Martin

1941	Racing	1953	San Martin	1965	Estudiantes	1977	Estudiantes
1942	San Martin	1954	Estudiantes	1966	Estudiantes	1978	Loma Negra
1943	San Martin	1955	Estudiantes	1967	Estudiantes	1979	Estudiantes
1944	Ferrocarril Sud	1956	Racing	1968	Racing		
1945	San Martin	1957	San Martin	1969	Ferrocarril Sud	1980	Loma Negra
1946	Ferrocarril Sud	1958	Estudiantes			1981	Loma Negra
1947	Sierra Chica	1959	Estudiantes	1970	not held	1982	Loma Negra
1948	Sierra Chica			1971	Racing	1983	Loma Negra
1949	Loma Negra	1960	San Martin	1972	Estudiantes	1984	Loma Negra
		1961	Estudiantes	1973	Racing	1985	Estudiantes
1950	not held	1962	El Fortin	1974	San Martin	1986	Estudiantes
1951	San Martin	1963	Racing	1975	Loma Negra	1987	
1952	Racing	1964	Estudiantes	1976	Racing	1988	

LIGA PAMPEANA DE FUTBOL (GENERAL PICO)

1926	Racing Club (Eduardo Castex)	1939	Alvear FC (Intendente Alvear)	1956	Cultural Argentino	1972	Costa Brava
1927	Racing Club (Eduardo Castex)			1957	Cultural Argentino	1973	Ferrocarril Oeste (Intendente Alvear)
		1940	Costa Brava	1958	Cultural Argentino		
1928	Sportivo Independiente	1941	Ferrocarril Oeste	1959	Cultural Argentino	1974	Alvear FC (Intendente Alvear)
		1942	Costa Brava				or Ferrocarril Oeste
1929	Racing Club (Eduardo Castex)	1943	Sportivo Independiente	1960	Ferrocarril Oeste		(Intendente Alvear)
		1944	Sportivo Independiente	1961	Sportivo Independiente	1975	
1930	Ferrocarril Oeste (Intendente Alvear)	1945	Cultural Argentino	1962	Alvear FC (Intendente Alvear)	1976	Ferrocarril Oeste (Intendente Alvear)
1931	Sportivo Independiente	1946	Racing Club (Eduardo Castex)	1963	Alvear FC (Intendente Alvear)	1977	Ferrocarril Oeste
1932	Miguel Cane	1947	Racing Club (Eduardo Castex)	1964	Alvear FC (Intendente Alvear)	1978	Costa Brava
1933	Sportivo Independiente	1948	Ferrocarril Oeste	1965	Pico FC	1979	Costa Brava
1934	Sportivo Independiente	1949	Sportivo Realico	1966	Pico FC	1980	Ferrocarril Oeste
1935	Sportivo Independiente	1950	Sportivo Independiente	1967	Ferrocarril Oeste (Intendente Alvear)	1981	Ferrocarril Oeste
1936	Alvear FC (Intendente Alvear)	1951	Sportivo Independiente	1968	Ferrocarril Oeste (Intendente Alvear)	1982	Racing Club (Eduardo Castex)
1937	Alvear FC (Intendente Alvear)	1952	Cultural Argentino	1969	Estudiantil (Eduardo Castex)	1983	Ferrocarril Oeste
1938	Sportivo Independiente	1953	Cultural Argentino			1984	Ferrocarril Oeste
		1954	Cultural Argentino	1970	Racing Club (Eduardo Castex)	1985	Pico FC
		1955	Pico FC	1971	Costa Brava	1986	Costa Brava
						1987	
						1988	

LIGA PARANAENSE DE FUTBOL (PARANA)

1942	Patronato	1954	Patronato	1966	Sportivo Urquiza	1978	Atletico Parana
1943	Patronato	1955	Patronato	1967	Penarol	1979	Atletico Parana
1944	Belgrano	1956	Atletico Parana	1968	Patronato		
1945	Patronato	1957	Patronato	1969	Patronato	1980	Atletico Parana
1946	Ministerio	1958	Ministerio			1981	not held
1947	Ministerio	1959	Belgrano	1970	Belgrano	1982	Universitario
1948	Ministerio			1971	Atletico Parana	1983	Atletico Parana
1949	Belgrano	1960	Patronato	1972	Patronato	1984	Patronato
		1961	Atletico Parana	1973	Atletico Parana	1985	Belgrano
1950	Patronato	1962	Atletico Parana	1974	Penarol	1986	Belgrano
1951	Atletico Parana	1963	Atletico Parana	1975	Atletico Parana	1987	
1952	Universitario	1964	Ministerio	1976	Atletico Parana	1988	
1953	Patronato	1965	Patronato	1977	Patronato		

ARGENTINA

LIGA RIOJANA DE FUTBOL (LA RIOJA)

Year	Champion	Year	Champion	Year	Champion	Year	Champion
1919	Almirante Brown	1938	Sportivo San Vicente	1957	Americo Tesorieri	1974	Estudiantes
		1939	Sportivo San Vicente	1958	Rioja Juniors	1975	Americo Tesorieri
1920	Atletico Riojana			1959	Sportivo San Francisco	1976	Union
1921	Atletico Riojana	1940	Atletico Riojana			1977	Andino
1922	Sportivo Firpo	1941	Sportivo San Vicente			1978	Andino
1923	Sportivo Firpo	1942	Rioja Juniors	1960	Rioja Juniors	1979	Andino
1924	Sportivo Firpo	1943	Rioja Juniors	1961	Atletico San Isidro		
1925	Sportivo Firpo	1944	Independiente	1962	Atletico San Isidro	1980	San Lorenzo de Vargas
1926	Sportivo Firpo	1945	Rioja Juniors	1963	Rioja Juniors	1981	Estudiantes
1927	Atletico Riojana	1946	Americo Tesorieri	1964	San Lorenzo de Vargas	1982	Andino
1928	Atletico Riojana	1947	Tiro Federal	1965	Union	1983	Defensores de la Boca
1929	Atletico Riojana	1948	Rioja Juniors	1966	Americo Tesorieri		
		1949	Tiro Federal	1967	Americo Tesorieri	1984	Independiente
1930	Independiente			1968	Rioja Juniors	1985	Union
1931	Penarol	1950	Tiro Federal	1969	Americo Tesorieri	1986	Union
1932	Independiente	1951	Americo Tesorieri			1987	
1933	Atletico Riojana	1952	Americo Tesorieri			1988	
1934	Independiente	1953	Andino	1970	Union		
1935	Independiente	1954	Americo Tesorieri	1971	Rioja Juniors		
1936	Atletico Riojana	1955	Rioja Juniors	1972	Atletico Riojana		
1937	Sportivo San Vicente	1956	Americo Tesorieri	1973	Atletico Riojana		

LIGA SANTIAGUENA DE FUTBOL (SANTIAGO DEL ESTERO)

Year	Champion	Year	Champion	Year	Champion	Year	Champion
1906	La Banda	1928	Mitre	1947	Sarmiento	1969	Central Cordoba
1907	Santiago	1929	Santiago	1948	Santiago		
1908	Santiago			1949	Estudiantes	1970	Central Cordoba
1909	Sarmiento	1930	Union			1971	Central Cordoba
		1931	Mitre	1950	Union	1972	Agua y Energia
1910	Atletico	1932	Sarmiento	1951	Estudiantes	1973	Estudiantes
1911	Santiago	1933	Union	1952	Estudiantes	1974	Central Cordoba
1912	Atletico	1934	Union	1953	Central Argentino	1975	Central Cordoba
1913	Mitre	1935	Mitre	1954	Santiago	1976	Central Cordoba
1914	Santiago	1936	Mitre	1955	Union	1977	Estudiantes
1915	Santiago	1937	Sarmiento	1956	Union	1978	Central Cordoba
1916	Sarmiento	1938	Comercio Central Unidos	1957	Central Cordoba	1979	Guemes
1917	Sarmiento			1958	Central Argentino		
1918	Santiago	1939	Comercio Central Unidos	1959	Central Cordoba	1980	Estudiantes
1919	Central Argentino					1981	Estudiantes
				1960	Central Cordoba	1982	Estudiantes
1920	Sarmiento	1940	Comercio Central Unidos	1961	Central Cordoba	1983	Union-Santiago (amalgamation)
1921	Santiago	1941	Central Argentino	1962	Central Cordoba		
1922	Santiago	1942	Estudiantes	1963	Central Cordoba	1984	
1923	Santiago	1943	Central Argentino	1964	Central Cordoba	1985	Central Cordoba
1924	Santiago	1944	Estudiantes	1965	Central Cordoba	1986	Central Cordoba
1925	Santiago	1945	Central Cordoba	1966	Central Cordoba	1987	
1926	Mitre	1946	Union	1967	Central Cordoba	1988	
1927	Mitre			1968	Mitre		

LIGA TUCAMANA DE FUTBOL (SAN MIGUEL DE TUCUMAN)

Year	Champion	Year	Champion	Year	Champion	Year	Champion
1919	San Martin	1922	San Pablo	1926	San Pablo	1930	Atletico Tucuman
		1923	San Martin	1927	Atletico Tucuman	1931	Central Cordoba
1920	Atletico Tucuman	1924	Atletico Tucuman	1928	San Pablo	1932	All Boys
1921	Atletico Tucuman	1925	Central Norte	1929	Central Norte	1933	All Boys

Year	Winner	Year	Winner	Year	Winner	Year	Winner
1934	Central Norte	1948	Central Cordoba	1961	Atletico Tucuman	1975	Atletico Tucuman
1935	Atletico Tucuman	1949	San Martin	1962	Atletico Tucuman	1976	San Martin
1936	All Boys			1963	Atletico Tucuman	1977	Atletico Tucuman
1937	Atletico Tucuman	1950	Central Cordoba	1964	Atletico Tucuman	1978	Atletico Tucuman
1938	Atletico Tucuman	1951	Atletico Tucuman	1965	Sportivo Guzman	1979	Atletico Tucuman
1939	Central Norte	1952	Central Cordoba	1966	San Martin		
		1953	San Martin	1967	San Martin	1980	San Martin
1940	San Martin	1954	San Martin	1968	Sportivo Guzman	1981	San Martin
1941	San Martin	1955	San Martin	1969	San Martin	1982	San Martin
1942	Atletico Tucuman	1956	San Martin			1983	Atletico Tucuman
1943	San Martin	1957	Atletico Tucuman	1970	San Martin	1984	San Martin
1944	San Martin	1958	Atletico Tucuman	1971	San Martin	1985	San Martin
1945	San Martin	1959	Atletico Tucuman	1972	Atletico Tucuman	1986	Alletico Tucuman
1946	All Boys			1973	Atletico Tucuman	1987	
1947	San Martin	1960	Atletico Tucuman	1974	San Martin	1988	

LIGA SANJUANINA DE FUTBOL (SAN JUAN)

Year	Winner	Year	Winner	Year	Winner	Year	Winner
1923	Atletico de la Juventud	1942	Atletico Graffigna	1961	Atletico de la Juventud	1978	San Martin
1924	San Martin	1943	San Martin	1962	Los Andes	1979	Penarol
1925	San Martin	1944	not held	1963	Sportivo Desamporados		
1926	San Martin	1945	Atletico de la Juventud	1964	San Martin	1980	San Martin
1927	Atletico Graffigna	1946	Atletico de la Juventud	1965	Penarol	1981	Atletico de la Juventud/Alianza
1928	Sportivo Desamporados	1947	Penarol	1966	San Martin		
1929	Atletico de la Juventud	1948	San Martin	1967	San Martin	1982	Atletico de la Juventud/Alianza
		1949	Independiente	1968	Sportivo Desamporados		
1930	San Martin			1969	San Martin	1983	Sportivo Desamporados
1931	Atletico Graffigna	1950	Atletico de la Juventud			1984	Atletico de la Juventud/Alianza
1932	San Martin	1951	San Martin	1970	Sportivo Desamporados		
1933	San Martin	1952	Atletico de la Juventud	1971	Sportivo Desamporados	1985	Atletico de la Juventud/Alianza
1934	Atletico de la Juventud	1953	Atletico de la Juventud	1972	Sportivo Desamporados		
1935	Atletico de la Juventud	1954	San Martin	1973	Sportivo Desamporados	1986	Atletico de la Juventud/Alianza
1936	Atletico de la Juventud	1955	San Martin	1974	Atletico de la Juventud/Alianza	1987	
1937	San Martin	1956	San Martin	1975	Sportivo Desamporados	1988	
1938	Atletico Graffigna	1957	San Martin	1976	Sportivo Desamporados		
1939	Los Andes	1958	Los Andes	1977	San Martin		
		1959	Los Andes				
1940	San Martin						
1941	San Martin	1960	San Martin				

LIGA DEPORTIVA CONFLUENCIA DE RIO NEGRO (CIPOLLETTI)

TORNEO OFICIAL

Year	Winner	Year	Winner	Year	Winner	Year	Winner
1975	Atletico Cipolletti	1979	Atletico Cipolletti	1981	Deportivo Roca	1984	Atletico Cipolletti
1976	Deportivo Roca			1982	Atletico Regina	1985	Atletico Cipolletti
1977	Deportivo Roca	1980	Atletico Cipolletti	1983	Atletico Cipolletti	1986	Deportivo Roca
1978	Atletico Cipolletti						

LIGA TANDILENSE DE FUTBOL (TANDIL)

Year	Winner	Year	Winner	Year	Winner	Year	Winner
1919	Newbery	1922	Ferrocarril Sud	1926	Ramon Santamarina	1930	Ramon Santamarina
		1923	Ferrocarril Sud	1927	Ferrocarril Sud	1931	Ferrocarril Sud
1920	Newbery	1924	Ramon Santamarina	1928	Ramon Santamarina	1932	Ramon Santamarina
1921	Sarmiento	1925	Ramon Santamarina	1929	Independiente	1933	Defensa Tandil

ARGENTINA

1934 Ferrocarril Sud	1948 Ferrocarril Sud	1961 Ramon Santamarina	1975 Excursionistas
1935 Excursionistas	1949 Ferrocarril Sud	1962 Ramon Santamarina	1976 Ramon Santamarina
1936 Independiente		1963 Ramon Santamarina	1977 Ferrocarril Sud
1937 Excursionistas	1950 Ramon Santamarina	1964 Ramon Santamarina	1978 Ferrocarril Sud
1938 Ramon Santamarina	1951 Ferrocarril Sud	1965 Ramon Santamarina	1979 Ramon Santamarina
1939 Ferrocarril Sud	1952 not held	1966 Ramon Santamarina	
	1953 Ramon Santamarina	1967 Loma Negra	1980 Ramon Santamarina
1940 Ferrocarril Sud	1954 Ferrocarril Sud	1968 Ramon Santamarina	1981 La Movediza
1941 Newbery	1955 Ramon Santamarina	1969 Defensa de Napaleofu	1982 Independiente
1942 Atletico Juarense	1956 Ramon Santamarina		1983 Racing
1943 Excursionistas	1957 Ramon Santamarina	1970 Ramon Santamarina	1984 Ramon Santamarina
1944 Excursionistas	1958 Ferrocarril Sud	1971 Racing	1985 Independiente
1945 Newbery	1959 Ramon Santamarina	1972 Loma Negra	1986 Grupo Universitario
1946 Ferrocarril Sud		1973 Ramon Santamarina	1987
1947 Figueroa	1960 Ramon Santamarina	1974 Racing	1988

LIGA RIONEGRINA DE FUTBOL (VIEDMA)

1985 El Ciclon

LIGA DEPORTIVA DEL OESTE (JUNIN)

1917 Sarmiento	1935 Rivadavia (Junin)	1953 Sarmiento	1971 Rivadavia (Junin)
1918 Jorge Newbery	1936 Sarmiento	1954 Sarmiento	1972 Jorge Newbery
1919 Buenos Aires al Pacifico	1937 Sarmiento	1955 Mariano Moreno	1973 Jorge Newbery
	1938 River Plate	1956 Sarmiento	1974 Jorge Newbery
1920 Sarmiento	1939 Sarmiento	1957 Sarmiento	1975 Jorge Newbery
1921 Sarmiento		1958 River Plate	1976 Jorge Newbery
1922 Jorge Newbery	1940 Mariano Moreno	1959 River Plate	1977 Jorge Newbery
1923 Jorge Newbery	1941 Mariano Moreno		1978 Jorge Newbery
1924 Jorge Newbery	1942 Rivadavia (Junin)	1960 Sarmiento	1979 Jorge Newbery
1925 Buenos Aires al Pacifico	1943 Sarmiento	1961 Mariano Moreno	
1926 Jorge Newbery	1944 Sarmiento	1962 not held	1980 Villa Belgrano
1927 Buenos Aires al Pacifico	1945 Sarmiento	1963 Ambos Mundos	1981 Mariano Moreno
1928 Sarmiento	1946 Mariano Moreno	1964 Rivadavia (Junin)	1982 El Linqueno
1929 Sarmiento	1947 Mariano Moreno	1965 Rivadavia (Junin)	1983 Rivadavia de Lincoln
	1948 Mariano Moreno	1966 Mariano Moreno	1984 El Linqueno
1930 Mariano Moreno	1949 Mariano Moreno	1967 Ambos Mundos	1985 Rivadavia de Lincoln
1931 Junin		1968 Rivadavia (Junin)	1986 El Linqueno
1932 Sarmiento	1950 Sarmiento	1969 Jorge Newbery	1987
1933 Mariano Moreno	1951 Mariano Moreno		1988
1934 not held	1952 not held	1970 River Plate	

LIGA POSADENA DE FUTBOL (POSADES)

1934 America for Ever	1940 Guarani Antonio	1948 Bartolome Mitre	1955 Guarani Antonio
1935 Union	Franco	1949 Atletico Posades	Franco
1936 Union	1941 Union		1956 Guarani Antonio
1937 Guarani Antonio	1942 Union	1950 J.G.Brown	Franco
Franco	1943 Guarani Antonio	1951 Bartolome Mitre	1957 Guarani Antonio
1938 Guarani Antonio	Franco	1952 Atletico Posades	Franco
Franco	1944 Union	1953 Independiente	1958 Bartolome Mitre
1939 Union	1945 J.G.Brown	1954 Guarani Antonio	1959 Guarani Antonio
	1946 Independiente	Franco	Franco
	1947 Bartolome Mitre		

1960	Bartolome Mitre	1967	Guarani Antonio Franco	1974	Bartolome Mitre	1982	Guarani Antonio Franco
1961	Guarani Antonio Franco	1968	Guarani Antonio Franco	1975	Bartolome Mitre	1983	Guarani Antonio Franco
1962	Guarani Antonio Franco	1969	Bartolome Mitre	1976	Atletico Posades	1984	Guarani Antonio Franco
1963	Bartolome Mitre	1970	Guarani Antonio Franco	1977	Atletico Posades	1985	Guarani Antonio Franco
1964	Guarani Antonio Franco	1971	Bartolome Mitre	1978	Guarani Antonio Franco	1986	Atletico Posades
1965	Guarani Antonio Franco	1972	Guarani Antonio Franco	1979	Guarani Antonio Franco	1987	
1966	Guarani Antonio Franco	1973	Guarani Antonio Franco	1980	Bartolome Mitre	1988	
				1981	Guarani Antonio Franco		

FEATURED CLUBS IN COPA LIBERTADORES DE AMERICA

All clubs are from Buenos Aires unless stated

Independiente	**River Plate**	**Estudiantes La Plata**	**Boca Juniors**
Rosario Central	**Racing Club Avellaneda**	**San Lorenzo De Almagro**	**Huracan**
Newell's Old Boys Rosario	**Quilmes Athletic Club**	**Ferro Carril Oeste**	**Argentinos Juniors**
Velez Sarsfield			

CLUB ATLETICO INDEPENDIENTE

Founded 1st January 1905
Address Avenida Mitre 70, 1870 Avellaneda ☎ 201-0020/1875/6590
Colours red shirts with white trim, dark blue shorts
Stadium Cordero (68,930)
Champions 1922, 1926, 1938, 1939, 1948, 1960, 1963
Metropolitan Champions 1970, 1971; Primera 1983
National Champions 1967, 1977, 1978, 1987
Libertadores Winners 1964, 1965, 1972, 1973, 1974, 1975, 1984
World Club Champions 1973, 1984 World Club Finalists 1964, 1965, 1972, 1974
Inter America Cup Winners 1974, 1975

Season	Opponent	Home	Playoff Result	Away	Rnd
1961	Palmeiras Sao Paulo, Brazil	0-2		0-1	qf
1964	Millonarios Bogota, Colombia*	*disqualified		5-1	1
	Alianza Lima, Peru	4-0		2-2	1
	Santos FC Sao Paulo, Brazil	2-1		3-2	1
	Nacional, Uruguay	1-0		0-0	FINAL
1965	Boca Juniors, Argentina	2-0	0-0*	0-1	sf
					* goal difference
	Penarol, Uruguay	1-0	4-1 in Santiago	1-3	FINAL
1966	Boca Juniors, Argentina	2-0		0-0	1
	Guarani, Paraguay	2-1		2-0	sf
	River Plate, Argentina	1-1	1-2	2-4	sf
1968	Estudiantes La Plata, Argentina	2-4		0-2	1
	Millonarios Bogota, Colombia	3-1		2-1	1
	Deportivo Cali, Colombia	1-1	3-2	0-1	1
	Estudiantes La Plata, Argentina	1-2		0-1	qf
	Universitario Lima, Peru	3-0		3-0	qf
1972	Rosario Central, Argentina	2-0		2-2	1
	Nacional Medellin, Colombia	2-0		1-1	1
	Independiente Sante Fe, Colombia	2-0		2-4	1
	Barcelona Sporting Guayaquil, Ecuador	1-0		1-1	sf
	Sao Paulo FC, Brazil	2-0		0-1	sf
	Universitario Lima, Peru	2-1		0-0	FINAL
1973	Millonarios Bogota, Colombia	2-0		0-1	sf
	San Lorenzo, Argentina	1-0		2-2	sf

ARGENTINA

Year	Opponent	Home	Playoff	Away	Round
	Colo Colo, Chile	1-1	2-1 in Montevideo	0-0	FINAL
1974	Huracan, Argentina	3-0		1-1	sf
	Penarol, Uruguay	3-2		1-1	sf
	Sao Paulo FC, Brazil	1-0	1-0 in Santiago	1-2	FINAL
1975	Rosario Central, Argentina	2-0		0-2	sf
	Cruzeiro Belo Horizonte, Brazil	3-0		0-2	sf
	Union Espanola, Chile	3-1	2-0 in Asuncion	0-1	FINAL
1976	River Plate, Argentina	0-1	0-1	0-0	sf
	Penarol, Uruguay	1-0		1-0	sf
1978	River Plate, Argentina	0-0	1-4	0-0	1
	Nacional, Ecuador	2-0		2-1	1
	Liga Deportivo Universitaria Quito, Ecuador	2-0		0-1	1
1979	Quilmes, Argentina	2-0		2-1	1
	Millonarios Bogota, Colombia	4-1		3-3	1
	Deportivo Cali, Colombia	1-0		0-1	1
	Penarol, Uruguay	1-0		0-0	sf
	Boca Juniors, Argentina	1-0	0-1	0-2	sf
1984	Estudiantes La Plata, Argentina	4-1		1-1	1
	Olimpia, Paraguay	3-2		0-1	1
	Sportivo Luqueno Luque, Paraguay	2-0		1-0	1
	Nacional, Uruguay	1-0		1-1	sf
	Universidad Catolica, Chile	2-1		0-0	sf
	Gremio Porto Alegre, Brazil	0-0		1-0	FINAL
1985	Argentinos Juniors, Argentina	1-2		2-2	sf
	Blooming Santa Cruz, Bolivia	2-0		1-1	sf
1987	Rosario Central, Argentina	3-1		0-0	1
	Tachira San Cristobal, Venezuela	5-0		2-3	1
	Estudiantes Merida, Venezuela	2-0		1-0	1
	Penarol, Uruguay	2-4		0-3	sf
	River Plate, Argentina	2-1		0-0	sf
1990	River Plate, Argentina	1-0		0-0	1
	Pepeganga Margarita, Venezuela	3-0		6-0	2
	River Plate, Argentina	1-1		0-2	3

CLUB ATLETICO RIVER PLATE

Founded 25th May 1901
Address Figueroa Alcorta 7597 (1428) Buenos Aires ☎ 785-6868/7844/1019
Colours white shirts with red sash, black shorts
Stadium Antonio Liberti 'Monumental' de Nunez, Buenos Aires (85,050)
Champions 1920, 1932, 1936, 1937, 1941, 1942, 1945, 1947, 1952, 1953, 1955, 1956, 1957
Metropolitan Champions 1975, 1977, 1979, Cuarto Centenario 1980
National Champions 1975, 1979, 1981, 1990
Libertadores Winners 1986 Finalists 1966, 1976
World Champions 1986
Inter America Cup Winners 1986

Season	Opponent	Home	Playoff Result	Away	Round
1966	Boca Juniors, Argentina	2-1		0-2	1
	Italia Caracas, Venezuela	2-1		3-0	1
	Universitario Lima, Peru	5-0		1-1	1
	Alianza Lima, Peru	3-2		2-0	1
	Lara Basquimento, Venezuela	3-0		2-1	1
	Guarani, Paraguay	3-1		3-1	sf
	Boca Juniors, Argentina	2-2		0-1	sf
	Independiente, Argentina	4-2		1-1	sf
	Penarol, Uruguay	3-0	2-4 in Santiago	0-2	FINAL
1967	Racing Club Avellaneda, Argentina	0-0		1-2	1
	Bolivar, Bolivia	2-0		3-3	1
	31 de Octubre, Bolivia	7-0		4-0	1
	Deportivo Independiente Medellin, Colombia	6-2		1-0	1
	Independiente Santa Fe, Colombia	4-0		2-2	1
	Colo Colo, Chile	1-1		0-1	sf
	Racing Club Avellaneda, Argentina	0-0		1-3	sf
	Universitario Lima, Peru	0-1		2-2	sf

1970	Boca Juniors, Argentina	1-3		1-2	1
	Universitario La Paz, Bolivia	9-0		2-0	1
	Bolivar, Bolivia	1-0		1-1	1
	Boca Juniors, Argentina	1-1		1-0	qf
	Universitario Lima, Peru	5-3		2-1	qf
	Estudiantes La Plata, Argentina	0-1		1-3	sf
1973	San Lorenzo, Argentina	0-1		0-4	1
	Jorge Wilsterman Cochabamba, Bolivia	2-2		0-1	1
	Oriente Petrolero Santa Cruz, Bolivia	7-1		3-1	1
1976	Estudiantes La Plata, Argentina	1-0		0-1	1
	Galicia Caracas, Venezuela	4-1		1-0	1
	Portuguesa Acarigua, Venezuela	2-1		2-0	1
	Independiente, Argentina	0-0	1-0	1-0	sf
	Penarol, Uruguay	3-0		0-1	sf
	Cruzeiro Belo Horizonte, Brazil	2-1	2-3 in Santiago	1-4	FINAL
1977	Penarol, Uruguay	2-1		2-2	1
	Boca Juniors, Argentina	0-0		0-1	1
	Defensor Sporting, Uruguay	1-1		0-0	1
1978	Independiente, Argentina	0-0	4-1	0-0	1
	Nacional Quito, Ecuador	2-0		1-1	1
	Liga Deportivo Universitaria Quito, Ecuador	4-0		0-0	1
	Atletico Mineiro Belo Horizonte, Brazil	1-0		0-1	sf
	Boca Juniors, Argentina	0-2		0-0	sf
1980	Sporting Cristal, Peru	3-2		2-1	1
	Atletico Chalaco Callao, Peru	3-0		2-0	1
	Velez Sarsfield, Argentina	0-0		0-0	1
1981	Rosario Central, Argentina	3-2		1-0	1
	Junior Barranquilla, Colombia	3-0		0-0	1
	Deportivo Cali, Colombia	1-2		1-2	1
1982	Boca Juniors, Argentina	1-0		0-0	1
	The Strongest, Bolivia	4-1		0-1	1
	Jorge Wilsterman Cochabamba, Bolivia	3-0		1-0	1
	Flamengo Rio de Janeiro, Brazil	0-3		2-4	sf
	Penarol, Uruguay	2-4		1-2	sf
1986	Boca Juniors, Argentina	1-0		1-1	1
	Wanderers Montevideo, Uruguay	4-2		2-0	1
	Penarol, Uruguay	3-1		2-0	1
	Argentinos Juniors, Argentina	0-2	0-0	0-0	sf
	Barcelona Sporting Guayaquil, Ecuador	4-1		3-0	sf
	America de Cali, Colombia	1-0		2-1	FINAL
1987	Penarol, Uruguay	1-0		0-0	sf
	Independiente, Argentina	0-0		1-2	sf
1990	Independiente, Argentina	0-0		0-1	1
	Defensor Sportying, Uruguay	2-1		2-1	2
	Independients, Argentina	2-0		1-1	3
	Barcelona Guayaquil, Equdaor	1-0	3-4p	0-1	sf

CLUB ESTUDIANTES LA PLATA

Founded 4th August 1905
Address Avenida 53n 6200, 1900 La Plata ☎ 021-211137/38
Colours red and white striped shirts, black shorts
Stadium Paseo Bosque, Buenos Aires (25,000)
Champions 1913, 1931, 1934 (two Leagues in operation)
Metropolitan Champions 1967, Primera 1982
Libertadores Winners 1968, 1969, 1970 Finalists 1971
World Club Champions 1968 Finalists 1969, 1970
Inter America Cup Winners 1968

Season	Opponent	Home	Playoff Result	Away	Round
1968	Independiente, Argentina	2-0		4-2	1
	Millonarios Bogota, Colombia	0-0		1-0	1
	Deportivo Cali, Colombia	3-0		2-1	1
	Universitario Lima, Peru	1-0		0-1	qf
	Independiente, Argentina	1-0		2-1	qf

ARGENTINA

	Racing Club Avellaneda, Argentina	3-0	1-1	0-2	sf
	Palmeiras Sao Paulo, Brazil	2-1	2-0 in Montevideo	1-3	FINAL
1969	Universidad Catolica, Chile	3-1		3-1	sf
	Nacional, Uruguay	2-0		1-0	FINAL
1970	River Plate, Argentina	3-1		1-0	sf
	Penarol, Uruguay	1-0		0-0	FINAL
1971	Barcelona Sporting Guayaquil, Ecuador	0-1		1-0	sf
	Union Espanola, Chile	2-1		1-0	sf
	Nacional, Uruguay	1-0	0-2 in Lima	0-1	FINAL
1976	River Plate, Argentina	1-0		0-1	1
	Portuguesa Acarigua, Venezuela	3-0		2-2	1
	Galicia Caracas, Venezuela	4-0		1-0	1
1983	Cobreloa Calama, Chile	2-0		0-3	1
	Colo Colo, Chile	4-1		0-1	1
	FC Oeste, Argentina	0-0		2-1	1
	America de Cali, Colombia	2-0		0-0	sf
	Gremio Porto Alegre, Brazil	3-3		1-2	sf
1984	Independiente, Argentina	1-1		1-4	1
	Olimpia, Paraguay	0-1		1-2	1
	Sportivo Luqueno Luque, Paraguay	1-1		0-0	1

CLUB ATLETICO BOCA JUNIORS

Founded 3rd April 1905
Address Bradseb 805, 1161 Buenos Aires ☎ 362-2260/2551/2050
Colours all blue with broad yellow hoop on the shirt
Stadium La Bombonera, Buenos Aires (58,850)
Champions 1919, 1920, 1923, 1924, 1926*, 1930, 1931, 1934, 1935, 1940, 1943, 1944, 1954, 1962, 1964, 1965
Metropolitan Champions 1976, Primera 1981
National Champions 1969, 1970, 1976, 1986 (two Leagues in operation)
Libertadores Winners 1977, 1978 Finalists 1963, 1979
World Club Champions 1977
Inter America Cup Finalists 1977

Season	Opponent	Home	Playoff Result	Away	Round
1963	Olimpia, Paraguay	5-3		0-1	1
	Universidad de Chile, Chile	1-0		3-2	1
	Penarol, Uruguay	1-0		2-1	sf
	Santos Sao Paulo, Brazil	1-2		2-3	FINAL
1965	Deportivo Quito, Ecuador	4-0		2-1	1
	The Strongest, Bolivia	2-0		3-2	1
	Independiente, Argentina	1-0	0-0	0-2	sf
1966	River Plate, Argentina	2-0		1-2	1
	Italia Caracas, Venezuela	5-2		2-1	1
	Universitario Lima, Peru	2-0		1-2	1
	Alianza Lima, Peru	0-1		1-0	1
	Lara Basquimento, Venezuela	2-1		3-0	1
	Independiente, Argentina	0-0		0-2	sf
	Guarani, Paraguay	1-1		3-1	sf
	River Plate, Argentina	1-0		2-2	sf
1970	River Plate, Argentina	2-1		3-1	1
	Bolivar, Bolivia	2-0		3-2	1
	Universitario La Paz, Bolivia	4-0		0-0	1
	Universitario Lima, Peru	1-0		3-1	qf
	River Plate, Argentina	0-1		1-1	qf
1971	Rosario Central, Argentina	2-1		lost walkover	1
	Universitario Lima, Peru	lost walkover		0-0	1
	Sporting Cristal, Peru	2-2		0-2	1
1977	Defensor Sporting, Uruguay	2-0		0-0	1
	Penarol, Uruguay	1-0		1-0	1
	River Plate, Argentina	1-0		0-0	1
	Deportivo Cali, Colombia	1-1		1-1	sf
	Libertad, Paraguay	1-0		1-0	sf
	Cruzeiro Belo Horizonte, Brazil	1-0	0-0 5-4 pens*	0-1	FINAL

* Montevideo

1978	Atletico Mineiro Belo Horizonte, Brazil	3-1		2-1	sf
	River Plate, Argentina	0-0		2-0	sf
	Deportivo Cali, Colombia	4-0		0-0	FINAL
1979	Penarol, Uruguay	1-0		0-0	sf
	Independiente, Argentina	2-0	1-0	0-1	sf
	Olimpia, Paraguay	0-0		0-2	FINAL
1982	River Plate, Argentina	0-0		0-1	1
	Jorge Wilsterman Cochabamba, Bolivia	2-2		0-1	1
	The Strongest, Bolivia	1-0		0-1	1
1986	River Plate, Argentina	1-1		0-1	1
	Wanderers Montevideo, Uruguay	3-2		0-2	1
	Penarol, Uruguay	1-1		2-1	1
1989	Racing Club Avellaneda, Argentina	3-2	3-1	0-0	1
	Universitario Lima, Peru	2-0		0-1	1
	Sporting Cristal, Peru	4-3		0-1	1
	Olimpia, Paraguay	5-3	6-7p	0-2	2

CLUB ATLETICO ROSARIO CENTRAL

Founded 24th December 1889
Address Bvard Avellaneda v Avda Genova (2000) Rosario, Sante Fe ☎ 041-38317/390026
Colours blue and yellow striped shirts, blue shorts
Stadium Gigante de Arroyito/Cordoviola (41,634)
National Champions 1971, 1973, 1980, 1986

Season	Opponent	Home	Playoff Result	Away	Round
1971	Boca Juniors, Argentina	walk over		1-2	1
	Universitario Lima, Peru	2-2		2-3	1
	Sporting Cristal, Peru	4-0		2-1	1
1972	Independiente, Argentina	2-2		0-2	1
	Nacional Medellin, Colombia	3-1		0-1	1
	Independiente Santa Fe, Colombia	2-0		0-0	1
1974	Huracan, Argentina	1-0		0-1	1
	Union Espanola, Chile	4-0		1-0	1
	Colo Colo, Chile	2-0		3-2	1
1975	Newell's Old Boys Rosario, Argentina	1-1	1-0	1-1	1
	Cerro Porteno, Paraguay	2-1		3-1	1
	Olimpia, Paraguay	1-1		0-0	1
	Independiente, Argentina	2-0		0-2	sf
	Cruzeiro Belo Horizonte, Brazil	3-1		0-2	sf
1981	Junior Barranquilla, Colombia	5-0		2-1	1
	Deportivo Cali, Colombia	2-1		0-1	1
	River Plate, Argentina	0-1		2-3	1
1987	Independiente, Argentina	0-0		1-3	1
	Estudiantes Merida, Venezuela	5-2		3-0	1
	Tachira San Cristobal, Venezuela	3-2		0-0	1

RACING CLUB

Founded 25th March 1903
Address Avenida Mitre 934, 1870 Avellaneda ☎ 201-7258
Colours sky blue and white striped shirts, black shorts
Stadium Mozart y Cuyo, Avellaneda (70,100)
Champions 1913, 1914, 1915, 1916, 1917, 1918, 1919, 1921, 1925, 1949, 1950, 1951, 1958, 1961, 1966
World Club Champions 1967
South American Super Cup Winners 1988

Season	Opponent	Home	Playoff Result	Away	Round
1962	Sporting Cristal, Peru	2-1		1-2	1
	Nacional, Uruguay	2-2		2-3	qf

ARGENTINA

1967	Deportivo Independiente Medellin, Colombia	5-2		2-0	1
	Independiente Sante Fe, Colombia	4-1		2-1	1
	River Plate, Argentina	2-0		0-0	1
	Bolivar, Bolivia	6-0		2-0	1
	31 de Octubre, Bolivia	6-0		0-3	1
	Universitario Lima, Peru	1-2		2-1	sf
	River Plate, Argentina	3-1		0-0	sf
	Colo Colo, Chile	3-1		2-0	sf
	Nacional, Uruguay	0-0	2-1 in Santiago	0-0	FINAL
1968	Estudiantes La Plata, Argentina	2-0	1-1	0-3	sf
1989	Boca Juniors, Argentina	0-0	1-3	2-3	1
	Universitario Lima, Peru	2-0		1-2	1
	Sporting Cristal, Peru	2-0		2-1	1
	Nacional Medellin, Colombia	2-1		0-2	2

CLUB ATLETICO SAN LORENZO DE ALMAGRO

Founded 1st April 1908
Address Avenida La Plata 1782, 1250 Buenos Aires ☎ 923 9212
Colours red and blue broad striped shirts, blue shorts
Stadium Estadio Tomas A Duco, Buenos Aires (49,300)
Champions 1923, 1924, 1927, 1933, 1946, 1959
Metropolitan Champions 1968, 1972
National Champions 1972, 1974

Season	Opponent	Home	Playoff Result	Away	Round
1960	Sport Clube Bahia Salvador, Brazil	3-0		2-3	1
	Penarol, Uruguay	1-1	1-2	0-0	sf
1973	River Plate, Argentina	4-0		1-0	1
	Jorge Wilsterman Cochabamba, Bolivia	3-0		0-1	1
	Oriente Petrolero Santa Cruz, Bolivia	4-0		3-0	1
	Millonarios Bogota, Colombia	2-0		0-0	sf
	Independiente, Argentina	2-2		0-1	sf
1988	Newell's Old Boys Rosario, Argentina	0-0	0-1	0-0	1
	Barcelona Sporting Guayaquil, Ecuador	2-1		0-2	1
	Filanbanco Guayaquil, Ecuador	2-0		2-1	1
	Guarani Campinas, Brazil	1-1		1-0	2
	Penarol, Uruguay	1-0		0-0	qf
	Newell's Old Boys Rosario, Argentina	1-2		0-1	sf

CLUB ATLETICO HURACAN

Founded 1st November 1908
Address Avenida Caseros 3121, 1263 Buenos Aires
Colours white shirts with red trim, blue shorts
Stadium Tomas Adolfo Duco, Buenos Aires (48,500)
Champions 1921, 1922, 1925, 1928
Metropolitan Champions 1973

Season	Opponent	Home	Playoff Result	Away	Round
1974	Rosario Central, Argentina	1-0	4-0	0-1	1
	Union Espanola, Chile	5-1		3-1	1
	Colo Colo, Chile	2-0		2-1	1
	Independiente, Argentina	1-1		0-3	sf
	Penarol, Uruguay	0-3		1-1	sf

CLUB ATLETICO NEWELL'S OLD BOYS

Founded 3rd November 1903
Address Parque Independencia, 2000 Rosario ☎ 041-499661/21180
Colours red and black halved shirts, black shorts
Stadium Parque Independencia (35,000)
Metropolitan Champions 1974
Libertadores Finalists 1988

Season	Opponent	Home	Playoff Result	Away	Round
1975	Rosario Central, Argentina	1-1	0-1	1-1	1
	Olimpia, Paraguay	3-2		0-2	1
	Cerro Porteno, Paraguay	3-2		1-0	1
1988	San Lorenzo, Argentina	0-0	1-0	0-0	1
	Barcelona Sporting Guayaquil, Ecuador	3-0		0-0	1
	Filanbanco Guayaquil, Ecuador	1-0		1-1	1
	Bolivar, Bolivia	1-0	3-2p	0-1	2
	Nacional, Uruguay	1-1		1-2	qf
	San Lorenzo, Argentina	1-0		2-1	sf
	Nacional, Uruguay	1-0		0-3 aet	FINAL

QUILMES ATHLETIC CLUB

Founded 27th November 1887
Address Guidoy Paz, 1878 Quilmes
Colours white shorts with blue trim, blue shorts
Stadium Sarmiento (20,000)
Metropolitan Champions 1978

Season	Opponent	Home	Result	Away	Round
1979	Independiente, Argentina	1-2		0-2	1
	Deportivo Cali, Colombia	3-1		2-3	1
	Millonarios Bogota, Colombia	1-2		0-1	1

CLUB FERRO CARRIL OESTE

Founded 28th July 1904
Address Cucha Cucha 350, 1405 Buenos Aires ☎ 431 8282/6673
Colours green shirts with white trim, white shorts
Stadium Martin de Gainza, Buenos Aires (24,812)
National Champions 1982, 1984

Season	Opponent	Home	Playoff Result	Away	Round
1985	Fluminense Rio de Janeiro, Brazil	1-0		0-0	1
	Vasco da Gama Rio de Janeiro, Brazil	2-0		2-0	1
	Argentinos Juniors, Argentina	1-3	1-3	1-0	1

ARGENTINA

ASOCIACION ATLETICA ARGENTINOS JUNIORS

Founded 15th August 1904 by merger of Soldela Victoria, Martires de Chicago and Catedral Porteno
Address Punta Arenas 1271, 1427 Buenos Aires ☎ 581-8949
Stadium Estadio Martin de Gainza, Buenos Aires (24,812)
Colours all red with white trim
Metropolitan Champions 1984, 1985
National Champions 1985
Libertadores Winners 1985
World Club Champions 1985

Season	Opponent	Home	Playoff Result	Away	Round
1985	Vasco da Gama Rio de Janeiro, Brazil	2-2		2-1	1
	Fluminense Rio de Janeiro, Brazil	1-0		1-0	1
	FC Oeste, Argentina	0-1	3-1	3-1	1
	Independiente, Argentina	2-2		2-1	sf
	Blooming Santa Cruz, Bolivia	1-0		1-1	sf
	America de Cali, Colombia	1-0	1-1 in Asuncion	0-1 5-4 pens	FINAL
1986	River Plate, Argentina	0-0		2-0	sf
	Barcelona Sporting Guayaquil, Ecuador	1-0		0-1	sf

CLUB ATLETICO VELEZ SARSFIELD

Founded 1st January 1910
Address Juan B Justo 9200, 1408 Buenos Aires ☎ 641-5663/5763/3310
Colours white shirts with blue V, blue shorts
Stadium Jose Amalfitani, Buenos Aires (49,806)
National Champions 1968

Season	Opponent	Home	Result	Away	Round
1980	Sporting Cristal, Peru	2-0		1-0	1
	Atletico Chalaco Callao, Peru	5-2		2-0	1
	River Plate, Argentina	0-0		0-0	1
	Internacional Porto Alegre, Brazil	0-1		1-3	sf
	America de Cali, Colombia	0-0		0-0	sf

BOLIVIA

Founded 1925
Federacion Boliviana de Football, Av 16 de Julio n.0782, CP 0782 Cochabamba Casilla Postal No 484
☎ **010 591-42 4 5064/4 7950 Telex 6239 Fedbol Fax (591-42) 47951**
National colours white shirts, black shorts
Language Spanish
Season February to December

PRE WAR CHAMPIONS

1926	Sucre, Cochabamba F.A.	**1930**	no competition
1927	Potosi, Asociacion de Football Potosi	**1931**	Uyuni, Cochabamba F.A.
1928	La Paz, Cochabamba F.A.	**1932-35**	not contested owing to war
1929	Oruro, Liga Deportiva de Oruro		

LEAGUE CHAMPIONS

1914	The Strongest	**1930**	The Strongest	**1947**	Litoral	**1960**	Jorge Wilsterman
1915	Colego Militar	**1931**	Nimbles Rail	**1948**	Litoral	**1961**	Deportivo Municipal
1916	The Strongest	**1932**	The Strongest	**1949**	Litoral	**1962**	Chaco Petrolero
1917	The Strongest	**1933**	not held			**1963**	Aurora
1918	not held	**1934**	not held	**1950**	Bolivar	**1964**	The Strongest
1919	not held	**1935**	The Strongest	**1951**	Always Ready	**1965**	Deportivo Municipal
		1936	Ayacucho	**1952**	The Strongest	**1966**	Bolivar
1920	The Strongest	**1937**	The Strongest	**1953**	Bolivar	**1967**	Jorge Wilsterman
1921	not held	**1938**	The Strongest	**1954**	Litoral	**1968**	Bolivar
1922	not held	**1939**	Bolivar	**1955**	San Jose Oruro	**1969**	Universitario
1923	Universitario			**1956**	Bolivar		
1924	The Strongest	**1940**	Bolivar	**1957**	Always Ready	**1970**	Chaco Petrolero
1925	not held	**1941**	Bolivar	**1958**	Deportivo Municipal	**1971**	Oriente Petrolero
1926	Universitario	**1942**	Bolivar	**1959**	Jorge Wilsterman	**1972**	Jorge Wilsterman
1927	Nimbles Sport	**1943**	The Strongest			**1973**	Jorge Wilsterman
1928	Deportivo Militar	**1944**	Ferroviario			**1974**	The Strongest
1929	The Strongest	**1945**	The Strongest			**1975**	Guabira
		1946	not held			**1976**	Bolivar

PROFESIONAL LEAGUE

1977	The Strongest	**1983**	Bolivar
1978	Bolivar	**1984**	Blooming
1979	Oriente Petrolero	**1985**	Bolivar
		1986	The Strongest
1980	Jorge Wilsterman	**1987**	Bolivar
1981	Jorge Wilsterman	**1988**	The Strongest
1982	Bolivar	**1989**	The Strongest
		1990	Oriente Petrolero

BOLIVIA

FEATURED CLUBS IN COPA LIBERTADORES DE AMERICA

Jorge Wilsterman Cochbamba	Deportivo Municipal La Paz	31st de Octubre	Bolivar La Paz
The Strongest La Paz	Oriente Petrolero Santa Cruz	Always Ready	Litoral
Universitario	Guabira Santa Cruz de la Sierra		Chaco Petrolero La Paz
Blooming Santa Cruz de la Sierra		Club Aurora Cochabamba	

CLUB JORGE WILSTERMAN

Founded 1949
Address San Martin S-0348, Cochabamba
Colours dark red shirts, blue shorts
Stadium Felix Capriles, Cochabamba (35,000)
Champions 1958, 1959, 1966, 1967, 1972, 1973, 1980, 1981

Season	Opponent	Home	Playoff Result	Away	Rnd
1960	Penarol, Uruguay	1-1		1-7	1
1961	Independiente Santa Fe, Colombia	3-2	lag	0-1	2
1966	Penarol, Uruguay	1-0		0-2	1
	Nacional, Uruguay	0-0		0-3	1
	Deportivo Municipal La Paz, Bolivia	2-1		1-1	1
	Emelec Guayaquil, Ecuador	2-1		1-3	1
	Nueve de Octubre Guayaquil, Ecuador	4-1		2-3	1
1968	Sporting Cristal, Peru	0-1		0-2	1
	Always Ready, Bolivia	3-0		not played	1
	Universitario Lima, Peru	0-0		5-1	1
1973	San Lorenzo, Argentina	1-0		0-3	1
	River Plate, Argentina	1-0		2-2	1
	Oriente Petrolero Santa Cruz, Bolivia	3-1		0-1	1
1974	Palmeiras Sao Paulo, Brazil	1-0		0-2	1
	Sao Paulo FC, Brazil	0-1		0-5	1
	Deportivo Municipal La Paz, Bolivia	1-0		not played	1
1975	The Strongest, Bolivia	1-1		1-3	1
	Huachipato Talcahuano, Chile	0-0		0-4	1
	Union Espanola, Chile	1-1		1-4	1
1979	Bolivar, Bolivia	0-6		0-4	1
	Olimpia, Paraguay	0-2		2-4	1
	Sol de America, Paraguay	2-3		1-2	1
1981	Barcelona Sporting Guayaquil, Ecuador	1-0		0-3	1
	Tecnico Universitario de Ambato, Ecuador	3-1		2-1	1
	The Strongest, Bolivia	3-2		0-2	1
	Flamengo Rio de Janeiro, Brazil	1-2		1-4	sf
	Deportivo Cali, Colombia	1-1		0-1	sf
1982	The Strongest, Bolivia	1-2		1-1	1
	Boca Juniors, Argentina	1-0		2-2	1
	River Plate, Argentina	0-1		0-3	1
1986	Bolivar, Bolivia	1-2		0-2	1
	Universitario Lima, Peru	4-0		2-1	1
	Universidad Tecnica Cajarmarca, Peru	2-0		2-3	1

DEPORTIVO MUNICIPAL

Founded 1944
Colours crimson shirts with green and white trim, white shorts
Stadium Luis Lastra, La Paz (10,000)
Champions 1960, 1961, 1965

Season	Opponents	Home	Result	Away	Round
1962	Cerro Porteno, Paraguay	1-2		2-3	1
	Santos Sao Paulo, Brazil	3-4		1-6	1
1966	Penarol, Uruguay	1-2		1-3	1
	Nacional, Uruguay	3-2		1-4	1
	Jorge Wilsterman Cochabamba, Bolivia	1-1		1-2	1
	Emelec Guayaquil, Ecuador	4-1		1-2	1
	Nueve de Octubre, Ecuador	5-1		4-3	1
1974	Palmeiras Sao Paulo, Brazil	0-1		0-3	1
	Sao Paulo FC, Brazil	1-1		3-3	1
	Jorge Wilsterman Cochabamba, Bolivia	not played		0-1	1

31st de OCTUBRE

Founded
Colours white shirts with 31 in black on the chest, and black trim
Stadium

Season	Opponents	Home	Result	Away	Round
1967	Deportivo Independiente Medellin, Colombia	1-2		1-2	1
	Independiente Santa Fe, Colombia	6-2		0-2	1
	Racing Club Avellaneda, Argentina	3-0		0-6	1
	River Plate, Argentina	0-4		0-7	1
	Bolivar, Bolivia	2-2		0-1	1

BOLIVAR INDEPEDIENTE UNIFICADA

Founded 1925
Colours all sky blue
Stadium main matches played at Estadio Nacional, Quito (65,000)
Address Ed. Litoral, Calle Colon, La Paz
Champions 1939, 1940, 1941, 1942, 1950, 1953, 1956, 1968, 1976, 1978, 1982, 1983, 1985, 1987

Season	Opponents	Home	Playoff Result	Away	Round
1967	Deportivo Independiente Medellin, Colombia	2-2		0-2	1
	Independiente Santa Fe, Colombia	2-2		2-1	1
	Racing Club Avellaneda, Argentina	0-2		0-6	1
	River Plate, Argentina	3-3		0-2	1
	31st de Octubre, Bolivia	1-0		2-2	1
1969	Litoral, Bolivia	1-0		1-1	1
	Cerro Porteno, Paraguay	2-1		1-1	1
	Olimpia, Paraguay	1-1	1-2	0-4	1
1970	Universitario La Paz, Bolivia	2-0		2-2	1
	Boca Juniors, Argentina	2-3		0-2	1
	River Plate, Argentina	1-1		0-1	1
1976	Guabira Santa Cruz, Bolivia	7-1		0-1	1
	Liga Deportivo Universitaria, Ecuador	3-2		1-2	1
	Deportivo Cuenca, Ecuador	4-2		1-3	1
1977	Oriente Petrolero Santa Cruz, Bolivia	1-0		0-0	1
	Nacional Medellin, Colombia	3-0		0-1	1
	Deportivo Cali, Colombia	3-0		0-3	1

BOLIVIA

1979	Jorge Wilsterman Cochabamba, Bolivia	4-0		6-0	1
	Sol de America, Paraguay	4-1		2-2	1
	Olimpia, Paraguay	2-1		0-3	1
1983	Gremio Porto Alegre, Brazil	1-2		1-3	1
	Flamengo Rio de Janeiro, Brazil	3-1		2-5	1
	Blooming Santa Cruz, Bolivia	6-0		0-3	1
1984	Universidad Catolica, Chile	3-2		1-3	1
	O'Higgins Rancagua, Chile	5-1		0-0	1
	Blooming Santa Cruz, Bolivia	0-0		1-2	1
1986	Jorge Wilsterman Cochabamba, Bolivia	2-0		2-1	1
	Universitario Lima, Peru	4-0		0-3	1
	Universidad Tecnica Cajarmarca, Peru	2-1		2-2	1
	Olimpia, Paraguay	1-1		1-3	sf
	America de Cali, Colombia	2-0		1-2	sf
1988	Oriente Petrolero Santa Cruz, Bolivia	3-1		1-2	1
	Olimpia, Paraguay	2-0		2-4	1
	Cerro Porteno, Paraguay	2-0		2-3	1
	Newell's Old Boys Rosario, Argentina	1-0	2-3p	0-1	2
1989	The Strongest, Bolivia	0-0		0-0	1
	Penarol, Uruguay	3-0		0-5	1
	Danubio, Uruguay	3-1		0-1	1
	Millonarios Bogota, Colombia	1-0	3-4p	2-3	2

ORIENTE PETROLERO

Founded 1955
Colours green shirts, white shorts
Stadium Ramon "Tauhichi" Aguilera, Santa Cruz de la Sierra (40,000)
Address YPFB, Santa Cruz de la Sierra
Champions 1971, 1979, 1990

Season	Opponents	Home	Result	Away	Round
1972	Barcelona Sporting Guayaquil, Ecuador	0-0		1-1	1
	Chaco Petrolero, Bolivia	5-0		0-1	1
	America Quito, Ecuador	4-2		0-3	1
1973	San Lorenzo, Argentina	0-3		0-4	1
	River Plate, Argentina	1-3		1-7	1
	Jorge Wilsterman Cochabamba, Bolivia	3-1		0-1	1
1977	Bolivar, Bolivia	0-0		0-1	1
	Nacional Medellin, Colombia	4-0		1-3	1
	Deportivo Cali, Colombia	1-0		0-3	1
1978	The Strongest, Bolivia	4-0		0-2	1
	Alianza Lima, Peru	0-4		1-5	1
	Sporting Cristal, Peru	0-1		0-1	1
1980	The Strongest, Bolivia	1-0		2-3	1
	Nacional, Uruguay	1-3		0-5	1
	Defensor Sporting, Uruguay	0-1		1-1	
1985	Blooming Santa Cruz, Bolivia	0-1		1-1	1
	Tachira San Cristobal, Venezuela	3-2		1-1	1
	Italia Caracas, Venezuela	3-1		3-0	1
1987	The Strongest, Bolivia	2-1		2-3	1
	Deportivo Cali, Colombia	0-1		1-5	1
	America de Cali, Colombia	1-1		1-3	1
1988	Bolivar, Bolivia	2-1		1-3	1
	Olimpia, Paraguay	1-0		2-1	
	Cerro Porteno, Paraguay	2-2		0-1	1
	Colo Colo, Chile	2-1		0-0	2
	America de Cali, Colombia	1-1		0-2	qf
1990	The Strongest, Bolivia	1-0		0-2	1
	Emelec, Ecudaro	1-0		0-0	1
	Barcelona Guayaquil, Ecuador	1-1		1-2	1
	Barcelona Guayaquil, Ecuador	3-2	lag	1-3	1 po

THE STRONGEST

Founded 8th April 1908
Colours black and yellow striped shirts, black shorts
Stadium Rafael Mendoza, La Plaz (40,000)
Address Comercio Esquerda 512, La Paz
Champions 1914, 1916, 1917, 1920, 1924, 1929, 1930, 1932, 1935, 1937, 1938, 1943, 1945, 1952, 1963, 1964, 1974, 1977, 1986, 1988, 1989

Season	Opponents	Home	Result	Away	Round
1965	Deportivo Quito, Ecuador	2-2		1-0	1
	Boca Juniors, Argentina	2-3		0-2	
1971	Chaco Petrolero, Bolivia	2-1		1-3	1
	Penarol, Uruguay	1-2		0-9	1
	Nacional, Uruguay	1-1		0-5	1
1975	Jorge Wilsterman Cochabamba, Bolivia	3-1		1-1	1
	Hauchipato Talcahuano, Chile	1-0		2-4	1
	Union Espanola, Chile	1-1		0-4	1
1978	Alianza Lima, Peru	2-2		1-4	1
	Oriente Petrolero Santa Cruz, Bolivia	2-0		0-4	1
	Sporting Cristal, Peru	3-1		0-2	1
1980	Oriente Petrolero Santa Cruz, Bolivia	3-2		0-1	1
	Nacional, Uruguay	3-0		0-2	1
	Defensor Sporting, Uruguay	2-0		1-1	1
1981	Barcelona Sporting Guayaquil, Ecuador	1-0		1-2	1
	Universitario Tecnico Ambata, Ecuador	4-2		3-2	1
	Jorge Wilsterman Cochabamba, Bolivia	2-0		2-3	1
1982	Jorge Wilsterman Cochabamba, Bolivia	1-1		2-1	1
	River Plate, Argentina	1-0		1-4	1
	Boca Juniors, Argentina	1-0		0-1	1
1987	Oriente Petrolero Santa Cruz, Bolivia	3-2		1-2	1
	Deportivo Cali, Colombia	2-1		0-4	1
	America de Cali, Colombia	1-1		0-6	1
1989	Bolivar, Bolivia	0-0		0-0	1
	Penarol, Uruguay	1-2		1-1	1
	Danubio, Uruguay	1-0		0-1	1
1990	Oriente Petrolero, Bolivia	2-0		0-1	1
	Emelec, Ecuador	4-3		0-1	1
	Barcelona Guayaquil, Ecuador	2-1		0-1	1
	Universidad Catolica, Chile	1-1		1-3	2

CLUB ALWAYS READY

Founded
Colours all white with red sash and trim
Stadium Olimpico de Hernanda Siles, La Plaz (55,000) or Achumani (40,000)
Champions 1951, 1957

Season	Opponents	Home	Result	Away	Round
1968	Sporting Cristal, Peru	1-4		1-1	1
	Jorge Wilsterman Cochabamba, Bolivia	not played		0-3	1
	Universitario Lima, Peru	0-3		0-6	1

BOLIVIA

CLUB LITORAL

Founded
Colours all white with sky blue trim
Stadium Olimpico de Hernanda Siles, La Plaz (55,000) or Achumani (40,000)
Champions 1947, 1948, 1949, 1954

Season	Opponents	Home	Result	Away	Round
1969	Bolivar, Bolivia	1-1		0-1	1
	Olimpia, Paraguay	0-3		0-2	1
	Cerro Porteno, Paraguay	0-1		0-6	1

UNIVERSITARIO

Founded
Coloursall blue with white trim
Stadium Olimpicode Hernando Siles, La Plaz (55,000)
Champions 1923, 1926, 1969

Season	Opponents	Home	Result	Away	Round
1970	Bolivar, Bolivia	2-2		0-2	1
	Boca Juniors, Argentina	0-0		0-4	1
	River Plate, Argentina	0-2		0-9	1

GUABIRA

Founded 1962
Colours Red shirts, Blue shorts
Stadium Ramon "Tauhichi" Aguilera (40,000)
Address Ingenio Azucarero Guabira, Santa Cruz
Champions 1975

Season	Opponents	Home	Result	Away	Round
1976	Bolivar, Bolivia	1-0		1-7	1
	Liga Deportivo Universitaria, Ecuador	0-1		0-4	1
	Deportivo Cuenca, Ecuador	0-2		0-1	1

CHACO PETROLERO

Founded 1944
Colours green and white striped shirts, white shorts
Stadium Estadio Nacional Olimpico, La Plaz (55,000)
Champions 1962, 1970

Season	Opponents	Home	Result	Away	Round
1963	withdrew				
1971	The Strongest, Bolivia	3-1		1-2	1
	Nacional, Uruguay	0-1		0-3	1
	Penarol, Uruguay	1-1		0-1	1
1972	Barcelona Sporting Guayaquil, Ecuador	1-2		0-3	1
	Oriente Petrolero Santa Cruz, Bolivia	1-0		0-5	1
	America Quito, Ecuador	1-2		0-1	1

78

CLUB BLOOMING

Founded 1946
Colours sky blue shirts, white shorts
Stadium Ramon "Tauhichi" Aquilera, Santa Cuz de la Sierra (40,000)
Address 24 de Septembre, Santa Cruz de la Sierra
Champions 1984

Season	Opponents	Home	Result	Away	Round
1983	Gremio Porto Alegre, Brazil	0-2		0-2	1
	Flamengo Rio de Janeiro, Brazil	0-0		1-7	1
	Bolivar, Bolivia	3-0		0-6	1
1984	Universidad Catolica, Chile	1-2		0-0	1
	Bolivar, Bolivia	2-1		0-0	1
	O'Higgins Rancagua, Chile	3-0		4-3	1
1985	Oriente Petrolero Santa Cruz, Bolivia	1-1		1-0	1
	Italia Caracas, Venezuela	8-0		3-0	1
	Tachira San Cristobal, Venezuela	6-1		1-0	1
	Argentinos Juniors, Argentina	1-1		0-1	sf
	Independiente, Argentina	1-1		0-2	sf

CLUB AURORA

Founded 1935
Colours sky blue shirts, white shorts
Stadium Felix Capriles, Cochabamba (35,000)
Address Jordan 3797, Cochabamba

Season	Opponents	Home	Result	Away	Round
1964	Nacional, Uruguay	0-3		0-2	1
	Cerro Porteno, Paraguay	2-2		0-7	1

1968 **Estudiantes** (Argentina)

1970 **Estudiantes** (Argentina)

1975 **Independiente** (Argentina)

BRAZIL

Founded 1914
Confederacao Brasileira De Futebol (CBF), P.O.Box 1078, Rua de Alfandega 70, 20700 CEP, Rio de Janeiro
☎ 010 55-21 221 5937 Telex 2121509 Fax (55-21) 2529294
National colours yellow shirts, green shorts
Language Spanish, French, English

No country in the world is as chaotically disorganised at national level.

Domestic competition is split into two spheres. On the one hand is the national championship, which brings 'together' around 36 of the top clubs of all Brazil's provinces; then, and of far greater importance to the vast majority of fans, come the provincial championships.

The national championship was inaugurated in the 1970s in answer to pressure from the great provincial (ie NOT Rio de Janeiro and Sao Paulo) clubs who wanted to contest the traditional power of Rio and Sao Paulo. Clubs such as Gremio and Internacional of Porto Alegre and Atletico Mineiro and Cruzeiro of Belo Horizonte have, since their 'emergence', proved among the most successful of Brazilian clubs in the South American club cup.

Thr national championship is not run on a traditional European home-and-away league basis. The various rounds are based on mini-leagues of five or six clubs. The teams play each other home and away with the bottom club being eliminated. The survivors are then reorganised in a new set of mini-league in the next round, and so on. The final is a home-and-away affair between the two survivors of this whittling-down process.

It's a system specifically designed to protect the giants (Flamengo, Vasco, Botafogo and Fluminense of Rio; Sao Paulo FC and Corinthians from Sao Paulo).

Even so, the big clubs hate the championship because the costs of flying thousands of miles round Brazil are enormous, even though they receive sponsorship subsidies through the confederation. The big clubs also complain that though they draw big crowds in the provinces, the provincial clubs are anything but crowd-pullers when they come to Rio and Sao Paulo.

Thus the big clubs prefer the state tournaments where travel costs are minimal and the old derby rivalries guarantee far better average attendances.

Yet even the state leagues are articially reorganised to try to maintain interest - often with a big fuss being made over the leaders at halfway. They either win a big trophy (such as the Guanabara Cup in Rio) or are guaranteed a place in the end-of-league title play-off against the team which is top at the end of the championship.

The formats are changed and varied each year and, sometimes, even halfway through the championships themselves. This happened in the 1990 Rio (Carioca) championship and resulted in Botafogo going to court after Vasco da Gama claimed that they - under a midseason rule change - should have been crowned champions instead!

NATIONAL CHAMPIONS

1967	Palmeiras, Sao Paulo		**1980**	Flamengo, Rio de Janeiro v Atletico Mineiro	
1968	Santos FC, Sao Paulo			Belo Horizonte	
1969	Palmeiras, Sao Paulo		**1981**	Gremio, Porto Alegre v Sao Paulo FC	
			1982	Flamengo, Rio de Janeiro v Gremio, Belo Horizonte	
1970	Fluminense, Rio de Janeiro		**1983**	Flamengo, Rio de Janeiro v Santos FC, Sao Paulo	
1971	Atletico Mineiro Belo Horizonte v Sao Paulo FC		**1984**	Fluminense, Rio de Janeiro v Vasco de Gama,	
1972	Palmeiras, Sao Paulo v Botafogo, Rio de Janeiro			Rio de Janeiro	
1973	Palmeiras, Sao Paulo v Sao Paulo FC		**1985**	Coritiba, Curitiba v Bangu, Rio de Janeiro	
1974	Vasco de Gama, Rio v Cruzeiro, Belo Horizonte		**1986**	Sao Paulo FC v Guarani, Sao Paulo	
1975	Internacional, Porto Alegre v Cruzeiro, Belo Horizonte		**1987**	Flamengo, Rio de Janeiro v Internacional Porto Alegre	
1976	Internacional, Porto Alegre v Corinthians, Sao Paulo		**1988**	Esporte Clube Bahia, Salvador v Internacional Porto	
1977	Sao Paulo FC v Atletico Mineiro, Belo Horizonte			Alegre	0-0 2-1
1978	Guarani, Sao Paulo v Palmeiras, Sao Paulo		**1989**	Vasco da Gama, Rio v Sao Paulo FC	1-0
1979	Internacional Porto Alegre v Vasco de Gama,				
	Rio de Janeiro		**1990**	Corinthiens Sao Paulo v Sao Paulo FC	1-0 1-0

81

BRAZIL

RIO DE JANEIRO (FEDERACAO CARIOCA de FUTEBOL)

Main Clubs
RIO: Fluminense FC, CR Flamengo, Botafogo, Vasco de Gama, AC Bangu, America FC, Olaria AC
CAMPOS: Americano FC, Goytacaz FC
ITAPERUMA: Porto Alegre FC

1906	Fluminense	1927	Flamengo	1947	Vasco de Gama	1970	Vasco de Gama
1907	Fluminense/Botafogo	1928	America	1948	Botafogo	1971	Fluminense
1908	Fluminense	1929	Vasco de Gama	1949	Vasco de Gama	1972	Flamengo
1909	Fluminense					1973	Fluminense
		1930	Botafogo	1950	Vasco de Gama	1974	Flamengo
1910	Botafogo	1931	America	1951	Fluminense	1975	Fluminense
1911	Fluminense	1932	Botafogo	1952	Vasco de Gama	1976	Fluminense
1912	Paissandu	1933	Bangu/Botafogo	1953	Flamengo	1977	Vasco de Gama
1913	America	1934	Vasco de Gama/	1954	Flamengo	1978	Flamengo
1914	Flamengo		Botafogo	1955	Flamengo	1979	Flamengo
1915	Flamengo	1935	Botafogo/America	1956	Vasco de Gama		
1916	America	1936	Vasco de Gama/	1957	Botafogo	1980	Fluminense
1917	Fluminense		Fluminense	1958	Vasco de Gama	1981	Flamengo
1918	Fluminense	1937	Fluminense	1959	Fluminense	1982	Vasco de Gama
1919	Fluminense	1938	Fluminense			1983	Fluminense
		1939	Flamengo	1960	America	1984	Fluminense
				1961	Botafogo	1985	Fluminense
1920	Flamengo			1962	Botafogo	1986	Flamengo
1921	Flamengo	1940	Fluminense	1963	Flamengo	1987	Vasco de Gama
1922	America	1941	Fluminense	1964	Fluminense	1988	Vasco de Gama
1923	Vasco de Gama	1942	Flamengo	1965	Flamengo		
1924	Vasco de Gama/	1943	Flamengo	1966	Bangu		
	Fluminense	1944	Flamengo	1967	Botafogo		
1925	Flamengo	1945	Vasco de Gama	1968	Botafogo		
1926	Sao Cristovao	1946	Fluminense	1969	Fluminense		

SAO PAULO (FEDERACAO PAULISTA de FUTEBOL)

Main Clubs
SAO PAULO: Santos FC, Sao Paulo FC, Corinthians, Palmeiras, Portuguesa de Deportes
CAMPINAS: Guarani FC, AA Ponte Preta
ARARAQUARA: Ferroviaria
SAO JOSE do RIO PRETO: America FC
LIMEIRA: Internacional

* Two rival Leagues in operation

1902	Sao Paulo AC	1918	Paulistano	1930	Corinthians	1946	Sao Paulo FC
1903	Sao Paulo AC	1919	Paulistano	1931	Sao Paulo FC	1947	Palmeiras
1904	Sao Paulo AC			1932	Palestra Italia	1948	Sao Paulo FC
1905	Paulistano	1920	Palestra Italia	1933	Palestra Italia	1949	Sao Paulo FC
1906	Germania	1921	Paulistano	1934	Palestra Italia		
1907	Internacional Limeira	1922	Corinthians	1935	Portuguesa/Santos FC*	1950	Palmeiras
1908	Paulistano	1923	Corinthians	1936	Portuguesa/	1951	Corinthians
1909	AA das Palmeiras	1924	Corinthians		Palestra Italia*	1952	Corinthians
		1925	Sao Bento	1937	Corinthians	1953	Sao Paulo FC
1910	AA das Palmeiras	1926	Palestra Italia/	1938	Corinthians	1954	Corinthians
1911	Sao Paulo AC		Paulistano*	1939	Corinthians	1955	Santos FC
1912	Americano	1927	Palestra Italia/			1956	Santos FC
1913	Americano/Paulistano*		Paulistano*	1940	Palestra Italia	1957	Sao Paulo FC
1914	Corinthians/Sao Bento*	1928	Corinthians/	1941	Corinthians	1958	Santos FC
1915	Germania/		Internacional SP*	1942	Palmeiras	1959	Palmeiras
	AA das Palmeiras*	1929	Corinthians/	1943	Sao Paulo FC		
1916	Corinthians/Paulistano*		Paulistano*	1944	Palmeiras	1960	Santos FC
1917	Paulistano			1945	Sao Paulo FC	1961	Santos FC

1962	Santos FC	1970	Sao Paulo FC	1978	Santos FC	1985	Sao Paulo FC
1963	Palmeiras	1971	Sao Paulo FC	1979	Corinthians	1986	Internacional Limeira
1964	Santos FC	1972	Palmeiras			1987	Sao Paulo FC
1965	Santos FC	1973	Santos FC/Portuguesa	1980	Sao Paulo FC	1988	Corinthians
1966	Palmeiras	1974	Palmeiras	1981	Sao Paulo FC		
1967	Santos FC	1975	Sao Paulo FC	1982	Corinthians		
1968	Santos FC	1976	Palmeiras	1983	Corinthians		
1969	Santos FC	1977	Corinthians	1984	Santos FC		

RIO/SAO PAULO CHAMPIONS

1950	Corinthians Sao Paulo	1957	Fluminense Rio De Janeiro	1960	Fluminense Rio de Janeiro	1965	Palmeiras Sao Paulo
1951	Palmeiras Sao Paulo					1966	Botafogo/Corinthians/
1952	Portuguesa Sao Paulo	1958	Vasco de Gama Rio de Janeiro	1961	Flamengo Rio de Janeiro		Santos FC/Vasco de Gama all shared
1953	Corinthians Sao Paulo			1962	Botafogo Rio de Janeiro		
1954	Corinthians Sao Paulo	1959	Santos FC Sao Paulo	1963	Santos FC Sao Paulo		
1955	Portuguesa Sao Paulo			1964	Botafogo Rio de Janeiro/ Santos FC Sao Paulo shared		
1956	not held						

MINAS GERAIS STATE CHAMPIONSHIP

Main Clubs
BELO HORIZONTE: Club Atletico Mineiro, Cruzeiro EC, America FC
UBERABA: Nacional FC, Uberaba SC
ITABIRA: Valerio EC
NOVA LIMA: Villa Nova AC
LAVRAS: Fabril EC

1914	Atletico Mineiro	1940	Palestra Italia	1960	Cruzeiro	1980	Atletico Mineiro
1915	not held	1941	Atletico Mineiro	1961	Cruzeiro	1981	Atletico Mineiro
1916	America	1942	Atletico Mineiro	1962	Atletico Mineiro	1982	Atletico Mineiro
1917	America	1943	Cruzeiro	1963	Atletico Mineiro	1983	Atletico Mineiro
1918	America	1944	Cruzeiro	1964	Siderurgica	1984	Cruzeiro
1919	America	1945	Cruzeiro	1965	Cruzeiro	1985	Atletico Mineiro
		1946	Atletico Mineiro	1966	Cruzeiro	1986	Atletico Mineiro
1920	America	1947	Atletico Mineiro	1967	Cruzeiro	1987	Cruzeiro
1921	America	1948	America	1968	Cruzeiro	1988	Atletico Mineiro
1922	America	1949	Atletico Mineiro	1969	Cruzeiro		
1923	America						
1924	America	1950	Atletico Mineiro	1970	Atletico Mineiro		
1925	America	1951	Vila Nova	1971	America		
1926	Atletico Mineiro	1952	Atletico Mineiro	1972	Cruzeiro		
1927	Atletico Mineiro	1953	Atletico Mineiro	1973	Cruzeiro		
1928	Palestra Italia	1954	Atletico Mineiro	1974	Cruzeiro		
1929	Palestra Italia	1955	Atletico Mineiro	1975	Cruzeiro		
		1956	Atletico Mineiro/ Cruzeiro	1976	Atletico Mineiro		
1930	Palestra Italia			1977	Cruzeiro		
1931	Atletico Mineiro	1957	America	1978	Atletico Mineiro		
1932	Atletico Mineiro/ Vila Nova	1958	Atletico Mineiro	1979	Atletico Mineiro		
1933	Vila Nova	1959	Cruzeiro				
1934	Vila Nova						
1935	Vila Nova						
1936	Atletico Mineiro						
1937	Siderurgica						
1938	Atletico Mineiro						
1939	Atletico Mineiro						

BRAZIL

BAHIA (FEDRACAO BAHIANA de FUTEBOL)

Main Club
SALVADOR: Esporte Clube Bahia, Vitoria, Botafogo SC, Ypiranga, Galicia EC
ITABUNA: CE Itabuna
ALAGOINHAS: Atletico Clube, AE Catuense
VITORIA de CONQUISTA: Serrano FC
FEIRA de SANTANA: Fluminense, AD Bahia
SIMOES FILHO: AD Leonico

Year	Champion	Year	Champion	Year	Champion	Year	Champion
1905	Inter de Cricket	1927	Baiano de tenis	1950	Bahia	1970	Bahia
1906	Sao Salvador	1928	Ipiranga	1951	Ipiranga	1971	Bahia
1907	Sao Salvador	1929	Ipiranga	1952	Bahia	1972	Vitoria
1908	Vitoria			1953	Vitoria	1973	Bahia
1909	Vitoria	1930	Botafogo	1954	Bahia	1974	Bahia
		1931	Bahia	1955	Vitoria	1975	Bahia
1910	Santos Dumont	1932	Ipiranga	1956	Bahia	1976	Bahia
1911	SC Bahia	1933	Bahia	1957	Vitoria	1977	Bahia
1912	Atletico	1934	Bahia	1958	Bahia	1978	Bahia
1913	Fluminense	1935	Botafogo	1959	Bahia	1979	Bahia
1914	Internacional	1936	Bahia				
1915	Fluminense	1937	Galicia	1960	Bahia	1980	Vitoria
1916	Republica	1938	Botafogo/Bahia	1961	Bahia	1981	Bahia
1917	Ipiranga	1939	Ipiranga	1962	Bahia	1982	Bahia
1918	Ipiranga			1963	Flumin de Feira	1983	Bahia
1919	Botafogo	1940	Bahia	1964	Vitoria	1984	Bahia
		1941	Galicia	1965	Vitoria	1985	Vitoria
1920	Ipiranga	1942	Galicia	1966	Leonico	1986	Bahia
1921	Ipiranga	1943	Galicia	1967	Bahia	1987	EC Bahia
1922	Botafogo	1944	Bahia	1968	Galicia	1988	EC Bahia
1923	Botafogo	1945	Bahia	1969	Fluminense		
1924	AA de Bahia	1946	Guarani				
1925	Ipiranga	1947	Bahia				
1926	Botafogo	1948	Bahia				
		1949	Bahia				

ALAGOAS (FEDERACAO ALAGOANA de DESPORTES)

Main Clubs
MACEIO: CSA (Centro Sportivo Alagoana), CRB (CR Brasil), Ferroviario AC, Sao Domingos
CAPELA: EC Capelense
PALMEIRA dos INDIOS: CSE (Centro Social Esportiva)
PENEDA: SC Penedense
ARAPIRACA: Cruzeiro, AS Arapiraca
VICOSA: Comercial

Year	Champion	Year	Champion	Year	Champion	Year	Champion
1927	CRB	1943	not held	1960	CSA	1975	CSA
1928	CSA	1944	CSA	1961	CSA	1976	CRB
1929	CSA	1945	Santa Cruz	1962	EC Capelense Capela	1977	CRB
		1946	Barroso	1963	CSA	1978	CSA
1930	CRB	1947	Alexandria	1964	CRB	1979	CRB
1931	not held	1948	Santa Cruz	1965	CSA		
1932	not held	1949	CSA	1966	CSA	1980	CSA
1933	CSA			1967	CSA	1981	CSA
1934	not held	1950	CRB	1968	CSA	1982	CSA
1935	CSA	1951	CRB	1969	CRB	1983	CRB
1936	CSA	1952	CSA			1984	CSA
1937	CRB	1953	Ferroviario AC Maceio	1970	CRB	1985	CSA
1938	CRB	1954	Ferroviario AC Maceio	1971	CSA	1986	CRB
1939	CRB	1955	CSA	1972	CRB	1987	CRB
		1956	CSA	1973	CRB	1988	CSA
1940	CRB	1957	CSA	1974	CSA		
1941	CSA	1958	CSA				
1942	CSA	1959	EC Capelense Capela				

AMAZONAS (FEDERACAO AMAZONENSE de FUTEBOL)

Main Clubs
MANAUS: Nacional FC, CA Rio Negro, Sao Raimundo EC, America, Libermorro, Sul America, Fast Club
ITACOATIARA: Penarol
MANACAPURU: Princess dos Solimoes

1914	Manaus Atletic	1934	Portuguesa	1954	Fast		
1915	Manaus Atletic	1935	Portuguesa	1955	Fast		
1916	Nacional	1936	Nacional	1956	Auto Esporte		
1917	Nacional	1937	Nacional	1957	Nacional	1974	Nacional
1918	Nacional	1938	Rio Negro	1958	Santos	1975	Rio Negro
1919	Nacional	1939	Nacional	1959	Auto Esporte	1976	Nacional
						1977	Nacional
1920	Nacional	1940	Rio Negro	1960	Fast	1978	Nacional
1921	Rio Negro	1941	Nacional	1961	Sao Raimundo	1979	Nacional
1922	Nacional	1942	Nacional	1962	Rio Negro		
1923	Nacional	1943	Rio Negro	1963	Nacional	1980	Nacional
1924	not held	1944	Olimpico	1964	Nacional	1981	Nacional
1925	not held	1945	Nacional	1965	Rio Negro	1982	Rio Negro
1926	not held	1946	Nacional	1966	Olimpico	1983	Nacional
1927	Rio Negro	1947	Olimpico	1967	Olimpico	1984	Nacional
1928	Cruzeiro do Sol	1948	Fast	1968	Nacional	1985	Nacional
1929	Manaus Sporting	1949	Fast	1969	Nacional	1986	Nacional
						1987	Rio Negro
1930	Cruzeiro do Sol	1950	Nacional	1970	Fast	1988	Rio Negro
1931	Rio Negro	1951	America	1971	Fast		
1932	Rio Negro	1952	America	1972	Nacional		
1933	Nacional	1953	America	1973	Rodoviaria		

CEARA (FEDERACAO CEARENSE de FUTEBOL)

Main Clubs
FORTALEZA: Ceara SC, Fortaleza FC, Ferroviario AC, America FC, Tiradentes, Calouros do Ar
QUIXADA: Quixada
SOBRAL: Guarany
JAUZEIRO do NORTE: Guarani, Icasa

1920	Fortaleza	1940	Tramways	1960	Fortaleza	1980	Ceara
1921	Fortaleza	1941	Ceara	1961	Ceara	1981	Ceara
1922	Ceara	1942	Ceara	1962	Ceara	1982	Fortaleza
1923	Fortaleza	1943	Maguari	1963	Ceara	1983	Fortaleza
1924	Fortaleza	1944	Maguari	1964	Fortaleza	1984	Ceara
1925	Ceara	1945	Ferroviario	1965	America	1985	Fortaleza
1926	Fortaleza	1946	Fortaleza	1966	America	1986	Ceara
1927	Fortaleza	1947	Fortaleza	1967	Fortaleza	1987	Fortaleza
1928	Fortaleza	1948	Ceara	1968	Ferroviario	1988	Ferroviario
1929	Maguari	1949	Fortaleza	1969	Fortaleza		
1930	Orion	1950	Ferroviario	1970	Ferroviario		
1931	Ceara	1951	Ceara	1971	Ceara		
1932	Ceara	1952	Ferroviario	1972	Ceara		
1933	Fortaleza	1953	Fortaleza	1973	Fortaleza		
1934	Fortaleza	1954	Fortaleza	1974	Fortaleza		
1935	America	1955	Calouros do Ar	1975	Fortaleza		
1936	Maguari	1956	Gentilandia	1976	Ceara		
1937	Fortaleza	1957	Ceara	1977	Ceara		
1938	Fortaleza	1958	Fortaleza	1978	Ceara		
1939	Ceara	1959	Fortaleza	1979	Ferroviario		

BRAZIL

DISTRITO FEDERAL (FEDERACAO DESPORTIVA de BRASILIA)

Main Clubs
BRASILIA: Brasilia EC, Taguatinga EC, AD Gama, Guara, Ceilandia, Planaltina, Tiradentes
SOBRADINHO: Titadentes, Sobradinho EC

1973	CEUB	**1978**	Brasilia EC	**1982**	Brasilia EC	**1987**	Brasilia EC
1974	Pioneira	**1979**	AD Gama	**1983**	Brasilia EC	**1988**	Tiradentes Brasilia
1975	not held			**1984**	Brasilia EC		
1976	Brasilia EC	**1980**	Brasilia EC	**1985**	Sobradinho		
1977	Brasilia EC	**1981**	Taguantiga EC	**1986**	Sobradinho		

ESPIRITO SANTO (FEDERACAO CAPIXABA de DESPORTES)

Main Clubs
VITORIA: Rio Branco AC, Deportiva Ferroviaria, Vitoria FC, Guarapari
BOM JESUS: Ordem e Progresso
CACHOEIRO do ITAPEMIRIM: Estrela do Norte

1965	Desportiva Ferroviaria	**1972**	Desportiva Ferroviaria	**1980**	Desportiva Ferroviaria	**1985**	Rio Branco AC
1966	Rio Branco AC	**1973**	Rio Branco AC	**1981**	Desportiva Ferroviaria	**1986**	Desportiva Ferroviaria
1967	Desportiva Ferroviaria	**1974**	Desportiva Ferroviaria	**1982**	Rio Branco AC	**1987**	Guarapari
1968	Rio Branco AC	**1975**	Rio Branco AC	**1983**	Rio Branco AC	**1988**	Iboraci
1969	Rio Branco AC	**1976**	Vitoria FC	**1984**	Desportiva Ferroviaria		
		1977	Desportiva Ferroviaria				
1970	Rio Branco AC	**1978**	Rio Branco AC				
1971	not held	**1979**	Desportiva Ferroviaria				

GOIAS (FEDERACAO GOIANA de DESPORTES)

Main Clubs
GOIANIA: Vila Nova FC, Goias EC, Goiania, Atletico Clube Goianiense
ANAPOUS: Anapolis FC, AA Anapolina

1944	Atletico Goianiense	**1956**	Goiania	**1968**	Goiania	**1980**	Vila Nova FC
1945	Goiania	**1957**	Atletico Goianiense	**1969**	Vila Nova FC	**1981**	Goias AC
1946	Goiania	**1958**	Goiania			**1982**	Vila Nova FC
1947	Atletico Goianiense	**1959**	Goiania	**1970**	Atletico Goianiense	**1983**	Goias AC
1948	Goiania			**1971**	Goias AC	**1984**	Vila Nova FC
1949	Atletico Goianiense	**1960**	Goiania	**1972**	Goias AC	**1985**	Atletico Goianiense
		1961	Vila Nova FC	**1973**	Vila Nova FC	**1986**	Goias AC
1950	Goiania	**1962**	Vila Nova FC	**1974**	Goiania	**1987**	Goias AC
1951	Goiania	**1963**	Vila Nova FC	**1975**	Goias AC	**1988**	Atletico Goianiense
1952	Goiania	**1964**	Atletico Goianiense	**1976**	Goias AC		
1953	Goiania	**1965**	Anapolis	**1977**	Vila Nova FC		
1954	Goiania	**1966**	Goias AC	**1978**	Vila Nova FC		
1955	Atletico Goianiense	**1967**	Crac	**1979**	Vila Nova FC		

MARANHAO (FEDERACAO MARANHAENSE de DESPORTES)

Main Clubs
SAO LUIS: Moto Clube, Sampaio Correa FC, Expressinho, Maranhao AC, Boa Vontade, Tupa, Vitoria do Mar, AA Tocantins
BACABAL: Americano

1918 Fenix	1937 Maranhao AC	1956 Sampaio Correa FC	1974 Moto Clube
1919 Luso	1938 Tupa	1957 Ferroviario	1975 Sampaio Correa FC
	1939 Maranhao AC	1958 Ferroviario	1976 Sampaio Correa FC
1920 Luso		1959 Moto Clube	1977 Moto Clube
1921 FAC	1940 Sampaio Correa FC		1978 Sampaio Correa FC
1922 Fenix	1941 Maranhao AC	1960 Moto Clube	1979 Maranhao AC
1923 FAC	1942 Sampaio Correa FC	1961 Sampaio Correa FC	
1924 Luso	1943 Maranhao AC	1962 Sampaio Correa FC	1980 Sampaio Correa FC
1925 Luso	1944 Moto Clube	1963 Maranhao AC	1981 Moto Clube
1926 Luso	1945 Moto Clube	1964 Sampaio Correa FC	1982 Moto Clube
1927 Luso	1946 Moto Clube	1965 Sampaio Correa FC	1983 Moto Clube
1928 Vasco	1947 Moto Clube	1966 Moto Clube	1984 Sampaio Correa FC
1929 not held	1948 Moto Clube	1967 Moto Clube	1985 Sampaio Correa FC
	1949 Moto Clube	1968 Moto Clube	1986 Sampaio Correa FC
1930 Sampaio Correa FC		1969 Maranhao AC	1987 Sampaio Correa FC
1931 Sirio	1950 Moto Clube		1988 Sampaio Correa FC
1932 Tupa	1951 Maranhao AC	1970 Maranhao AC	
1933 Sampaio Correa FC	1952 Vitoria do Mar	1971 Ferroviario	
1934 Sampaio Correa FC	1953 Sampaio Correa FC	1972 Sampaio Correa FC	
1935 Tupa	1954 Sampaio Correa FC	1973 Ferroviario	
1936 not held	1955 Moto Clube		

MATO GROSSO (FEDERACAO MATO-GROSSENSE de DESPORTES)

State divided in 1979
Main Clubs
CUIABA: Mixto EC, Palmeiras, Atletico, Dom Bosco
RONDONOPOLIS: Uniao
VARZEA GRANDE: CE Operario

1974 Operario Campo Grande	1978 Operario Campo Grande	1983 Operario Varzea Grande	1986 Operario Varzea Grande
1975 Comercial Campo Grande	1979 Mixto Cuiaba	1984 Mixto Cuiaba	1987 Operario Varzea Grande
1976 Operario Campo Grande	1980 Mixto Cuiaba	1985 Operario Varzea Grande	1988 Mixto Cuiaba
1977 Operario Campo Grande	1981 Mixto Cuiaba		
	1982 Mixto Cuiaba		

MATO GROSSO DO SOL STATE CHAMPIONSHIPS

Prior to 1979 Operario and Comercial played in the Mato-Grosso state which split in 1979
Main Clubs
CAMPO GRANDE: Operario FC, Comercial EC, Aquidauana, Taveiropolis
DOURADOS: CA Douradense, Ubiratan
CORUMBA: Corumbaense
PONTE PORA: Comercial

1979 Operario Campo Grande	1983 Operario Campo Grande	1986 Operario Campo Grande	1988 Operario Campo Grande
1980 Operario Campo Grande	1984 Corumbaense Corumba	1987 Comercial Campo Grande	
1981 Operario Campo Grande	1985 Comercial Campo Grande		
1982 Comercial Campo Grande			

BRAZIL

PARA (FEDERACAO PARAENSE de FUTEBOL)

Main Clubs
BELEM: Club do Remo, Tuna Luso Brasileira, Sport Clube, Yamada, Pinheirense, Tiradentes, Independiente
SANTA ISABEL: Isabelense
CONRACI: Santa Rosa

1913	Remo	1933	Remo	1953	Remo	1972	Paysandu
1914	Remo	1934	Paysandu	1954	Remo	1973	Remo
1915	Remo	1935	not held	1955	Tuna Laso	1974	Remo
1916	Remo	1936	Remo	1956	Paysandu	1975	Remo
1917	Remo	1937	Tuna Luso	1957	Paysandu	1976	Paysandu
1918	Remo	1938	Tuna Luso	1958	Tuna Luso	1977	Remo
1919	Remo	1939	Tuna Luso	1959	Paysandu	1978	Remo
						1979	Remo
1920	Paysandu	1940	Remo	1960	Remo		
1921	Paysandu	1941	Tuna Luso	1961	Paysandu	1980	Paysandu
1922	Paysandu	1942	Paysandu	1962	Paysandu	1981	Paysandu
1923	Paysandu	1943	Paysandu	1963	Paysandu	1982	Paysandu
1924	Remo	1944	Paysandu	1964	Remo	1983	Tuna Luso
1925	Remo	1945	Paysandu	1965	Paysandu	1984	Paysandu
1926	Remo	1946	not held	1966	Paysandu	1985	Paysandu
1927	Paysandu	1947	Paysandu	1967	Paysandu	1986	Remo
1928	Paysandu	1948	Tuna Luso	1968	Remo	1987	Paysandu
1929	Paysandu	1949	Remo	1969	Paysandu	1988	Tuna Luso or Paysandu
1930	Remo	1950	Remo	1970	Tuna Luso		
1931	Paysandu	1951	Tuna Luso	1971	Remo		
1932	Remo	1952	Remo				

PARAIBA (FEDERACAO PARAIBANA de FUTEBOL)

Main Clubs
CAMPINA GRANDE: Treze FC, Campinense Clube
JOAO PESSOA: Botafogo, Auto Esporte, Santos
PATOS: Esporte, Nacional
SANTA RITA: Santa Cruz

1917	Colegio Pio X	1936	Botafogo	1954	Botafogo	1973	Campinense Clube
1918	Cabo Branco	1937	Botafogo	1955	Botafogo	1974	Campinense Clube
1919	Palmeiras	1938	Botafogo	1956	Auto Esporte	1975	Botafogo/Treze
		1939	Auto Esporte	1957	Botafogo	1976	Botafogo
1920	Cabo Branco			1958	Auto Esporte	1977	Botafogo
1921	Palmeiras	1940	Treze	1959	Estrela do Mar	1978	Botafogo
1922	Pytaguares	1941	Treze			1979	Botafogo
1923	America	1942	Astrea	1960	Campinense Clube		
1924	Cabo Branco	1943	Astrea	1961	Campinense Clube	1980	Campinense Clube
1925	America	1944	Botafogo	1962	Campinense Clube	1981	Treze FC
1926	Cabo Branco	1945	Botafogo	1963	Campinense Clube	1982	Treze FC
1927	Cabo Branco	1946	Filipeia	1964	Campinense Clube	1983	Treze FC
1928	Palmeiras	1947	Botafogo	1965	Campinense Clube	1984	Botafogo
1929	Cabo Branco	1948	Botafogo	1966	Treze FC	1985	undecided
		1949	Botafogo	1967	Campinense Clube	1986	Botafogo
1930	not held			1968	Botafogo	1987	Auto Esporte
1931	Cabo Branco	1950	Treze	1969	Botafogo	1988	Botafogo
1932	Cabo Branco	1951	not held				
1933	Palmeiras	1952	Red Cross	1970	Botafogo		
1934	Cabo Branco	1953	Botafogo	1971	Campinense Clube		
1935	Palmeiras			1972	Campinense Clube		

PARANA (FEDERACAO PARANENSE de FUTEBOL)

Main Clubs
CURITIBA: CA Paranaense, Coritiba FC, Pinheiros, Colorado EC

1915	America	1934	Atletico Paranaense	1953	Ferroviario	1972	Coritiba
1916	Coritiba	1935	Coritiba	1954	Coritiba	1973	Coritiba
1917	Internacional	1936	Atletico Paranaense	1955	Monte Alegre	1974	Coritiba
1918	Britania	1937	Ferroviario	1956	Coritiba	1975	Coritiba
1919	Britania	1938	Ferroviario	1957	Coritiba	1976	Coritiba
		1939	Coritiba	1958	Atletico Paranaense	1977	Maringa
1920	Britania			1959	Coritiba	1978	Coritiba
1921	Britania	1940	Atletico Paranaense			1979	Coritiba
1922	Britania	1941	Coritiba	1960	Coritiba		
1923	Britania	1942	Coritiba	1961	Comercial	1980	Cascavel
1924	Palestra Italia	1943	Atletico Paranaense	1962	Londrina	1981	Londrina
1925	Atletico Paranaense	1944	Ferroviario	1963	Maringa	1982	Atletico Paranaense
1926	Palestra Italia	1945	Atletico Paranaense	1964	Maringa	1983	Atletico Paranaense
1927	Coritiba	1946	Coritiba	1965	Ferroviario	1984	Pinheiros
1928	Britania	1947	Coritiba	1966	Ferroviario	1985	Atletico Paranaense
1929	Atletico Paranaense	1948	Ferroviario	1967	Agua Verde	1986	Coritiba
		1949	Atletico Paranaense	1968	Coritiba	1987	Pinheiros
1930	Atletico Paranaense			1969	Coritiba	1988	Atletico Paranaense
1931	Coritiba	1950	Ferroviario				
1932	Palestra Italia	1951	Coritiba	1970	Atletico Paranaense		
1933	Coritiba	1952	Coritiba	1971	Coritiba		

PERNAMBUCO (FEDERACAO PERNAMBUCHANA de FUTEBOL)

Main Clubs
RECIFE: Santa Cruz FC, Clube Nautico Capibaribe, Sport Clube, America CF, Clube Ferroviario, Ibis
PAULISTA: Paulistano FC, AA santo Amaro
CARUARU: Central SC, Atletico Clube

1915	Flamengo	1934	Nautico	1954	Nautico	1972	Santa Cruz
1916	Sport	1935	Santa Cruz	1955	Sport	1973	Santa Cruz
1917	Sport	1936	Tramways	1956	Sport	1974	Nautico
1918	America	1937	Tramways	1957	Santa Cruz	1975	Sport
1919	America	1938	Sport	1958	Sport	1976	Santa Cruz
		1939	Nautico	1959	Santa Cruz	1977	Sport
1920	Sport					1978	Santa Cruz
1921	America	1940	Santa Cruz	1960	Nautico	1979	Santa Cruz
1922	America	1941	Sport	1961	Sport		
1923	Sport	1942	Sport	1962	Sport	1980	Sport
1924	Sport	1943	Sport	1963	Nautico	1981	Sport
1925	Sport	1944	America	1964	Nautico	1982	Sport
1926	Torre	1945	Nautico	1965	Nautico	1983	Santa Cruz
1927	America	1946	Santa Cruz	1966	Nautico	1984	Nautico
1928	Sport	1947	Santa Cruz	1967	Nautico	1985	Nautico
1929	Torre	1948	Sport	1968	Nautico	1986	Santa Cruz
		1949	Sport	1969	Santa Cruz	1987	Santa Cruz
1930	Torre					1988	Sport
1931	Santa Cruz	1950	Nautico	1970	Santa Cruz		
1932	Santa Cruz	1951	Nautico	1971	Santa Cruz		
1933	Santa Cruz	1952	Nautico				
		1953	Sport				

PIAUI (FEDERACAO PIAUIENSE de DESPORTES)

Main Clubs
TERESINA: Auto Esporte, AE Tiradentes, Flamengo, River AC, Piaui EC
CAMPO MAIOR: Caicara, Commercial

1918	Palmeiras	1937	Militar	1955	River	1973	River
1919	Teresinense	1938	Botafogo	1956	River	1974	Tiradentes
		1939	Flamengo	1957	Botafogo	1975	Tiradentes/River
1920	Artistico			1958	River	1976	Flamengo
1921	Militar	1940	Botafogo	1959	River	1977	River
1922	Teresinense	1941	Botafogo			1978	River
1923	Artistico	1942	Flamengo	1960	River	1979	Flamengo
1924	Tiradentes	1943	Botafogo	1961	River		
1925	Tiradentes	1944	Flamengo	1962	River	1980	River
1926	Tiradentes	1945	Flamengo	1963	River	1981	River
1927	Tiradentes	1946	Flamengo	1964	Flamengo	1982	Tiradentes
1928	Tiradentes	1947	Botafogo	1965	Flamengo	1983	Auto Esporte
1929	Artistico	1948	River	1966	Piaui	1984	Flamengo
		1949	Botafogo	1967	Piaui	1985	Piaui
1930	Artistico			1968	Piaui	1986	Flamengo
1931	Militar	1950	River	1969	Piaui	1987	Flamengo
1932	Militar	1951	River			1988	Flamengo
1933	Artistico	1952	River	1970	Flamengo		
1934	Tiradentes	1953	River	1971	Flamengo		
1935	Militar	1954	River	1972	Tiradentes		
1936	Militar						

RIO GRANDE DO NORTE (FEDERACAO PORTIGUAR de DEPORTES)

Main Clubs
NATAL: Alecrim FC, America, ABC, Riachuelo, Atletico

1920	ABC	1940	ABC	1960	ABC	1980	America
1921	ABC	1941	ABC	1961	ABC	1981	America
1922	America	1942	not held	1962	ABC	1982	America
1923	ABC	1943	America	1963	America	1983	ABC
1924	America	1944	ABC	1964	Alecrim	1984	ABC
1925	ABC	1945	ABC	1965	ABC	1985	Alecrim
1926	ABC	1946	Santa Cruz	1966	ABC	1986	Alecrim
1927	America	1947	ABC	1967	Alecrim	1987	America
1928	ABC	1948	America	1968	Alecrim	1988	America
1929	ABC	1949	America	1969	America		
1930	America	1950	ABC	1970	ABC		
1931	America	1951	not held	1971	ABC		
1932	ABC	1952	America	1972	ABC		
1933	ABC	1953	ABC	1973	ABC		
1934	ABC	1954	ABC	1974	America		
1935	ABC	1955	ABC	1975	America		
1936	ABC	1956	America	1976	ABC		
1937	ABC	1957	America	1977	America		
1938	ABC	1958	ABC	1978	ABC		
1939	ABC	1959	ABC	1979	America		

RIO GRANDE DO SUL (FEDERACAO GUACHA de FUTEBOL)

Main Clubs
PORTO ALEGRE: SC Internacional, Gremio

1919	Brasil	**1940**	Internacional	**1960**	Gremio	**1980**	Gremio
		1941	Internacional	**1961**	Internacional	**1981**	Internacional
1920	Guarani	**1942**	Internacional	**1962**	Gremio	**1982**	Internacional
1921	Gremio	**1943**	Internacional	**1963**	Gremio	**1983**	Internacional
1922	Internacional	**1944**	Internacional	**1964**	Gremio	**1984**	Internacional
1923	not held	**1945**	Internacional	**1965**	Gremio	**1985**	Gremio
1924	not held	**1946**	Gremio	**1966**	Gremio	**1986**	Gremio
1925	Gremio	**1947**	Internacional	**1967**	Gremio	**1987**	Gremio
1926	Gremio	**1948**	Internacional	**1968**	Gremio	**1988**	Gremio
1927	Internacional	**1949**	Gremio	**1969**	Internacional		
1928	Americano						
1929	Cruzeiro	**1950**	Internacional	**1970**	Internacional		
		1951	Internacional	**1971**	Internacional		
1930	Pelotas	**1952**	Internacional	**1972**	Internacional		
1931	Gremio	**1953**	Internacional	**1973**	Internacional		
1932	Gremio	**1954**	Renner	**1974**	Internacional		
1933	Sao Paulo	**1955**	Internacional	**1975**	Internacional		
1934	Internacional	**1956**	Gremio	**1976**	Internacional		
1935	Farraoupilha	**1957**	Gremio	**1977**	Gremio		
1936	Rio Grande	**1958**	Gremio	**1978**	Internacional		
1937	Santanense	**1959**	Gremio	**1979**	Gremio		
1938	Guarani						
1939	Rio Grande						

SANTA CATARINA (FEDERACAO CATARINENSE de FUTBOL)

Main Clubs
JOINVILLE: Joinville, Operario
BRUSQUE: CE Paysandu
FLORIANOPOLIS: Atletico, Avai FC, Paula Ramos
ITAJAI: CIP, Club Nautico Marcilo Dias

1927	Avai	**1943**	Avai	**1960**	Metropol	**1976**	Joinville
1928	Avai	**1944**	Avai	**1961**	Metropol	**1977**	Chapecoense
1929	Caxiass	**1945**	Avai	**1962**	Metropol	**1978**	Joinville
		1946	not held	**1963**	not held	**1979**	Joinville
1930	Avai	**1947**	America	**1964**	Olimpico		
1931	Lauro Muller	**1948**	America	**1965**	Internacional	**1980**	Joinville
1932	Figueirense	**1949**	Olimpico	**1966**	Perdigao	**1981**	Joinville
1933	not held			**1967**	Metrpol	**1982**	Joinville
1934	Atletico Florianap	**1950**	Carlos Renaux	**1968**	Comerciario	**1983**	Joinville
1935	Figueirense	**1951**	America	**1969**	Metropol	**1984**	Joinville
1936	Figueirense	**1952**	America			**1985**	Joinville
1937	Figueirense	**1953**	Carlos Renaux	**1970**	Ferroviario	**1986**	Criciuma
1938	CIP de Itajal	**1954**	Caxias	**1971**	America	**1987**	Joinville
1939	Figueirense	**1955**	Caxias	**1972**	Figueirense	**1988**	Avai
		1956	Operario	**1973**	Avai		
1940	Ipiranga de SF	**1957**	Hercilio Luz	**1974**	Figueirense		
1941	Figueirense	**1958**	Hercilio Luz	**1975**	Avai		
1942	Avai	**1959**	Paula Ramos				

BRAZIL

SERGIPE (FEDERACAO SERGIPANA de DESPORTES)

Main Clubs
ARACAJU: Confianca, CS Sergipe, Vasco de Gama
ESTANCIA: Santa Cruz, Estanciano

1918 Continguiba	1936 Continguiba	1954 Confianca	1972 Sergipe
1919 not held	1937 Sergipe	1955 Sergipe	1973 Itabaiana
	1938 not held	1956 Santa Cruz	1974 Sergipe
1920 Continguiba	1939 Ipiranga	1957 Santa Cruz	1975 Sergipe
1921 Industrial		1958 Santa Cruz	1976 Confianca
1922 Sergipe	1940 Sergipe	1959 Santa Cruz	1977 Confianca
1923 Continguiba	1941 Riachuelo		1978 Itabaiana
1924 Sergipe	1942 Continguiba	1960 Santa Cruz	1979 Itabaiana
1925 not held	1943 Sergipe	1961 Sergipe	
1926 not held	1944 Vasco	1962 Confianca	1980 Itabaiana
1927 Sergipe	1945 Ipiranga	1963 Confianca	1981 Itabaiana
1928 Sergipe	1946 Olimpico	1964 Sergipe	1982 Sergipe
1929 Sergipe	1947 Olimpico	1965 Confianca	1983 Confianca
	1948 Vasco	1966 America	1984 Sergipe
1930 not held	1949 Palestra	1967 Sergipe	1985 Sergipe
1931 not held		1968 Confianca	1986 Confianca
1932 Sergipe	1950 Passagem	1969 Itabaiana	1987 Vasco
1933 Sergipe	1951 Confianca		1988 Confianca
1934 Palestra	1952 Continguiba	1970 Sergipe	
1935 Palestra	1953 Vasco	1971 Sergipe	

FEATURED CLUBS IN COPA LIBERTADORES DE AMERICA

Palmeiras Sao Paulo	Sao Paulo FC	Cruzeiro Belo Horizonte	Nautico Capiberibe Recife
Atletico Mineiro Belo Horizonte		Internacional Porto Alegre	Gremio Porto Alegre
Botafogo Rio de Janeiro	Santos FC Sao Paulo	Guarani Campinas	Vasco de Gama Rio de Janeiro
Esporte Clube Bahia	Corinthians Sao Paulo	Fluminense Rio de Janeiro	Coritiba Curitiba
Bangu Rio de Janeiro	Flamengo Rio de Janeiro	Sport Clube Recife	

SOCIEDADE ESPORTIVA PALMEIRAS (SAO PAULO)

Founded 24th August 1914 as Palestra Italia, 1942 Palmeiras
Address Rua Turiacu 1840, Agua Branca, Sao Paulo SP
Colours green shirts with white trim, white shorts
Stadium Parque Antartica (35,000) or Pacembeu (60,000)
Sao Paulo State Champions as Palestra Italia 1920, 1926, 1927, 1932, 1933, 1934, 1936, 1940 as Palmeiras 1942,
1944, 1947, 1950, 1959, 1963, 1966, 1972, 1974, 1976
Rio/Sao Paulo State Champions 1951, 1965
National Champions 1967, 1969, 1972, 1973
Libertadores Finalists 1961, 1968

Season	Opponent	Home	Playoff Result	Away	Rnd
1961	Independiente, Argentina	1-0		2-0	2
	Independiente Santa Fe, Colombia	4-1		2-2	sf
	Penarol, Uruguay	1-1		0-1	FINAL
1968	Nautico Capiberibe Recife, Brazil	0-0		3-1	1
	Portugues Caracas, Venezuela	3-0		2-1	1
	Galicia Caracas, Venezuela	2-0		2-1	1
	Guarani, Paraguay	2-1		0-2	qf
	Universidad Catolica, Chile	4-1		1-0	qf
	Penarol, Uruguay	1-0		1-1	sf
	Estudiantes La Plata, Argentina	3-1	0-2 in Montevideo	1-2	FINAL

1971	Fluminense Rio de Janeiro, Brazil	3-1		0-2	1
	Italia Caracas, Venezuela	1-0		3-0	1
	Galicia Caracas, Venezuela	3-0		3-2	1
	Nacional, Uruguay	0-3		1-3	sf
	Universitario Lima, Peru	3-0		2-1	sf
1973	Nacional, Uruguay	1-1		2-1	1
	Penarol, Uruguay	1-0		2-0	1
	Botafogo Rio de Janeiro, Brazil	2-1	1-2	0-2	1
1974	Sao Paulo FC, Brazil	1-2		0-2	1
	Jorge Wilsterman Cochabamba, Bolivia	2-0		0-1	1
	Deportivo Municipal La Paz, Bolivia	3-0		1-0	1
1979	Alianza Lima, Peru	4-0		4-2	1
	Universitario Lima, Peru	1-2		5-2	1
	Guarani Campinas, Brazil	1-4		0-1	1

SAO PAULO FUTEBOL CLUBE

Founded 17 December 1935
Colours all white shirts with one red and one black hoop, black shorts
Address Praca Gomes Pedrosa, Jardin Leoner, Sao Paulo
Stadium Estadio Cicero Pompeu de Toledo or Morumbi (150,000)
Sao Paulo State Champions as AC 1902, 1903, 1904, 1911, as FC 1931, 1943, 1945, 1946, 1948, 1949, 1953, 1957, 1970, 1971, 1975, 1980, 1981, 1985, 1987
National Champions 1977, 1986
Libertadores Finalists 1974

Season	Opponent	Home	Playoff Result	Away	Round
1972	Atletico Mineiro Belo Horizonte, Brazil	0-0		2-2	1
	Olimpia, Paraguay	3-1		1-0	1
	Cerro Porteno, Paraguay	4-0		2-3	1
	Independiente, Argentina	1-0		0-2	sf
	Barcelona Sporting Guayaquil, Ecuador	1-1		0-0	sf
1974	Palmeiras Sao Paulo, Brazil	2-0		2-1	1
	Jorge Wilsterman Cochabamba, Bolivia	5-0		1-0	1
	Deportivo Municipal La Paz, Bolivia	3-3		1-1	1
	Millonarios Bogota, Colombia	4-0		0-0	sf
	Defensor Lima, Peru	4-0		1-0	sf
	Independiente, Argentina	2-1	0-1 in Santiago	0-2	FINAL
1978	Atletico Mineiro Belo Horizonte, Brazil	1-1		1-2	1
	Union Espanola, Chile	1-1		1-1	1
	Palestino, Chile	1-2		1-0	1
1982	Gremio Porto Alegre, Brazil	2-2		0-0	1
	Defensor Sporting, Uruguay	2-1		3-1	1
	Penarol, Uruguay	0-1		0-1	1
1987	Guarani Campinas, Brazil	2-2		1-3	1
	Cobreloa Calama, Chile	2-1		1-3	1
	Colo Colo, Chile	1-2		2-2	1

BRAZIL

ESPORTE CLUBE CRUZEIRO (BELO HORIZONTE)

Founded 2nd January 1902 as Societa Sportiva Palestra Italia, 1942 Palestra Mineiro and Ypiranga, 1943 Cruzeiro
Address Cruzeiro Rua Guajajaras 1722, Barro Preto, CEP 30000 Belo Horizonte, Minas Gerais
Colours blue shirts, white shorts
Stadium Magalhaes Pinto Minerao (110,000)
Minas Gerais State Champions 1928, 1929, 1930, 1940, 1943, 1944, 1945, 1959, 1960, 1961, 1965, 1966, 1967, 1968,
1969, 1972, 1973, 1974, 1975, 1977, 1984, 1987
Libertadores Winners 1976 Finalists 1977
World Club Finalists 1976

Season	Opponent	Home	Playoff Result	Away	Round
1967	Italia Caracas, Venezuela	4-0		3-0	1
	Galicia Caracas, Venezuela	3-1		1-0	1
	Universitario Lima, Peru	2-2		4-1	1
	Sports Boys Callao, Peru	3-1		2-1	1
	Penarol, Uruguay	1-0		2-3	sf
	Nacional, Uruguay	2-1		0-2	sf
1975	Vasco da Gama Rio de Janeiro, Brazil	3-2		1-1	1
	Deportivo Cali, Colombia	2-1		0-1	1
	Nacional Medellin, Colombia	2-3		2-1	1
1976	Internacional Porto Alegre, Brazil	5-4		2-0	1
	Sportivo Luqueno Luque, Paraguay	4-1		3-1	1
	Olimpia, Paraguay	4-1		2-2	1
	Liga Deportivo Universitaria, Ecuador	4-1		3-1	sf
	Alianza Lima, Peru	7-1		4-0	sf
	River Plate, Argentina	4-1	3-2 nin Santiago	1-2	FINAL
1977	Internacional Porto Alegre, Brazil	0-0		1-0	sf
	Portuguesa Acarigua, Venezuela	2-1		4-0	sf
	Boca Juniors, Argentina	1-0	0-0 in Montevideo	0-1 4-5 pen	FINAL

NAUTICO CLUBE CAPIBERIBE (RECIFE)

Founded
Colours red and white striped shirts, white shorts
Stadium Estadio dos Aflitos
Address Avenida Conselheiro Rosa e Silva 1086, Aflitos, CEP 50000 Recife, Pernambuco PE
Pernambuco State Champions 1934, 1939, 1945, 1950, 1951, 1952, 1954, 1960, 1963, 1964, 1965, 1966, 1967, 1968,
1974, 1984, 1985

Season	Opponent	Home	Result	Away	Round
1968	Palmeiras Sao Paulo, Brazil	1-3		0-0	1
	Portuguesa Acarigua, Venezuela	3-2		1-1	1
	Galicia Caracas, Venezuela	1-0		1-2	1

CLUBE ATLETICO MINEIRO (BELO HORIZONTE)

Founded 25th March 1908
Address Avenida Olegario Maciel 1516, Lourdas, 30000 CEP Belo Horizonte, Minas Gerais MG
Colours black and white striped shirts, black shorts
Stadium Magalhaes-Mineiro Pinto (110,000)
Minas Gerais State Champions 1914, 1925, 1926, 1931, 1932, 1936, 1938, 1939, 1941, 1942, 1946, 1947, 1949, 1950, 1952, 1953, 1954, 1955, 1956, 1958, 1962, 1963, 1970, 1976, 1978, 1979, 1980, 1981, 1982, 1983, 1985, 1986, 1988
National Champions 1971

Season	Opponent	Home	Playoff Result	Away	Round
1972	Sao Paulo FC, Brazil	2-2		0-0	1
	Olimpia, Paraguay	0-0		2-2	1
	Cerro Porteno, Paraguay	1-1		0-1	1
1978	Sao Paulo FC, Brazil	2-1		1-1	1
	Union Espanola, Chile	5-1		1-1	1
	Palestino, Chile	2-0		5-4	1
	Boca Juniors, Argentina	1-2		1-3	sf
	River Plate, Argentina	1-0		0-1	sf
1981	Cerro Porteno, Paraguay	1-0		2-2	1
	Olimpia, Paraguay	1-0		0-0	1
	Flamengo Rio de Janeiro, Brazil	2-2	0-0*	2-2	1

* in Goiania abd 35

SPORT CLUB INTERNACIONAL (PORTO ALEGRE)

Founded 4th April 1909
Address Sport Club Inter, Avenida Padre Carique, Manino Deus, Porto Alegre, RS Brasil
Colours red shirts with white trim and shorts
Stadium Estadio Beira Rio (100,000)
Rio Grande do Sul State Champions 1913*, 1914*, 1915*, 1916, 1917, 1920*, 1922, 1927, 1934, 1936, 1940, 1941, 1942, 1943, 1944, 1945, 1947, 1948, 1950, 1951, 1952, 1953, 1955, 1961, 1969, 1970, 1971, 1972, 1973, 1974, 1975, 1976, 1978, 1981, 1982, 1983, 1984
National Champions 1975, 1976, 1979
Libertadores Cup Finalists 1980
* shared

Season	Opponent	Home	Playoff Result	Away	Round
1976	Cruzeiro Belo Horizonte, Brazil	0-2		4-5	1
	Olimpia, Paraguay	1-0		1-1	1
	Sportivo Luqueno Luque, Paraguay	3-0		1-0	1
1977	Corinthians Sao Paulo, Brazil	1-0		1-1	1
	Deportivo Cuenca, Ecuador	3-1		2-0	1
	Nacional Quito, Ecuador	2-0		0-2	1
	Cruzeiro Belo Horizonte, Brazil	0-1		0-0	sf
	Portuguesa Acarigua, Venezuela	2-1		0-3	sf
1980	Galicia Caracas, Venezuela	2-0		1-2	1
	Tachira San Cristobal, Venezuela	4-0		1-0	1
	Vasco de Gama Rio de Janeiro, Brazil	2-1		0-0	1
	Velez Sarsfield, Argentina	3-1		1-0	sf
	America de Cali, Colombia	0-0		0-0	sf
	Nacional, Uruguay	0-0		0-1	FINAL
1989	Esporte Clube Bahia Salvador, Brazil	0-1		1-2	1
	Tachira San Cristobal, Venezuela	3-1		0-1	1
	Sport Maritimo Caracas, Venezuela	3-0		1-1*	1
				* behind closed doors, political dispute	
	Penarol, Uruguay	6-2		2-1	2
	Esporte Clube Bahia Salvador, Brazil	1-0		0-0	qf
	Olimpa, Paraguay	2-3aet	3-5p	1-0	sf

BRAZIL

GREMIO FOOT-BALL PORTO ALEGRENSE (PORTO ALEGRE)

Founded 15th September 1903 Address Gremio FC, Largo dos Campeoes, Azenha, Porto Alegre, RS Brasil
Colours mid blue and black and white thin striped shirts, black shorts
Stadium Estadio Olimpico (100,000)
Rio Grande do Sul State Champions 1911, 1912, 1913*, 1914*, 1915*, 1919, 1920*, 1921, 1923, 1925, 1926, 1930,
1931, 1932, 1933, 1935, 1937, 1938, 1939, 1946, 1949, 1956, 1957, 1958, 1959, 1960, 1962, 1963, 1964, 1965, 1966,
1967, 1968, 1977, 1979, 1980, 1985, 1986, 1987, 1988
National Champions 1981
* shared
Libertadores Cup Winners 1983 Finalists 1984
World Club Champions 1983

Season	Opponent	Home	Result	Away	Round
1982	Sao Paulo FC, Brazil	0-0		2-2	1
	Defensor Sporting, Uruguay	not played		0-0	1
	Penarol, Uruguay	3-1		0-1	1
1983	Blooming Santa Cruz, Bolivia	2-0		2-0	1
	Bolivar, Bolivia	3-1		2-1	1
	Flamengo Rio de Janeiro, Brazil	1-1		3-1	1
	America de Cali, Colombia	2-1		0-1	sf
	Estudiantes La Plata, Argentina	2-1		3-3	sf
	Penarol, Uruguay	2-1		1-1	FINAL
1984	Flamengo Rio de Janeiro, Brazil	5-1		1-3	sf
	Universidad de Los Andes (ULA) Merida, Venezuela	6-1		2-0	sf
	Independiente, Argentina	0-1		0-0	FINAL
1990	Vasco da Gama Rio, Brazil	2-0		0-0	1
	Olimpia, Paraguay	2-2		0-1	1
	Cerro Porteno, Paraguay	0-0		1-3	1

BOTAFOGO de FUTEBOL e REGATAS (RIO DE JANEIRO)

Founded 12th August 1904
Address Rua Xavier Curado 1705, 21610 Rio de Janeiro RJ
Colours black and white striped shirts, black shorts
Stadium Estadio General Severiano (Sugar Loaf) (23,000) or Maracana (200,000)
Rio State Champions 1910, 1930, 1932, 1933*, 1934*, 1935*, 1948, 1957, 1961, 1962, 1967, 1968
Rio/Sao Paulo Champions 1962, 1964*, 1966*
* shared

Season	Opponent	Home	Playoff Result	Away	Round
1963	Alianza Lima, Peru	2-1		1-0	1
	Millonarios Bogota, Colombia	2-0		2-0	1
	Santos FC Sao Paulo, Brazil	0-4		1-1	sf
1973	Nacional, Uruguay	3-2		2-1	1
	Penarol, Uruguay	4-1		2-2	1
	Palmeiras Sao Paulo, Brazil	2-0	2-0	1-2	1
	Colo Colo, Chile	1-2	..	3-3	sf
	Cerro Porteno, Paraguay	2-0		2-3	sf

SANTOS FUTEBOL CLUBE (SAO PAULO)

Founded 14th April 1912
Address Rua Principesa Isabel, Vila Belmiro, Santos SP
Colours all white
Stadium Vila Belmiro (20,000) or Morumbi (150,000)

Sao Paulo State Champions 1935†, 1955, 1956, 1958, 1960, 1961, 1962, 1964, 1965, 1967, 1968, 1969, 1973*, 1978, 1984
Rio/Sao Paulo Champions 1959, 1963, 1964*, 1966*
National Champions 1968
Libertadores Cup Winners 1962, 1963
World Club Champions 1962, 1963
* shared
† two Leagues in operation

Season	Opponent	Home	Playoff Result	Away	Round
1962	Deportivo Municipal La Paz, Bolivia	6-1		4-3	1
	Cerro Porteno, Paraguay	9-1		1-1	1
	Universidad Catolica, Chile	1-0		0-0	sf
	Penarol, Uruguay	2-1	3-0 in Buenos Aires	2-3	FINAL
1963	Botafogo Rio de Janeiro, Brazil	1-1		4-0	sf
	Boca Juniors, Argentina	3-2		2-1	FINAL
1964	Independiente, Argentina	2-3		1-2	sf
1965	Universidad de Chile, Chile	1-0		5-1	1
	Universitario Lima, Peru	2-1		2-1	1
	Penarol, Uruguay	5-4	1-2	2-3	sf
1984	Flamengo Rio de Janeiro, Brazil	0-5		1-4	1
	America de Cali, Colombia	0-1		0-1	1
	Juniors Barranquilla, Colombia	1-3		3-0	1

GUARANI FUTEBOL CLUBE (CAMPINAS)

Founded 2nd April 1911
Address Avenida Imperatriz D Teresa Cristina II-Campinas SP
Colours green shirts, white shorts
Stadium Brino de Ouro de Princesa (35,000)
Rio Grande do Sol State Champions 1920, 1938
National Champions 1978

Season	Opponent	Home	Result	Away	Round
1979	Alianza Lima, Peru	2-1		3-0	1
	Universitario Lima, Peru	6-1		0-3	1
	Palmeiras Sao Paulo, Brazil	1-0		4-1	1
	Palestino, Chile	2-2		0-0	sf
	Olimpia, Paraguay	1-1		1-2	sf
1987	Sao Paulo FC, Brazil	3-1		2-2	1
	Cobreloa Calama, Chile	0-0		1-3	1
	Colo Colo, Chile	0-0		0-2	1
1988	Sport Recife, Brazil	4-1		1-0	1
	Alianza Lima, Peru	1-0		1-2	1
	Universitario Lima, Peru	1-1		1-1	1
	San Lorenzo, Argentina	0-1		1-1	2

ATLETICO CLUBE BANGU (RIO DE JANEIRO)

Founded 17th April 1904
Address Rua Sul America 950, 21870 Rio de Janeiro RJ
Colours red and white striped shirts, white shorts
Stadium Estadio Proletario Guilherme da Silveira Filho "Moca Bonita" (15,000)
Rio State Champions 1933*, 1966
* shared

Season	Opponent	Home	Result	Away	Round
1986	Barcelona Sporting Guayaquil, Ecuador	1-2		0-1	1
	Deportivo Quito, Ecuador	3-3		1-3	1
	Coritiba FC Curitiba, Brazil	1-1		not played	1

BRAZIL

SPORT CLUB CORINTHIANS PAULISTA (SAO PAULO)

Founded 1st September 1910 Address Rua Sao Jorge 777, Tatuape, 0387 Sao Paulo SP
Colours white shirts, black shorts
Stadium Parque Sao Jorge (30,000) or Morumbi (150,000)
Sao Paulo State Champions 1914*, 1916*, 1922, 1923, 1924, 1928*, 1929*, 1930, 1937, 1938, 1939, 1941, 1951,
1952, 1954, 1977, 1979, 1982, 1988
* two Leagues in operation
Rio/Sao Paulo Champions 1950, 1953, 1954, 1966*
National Champions 1990

Season	Opponent	Home	Result	Away	Round
1977	Internacional Porto Alegre, Brazil	1-1		0-1	1
	Nacional Quito, Ecuador	3-0		1-2	1
	Deportivo Cuenca, Ecuador	4-0		1-2	1

FLUMINENSE FOOTBALL CLUB (RIO DE JANEIRO)

Founded 21st July 1902
Address Fluminense FC, Rua Alvaro Chaves 41, 22231 Rio de Janeiro RJ
Colours maroon, green and thin white striped shirts, white shorts
Stadium Estadio Laranjeiras (10,000) or Maracana (200,000)
Rio State Champions 1906, 1907*, 1908, 1909, 1911, 1917, 1918, 1919, 1924*, 1936*, 1937, 1938, 1940, 1941, 1946,
1951, 1959, 1964, 1969, 1971, 1973, 1975, 1976
Rio/Sao Paulo Champions 1957, 1960
National Champions 1970, 1984
* shared

Season	Opponent	Home	Result	Away	Round
1971	Palmeiras Sao Paulo, Brazil	2-0		1-3	1
	Galicia Caracas, Venezuela	3-1		4-1	1
	Italia Caracas, Venezuela	6-0		0-1	1
1985	Vasco da Gama Rio de Janeiro, Brazil	0-0		3-3	1
	FC Oeste, Argentina	0-0		0-1	1
	Argentinos Juniors, Argentina	0-1		0-1	1

ESPORTE CLUBE BAHIA (SALVADOR)

Founded 1st January 1931 by merger of AA de Bahia and Baiano de Tenis
Address Avenida Otavio Mangabeira S/N CEP 41700 Salvador BA
Colours white shirts, sky blue shorts
Stadium Fonte Nova (84,300)
Baiano State Champions 1931, 1933, 1934, 1936, 1938, 1940, 1944, 1945, 1947, 1948, 1949, 1950, 1952, 1954, 1956,
1958, 1959, 1960, 1961, 1962, 1967, 1970, 1971, 1973, 1974, 1975, 1976, 1977, 1978, 1979, 1981, 1982, 1983, 1984,
1986, 1987, 1988
National Champions 1988

Season	Opponent	Home	Result	Away	Round
1960	San Lorenzo, Argentina	3-2		0-3	1
1964	Italia Caracas, Venezuela	1-2		0-0	prelim
1989	Internacional Porto Alegre, Brazil	2-1		1-0	1
	Sport Maritimo Caracas, Venezuela	3-2		0-0*	1
				* behind closed doors, political dispute	
	Tachira San Cristobal, Venezuela	4-1		1-1	1
	Universitario Lima, Peru	2-1		1-1	2
	Internacional Porto Alegre, Brazil	0-0		0-1	qf

VASCO DA GAMA CLUBE de REGATAS (RIO DE JANEIRO)

Founded 21st August 1898
Address Club de Regatas Vasco de Gama, Rua General Americo De Moura 131, Rio de Janeiro 20921 RJ
Colours all white with black sash
Stadium Estadio de Sao Januario (50,000) or Maracana (200,000)
Rio State Champions 1923, 1924*, 1929, 1934*, 1936*, 1945, 1947, 1949, 1950, 1952, 1956, 1958, 1970, 1977, 1982, 1987, 1988
Rio/Sao Paulo Champions 1958, 1966 (shared)
National Champions 1974, 1989

Season	Opponent	Home	Result	Away	Round
1975	Cruzeiro Belo Horizonte, Brazil	1-1		2-3	1
	Nacional Medellin, Colombia	2-0		1-1	1
	Deportivo Cali, Colombia	0-0		1-2	1
1980	Galicia Caracas, Venezuela	4-0		0-0	1
	Tachira San Cristobal, Venezuela	1-0		1-0	1
	Internacional Porto Alegre, Brazil	0-0		1-2	1
1985	Argentinos Juniors, Argentina	1-2		2-2	1
	Fluminense Rio de Janeiro, Brazil	3-3		0-0	1
	FC Oeste, Argentina	0-2		0-2	1
1990	Gremio Porto Alegro, Brazil	0-0		0-2	1
	Cerro Porteno, Paraguay	2-0		1-1	1
	Olimpia, Paraguay	1-0		1-2	1
	Colo Colo, Chile	0-0	5-4p	3-3	2
	Nacional Medellin, Colombia	0-0	0-1	0-2*	3

* disputed match which need the replay

1963 **Santos** (Brazil)

BRAZIL

CLUB DE REGATAS FLAMENGO (RIO DE JANEIRO)

Founded 15th November 1885
Address Placa Nossa Senhora Auxilladora S/N 22441, Rio de Janeiro RJ
Colours black and red hooped shirts, white shorts
Stadium Estadio da Gavea (8,000) or Maracana (200,000)
Rio State Champions 1914, 1915, 1920, 1921, 1925, 1927, 1939, 1942, 1943, 1944, 1953, 1954, 1955, 1963, 1965, 1972, 1974, 1978, 1979
Rio/Sao Paulo Champions 1961
National Champions 1980, 1982, 1983, 1987
Libertadores Cup Winners 1981
World Club Champions 1981

Season	Opponent	Home	Playoff Result	Away	Round
1981	Cerro Porteno, Paraguay	5-2		4-2	1
	Olimpia, Paraguay	1-1		0-0	1
	Atletico Mineiro Belo Horizonte, Brazil	2-2	0-0 in Goiania	2-2	1
				abandoned after 35 mins	
	Deportivo Cali, Colombia	3-0		1-0	sf
	Jorge Wilsterman Cochabamba, Bolivia	4-1		2-1	sf
	Cobreloa Calama, Chile	2-1	2-0 in Montevideo	0-1	FINAL
1982	River Plate, Argentina	4-2		3-0	sf
	Penarol, Uruguay	0-1		0-1	sf
1983	Blooming Santa Cruz, Bolivia	7-1		0-0	1
	Bolivar, Bolivia	5-2		1-3	1
	Gremio Porto Alegre, Brazil	1-3		1-1	1
1984	Santos FC Sao Paulo, Brazil	4-1		5-0	1
	America de Cali, Colombia	4-2		1-1	1
	Junior Barranquilla, Colombia	3-1		2-1	1
	Universidad de Los Andes (ULA) Merida, Venezuela	2-1		3-0	sf
	Gremio Porto Alegre, Brazil	3-1	0-0	1-5	sf

SPORT CLUBE RECIFE

Founded 13th May 1905
Address Avenida Abdias de Carvalho S/N, Ilha do Retiro, CEP 50750, Recife, Pernambuco PE
Colours red and black hooped shirts, black shorts
Stadium Estadio Ilha do Retiro (50,000) or Coloso de Arruda (150,000)
Pernambuco State Champions 1916, 1917, 1920, 1923, 1924, 1925, 1928, 1938, 1941, 1942, 1943, 1948, 1949, 1953, 1955, 1956, 1958, 1961, 1962, 1975, 1977, 1980, 1981, 1982, 1988

Season	Opponent	Home	Result	Away	Round
1988	Guarani Campinas, Brazil	0-1		1-4	1
	Universitario Lima, Peru	1-1		0-1	1
	Alianza Lima, Peru	5-0		1-0	1

CORITIBA FC (CURITIBA)

Founded 12th October 1909
Address Rua Ubaldino do Amaral 37, CEP 80030 Curitiba, Parana PR
Colours white shirts with green trim and two green hoops, black shorts
Stadium Estadio Antonio de Couto Pereira (80,000) or Pinherao (130,000)
Parana State Champions 1916, 1927, 1931, 1933, 1935, 1939, 1941, 1942, 1946, 1947, 1951, 1952, 1954, 1956, 1957, 1959, 1960, 1968, 1969, 1971, 1972, 1973, 1974, 1975, 1976, 1978, 1979, 1986

Season	Opponent	Home	Result	Away	Round
1986	Barcelona Sporting Guayaquil, Ecuador	0-0		1-1	1
	Deportivo Quito, Ecuador	3-1		1-2	1
	Bangu Rio de Janeiro, Brazil	not played		1-1	1

CHILE

Founded 1895
Federacion de Football de Chile, Calle Erasmo Escalo n.1872, Casilla 3733 Santiago de Chile ☎ (56-2) 696 5381
Telex 440474 Febol.cz.Postal Fax (56-2) 698 7082
Language Spanish, English
National colours red shirts, blue shorts, grey socks
Season April to September
Founded 1893

LEAGUE CHAMPIONS

All clubs from Santiago unless stated

1931	Associacion Santiago	1946	Audax Italiano	1960	Colo Colo	1975	Union Espanola
1932	not held	1947	Colo Colo	1961	Universidad Catolica	1976	Everton
1933	Magallanes	1948	Audax Italiano	1962	Universidad de Chile	1977	Union Espanola
1934	Magallanes	1949	Universidad Catolica	1963	Colo Colo	1978	Palestino
1935	Magallanes			1964	Universidad de Chile	1979	Colo Colo
1936	Audax Italiano	1950	Everton	1965	Universidad de Chile	1980	Cobreloa Calama
1937	Colo Colo	1951	Union Espanola	1966	Universidad Catolica	1981	Colo Colo
1938	Magallanes	1952	Everton	1967	Universidad de Chile	1982	Cobreloa Calama
1939	Colo Colo	1953	Colo Colo	1968	Santiago Wanderers	1983	Colo Colo
		1954	Universidad Catolica	1969	Universidad de Chile	1984	Universidad Catolica
1940	Universidad de Chile	1955	Palestino			1985	Cobreloa Calama
1941	Colo Colo	1956	Colo Colo	1970	Colo Colo	1986	Colo Colo
1942	Santiago Morning	1957	Audax Italiano	1971	Union San Felipe	1987	Universidad Catolica
1943	Union Espanola	1958	Wanderers Valparaiso	1972	Colo Colo	1988	Cobreloa Calama
1944	Colo Colo	1959	Universidad de Chile	1973	Union Espanola	1989	Colo Colo
1945	Green Cross			1974	Huachipata, Talcahuano		
						1990	Colo Colo

FEATURED CLUBS IN COPA LIBERTADORES DE AMERICA

All clubs from Santiago unless stated

Universidad de Chile	Universidad Catolica	Union Espanola	Colo Colo
Santiago Wanderers	Palestino	Cobreloa Calama	Hauchipato Talcahuano
O'Higgins Rancagua	Union San Felipe	Everton Vina del Mar	Rangers Talca
Magallanes San Bernado	Cobresal El Salvador		

UNIVERSIDAD DE CHILE (SANTIAGO)

Founded 4th March 1911
Address Marin 0525, Santiago de Chile
Colours all blue with white trim and U on chest
Stadium Santa Laura (35,000) or Estadio Nacional (74,159)
Champions 1940, 1959, 1962, 1964, 1965, 1967, 1969

Season	Opponent	Home	Playoff Result	Away	Rnd
1960	Millonarios Bogota, Colombia	0-6		0-1	1
1963	Boca Juniors, Argentina	2-3		0-1	1
	Olimpia, Paraguay	4-1		1-2	1

1965	Santos FC Sao Paulo, Brazil	1-5		0-1	1
	Universitario Lima, Peru	5-2		0-1	1
1966	Universidad Catolica, Chile	0-0		2-2	1
	Guarani, Paraguay	2-0		1-1	1
	Olimpia, Paraguay	1-2		0-2	1
1968	Emelec Guayaquil, Ecuador	0-0		1-2	1
	Nacional Quito, Ecuador	1-0		1-3	1
	Universidad Catolica, Chile	2-3		1-2	1
1970	Deportivo Cali, Colombia	3-1		0-2	1
	America de Cali, Colombia	2-1		2-2	1
	Olimpia, Paraguay	2-1		1-1	1
	Guarani, Paraguay	0-0		0-1	1
	Rangers Talca, Chile	7-1		2-1	1
	Nacional, Uruguay	3-0	2-1*	0-2	qf
					* Porto Alegre
	Penarol, Uruguay	1-0	2-2*	0-2	sf
					* Buenos Aires lag
1972	Union San Felipe, Chile	2-1		2-3	1
	Alianza Lima, Peru	2-3		4-3	1
	Universitario Lima, Peru	1-0		1-2	1
1977	Everton Vina del Mar, Chile	1-0		0-0	1
	Libertad, Paraguay	1-0		0-3	1
	Olimpia, Paraguay	1-0		0-1	1
1981	Sporting Cristal, Peru	1-1		2-2	1
	Atletico Torino Talara, Peru	3-0		2-1	1
	Cobreloa Calama, Chile	0-0		0-1	1

CLUB de DEPORTES UNIVERSIDAD CATOLICA (SANTIAGO)

Founded 10th April 1937
Address Avenida Andres Bellol 2782, Santiago
Colours white shirts with blue hoop and U on chest, blue shorts
Stadium Santa Laura (35,000) or Estadio Nacional (74,159)
Champions 1949, 1954, 1961, 1966, 1984, 1987

Season	Opponents	Home	Playoff Result	Away	Round
1962	Emelec Guayaquil, Ecuador	3-0		2-7	1
	Millonarios Bogota, Colombia	4-1		1-1	1
	Santos FC Sao Paulo, Brazil	0-0		0-1	sf
1966	Guarani, Paraguay	2-0		1-3	1
	Olimpia, Paraguay	0-0		4-0	1
	Universidad de Chile, Chile	2-2		0-0	1
	Penarol, Uruguay	1-0		0-2	sf
	Nacional, Uruguay	1-0		2-3	sf
1967	Emelec Guayaquil, Ecuador	5-2		1-2	1
	Barcelona Sporting Guayaquil, Ecuador	3-1		2-0	1
	Nacional, Uruguay	0-3		0-0	1
	Cerro Porteno, Paraguay	3-1		0-1	1
	Guarani, Paraguay	1-1		1-1	1
	Colo Colo, Chile	5-2		2-4	1
1968	Nacional Quito, Ecuador	2-0		1-2	1
	Emelec Guayaquil, Ecuador	1-1		2-1	1
	Universidad de Chile, Chile	2-1		3-2	1
	Palmeiras Sao Paulo, Brazil	0-1		1-4	qf
	Guarani, Paraguay	4-2		1-2	qf
1969	Santiago Wanderers, Chile	3-2		1-3	1
	Juan Aurich de Chiclana, Peru	4-2	4-1	1-2	1
	Sporting Cristal, Peru	3-2	2-1	0-2	1
	Italia Caracas, Venezuela	4-0		2-3	qf
	Cerro Porteno, Paraguay	1-0		0-0	qf
	Estudiantes La Plata, Argentina	1-3		1-3	sf
1984	O'Higgins Rancagua, Chile	2-0		2-0	1
	Bolivar, Bolivia	3-1		2-3	1
	Blooming Santa Cruz, Bolivia	0-0		2-1	1
	Independiente, Argentina	0-0		1-2	sf

	Nacional, Uruguay	not played		0-2	sf
1986	America de Cali, Colombia	1-3		1-2	1
	Cobresal El Salvador, Chile	0-1		1-1	1
	Deportivo Cali, Colombia	1-3		1-3	1
1988	Colo Colo, Chile	1-0		2-2	1
	Sport Maritimo, Venezuela	2-1		0-0	1
	Tachira San Cristobal, Venezuela	3-1		1-0	1
	Nacional, Uruguay	1-1	lag	0-0	2
1990	Colo Colo, Chile	0-0		2-1	1
	Sporting Cristal, Peru	2-0		0-0	1
	Union Huaral, Peru	2-2		0-1	1
	The Strongest, Boliva	3-1		1-1	2
	Olimpia, Paraguay	4-4		0-2	3

UNION ESPANOLA (SANTIAGO del CHILE)

Founded 16th November 1909 as Iberico, 1924 Union Espanola
Address Carmen 102/110, Santiago de Chile
Colours red shirts, blue shorts
Stadium San Carlos (12,500) or Santa Laura (35,000)
Champions 1943, 1951, 1973, 1975, 1977
Libertadores Finalists 1975

Season	Opponents	Home	Playoff Result	Away	Round
1971	Cerro Porteno, Paraguay	0-0		1-2	1
	Guarani, Paraguay	2-1		1-1	1
	Colo Colo, Chile	2-1		1-1	1
	Barcelona Sporting Guayaquil, Ecuador	3-1		0-1	sf
	Estudiantes La Plata, Argentina	0-1		1-2	sf
1973	Colo Colo, Chile	0-0		0-5	1
	Emelec Guayaquil, Ecuador	1-1		0-1	1
	Nacional Quito, Ecuador	2-1		0-1	1
1974	Colo Colo, Chile	2-1		2-0	1
	Huracan, Argentina	1-3		1-5	1
	Rosario Central, Argentina	0-1		0-4	1
1975	Hauchipato Talcahuano, Chile	7-2		0-0	1
	The Strongest, Bolivia	4-0		1-1	1
	Jorge Wilsterman Cochabamba, Bolivia	4-1		1-1	1
	Liga Deportivo Universitaria Quito, Ecuador	2-0		2-4	sf
	Universitario Lima, Peru	2-1		1-1	sf
	Independiente, Argentina	1-0	0-2 in Asuncion	1-3	FINAL
1976	Palestino, Chile	1-0		1-0	1
	Penarol, Uruguay	0-0		0-2	1
	Nacional, Uruguay	2-0		1-1	1
1978	Palestino, Chile	0-0		3-2	1
	Sao Paulo FC, Brazil	1-1		1-1	1
	Atletico Mineiro Belo Horizonte, Brazil	1-1		1-5	1

COLO COLO (SANTIAGO del CHILE)

Founded 19th April 1925
Address Cienfuegos 41, Santiago de Chile
Colours white shirts, black shorts
Stadium David Orellano (45,000) expanding to (110,000)
Champions 1937, 1939, 1941, 1944, 1947, 1953, 1956, 1960, 1963, 1970, 1972, 1979, 1981, 1983, 1986, 1989, 1990
Libertadores Finalists 1973

Season	Opponents	Home	Playoff Result	Away	Round
1961	Olimpia, Paraguay	2-5		2-1	1
1964	Italia Caracas, Venezuela	4-0		2-1	1
	Barcelona Sporting Guayaquil, Ecuador	0-4		3-2	1
	Nacional, Uruguay	2-4		2-4	sf

1967	Emelec Guayaquil, Ecuador	3-2		3-4	1
	Barcelona Sporting Guayaquil, Ecuador	3-2		1-1	1
	Nacional, Uruguay	3-2		2-5	1
	Cerro Porteno, Paraguay	5-1		1-0	1
	Guarani, Paraguay	1-0		2-4	1
	Universidad Catolica, Chile	4-2		2-5	1
	Racing Club Avellaneda, Argentina	0-2		1-3	sf
	Universitario Lima, Peru	0-1		0-3	sf
	River Plate, Argentina	1-0		1-1	sf
1971	Cerro Porteno, Paraguay	1-0		0-0	1
	Guarani, Paraguay	3-2		0-2	1
	Union Espanola, Chile	1-1		1-2	1
1973	Union Espanola, Chile	5-0		0-0	1
	Emelec Guayaquil, Ecuador	5-1		0-1	1
	Nacional Quito, Ecuador	5-1		1-1	1
	Botafogo Rio de Janeiro, Brazil	3-3		2-1	sf
	Cerro Porteno, Paraguay	4-0		1-5	sf
	Independiente, Argentina	0-0	1-2 in Montevideo	1-1	FINAL
1974	Union Espanola, Chile	0-2		1-2	1
	Huracan, Argentina	1-2		0-2	1
	Rosario Central, Argentina	2-3		0-2	1
1980	O'Higgins Rancagua, Chile	1-1		1-3	1
	Sol de America, Paraguay	1-1		1-2	1
	Cerro Porteno, Paraguay	2-1		3-5	1
1982	Cobreloa Calama, Chile	0-0		0-2	1
	Liga Deportivo Universitaria Quito, Ecuador	1-0		2-2	1
	Barcelona Sporting Guayaquil, Ecuador	2-0		3-1	1
1983	Cobreloa Calama, Chile	2-1		0-2	1
	FC Oeste, Argentina	1-0		0-1	1
	Estudiantes La Plata, Argentina	1-0		1-4	1
1985	Magallanes San Bernado, Chile	2-0		3-1	1
	Bella Vista, Uruguay	2-0		1-2	1
	Penarol, Uruguay	1-2		1-3	1
1987	Cobreloa Calama, Chile	0-0		0-1	1
	Guarani Campinas, Brazil	2-0		0-0	1
	Sao Paulo FC, Brazil	2-2		2-1	1
1988	Universidad Catolica, Chile	2-2		0-1	1
	Sport Maritimo Caracas, Venezuela	1-0		1-0	1
	Tachira San Cristobal, Venezuela	2-0		1-0	1
	Oriente Petrolero Santa Cruz, Paraguay	0-0		1-2	2
1989	Cobreloa Calama, Chile	2-2		0-2	1
	Sol de America, Paraguay	3-1		0-1	1
	Olimpia, Paraguay	2-0		0-2	1
1990	Universidad Catolica, Chile	1-2		0-0	1
	Sporting Cristal, Peur	2-0		2-1	1
	Union Huaral, Peru	3-1		1-1	1
	Vasco da Gama Rio, Brazil	3-3	4-5	0-0	2

SANTIAGO WANDERERS (VALPARAISO)

Founded 15th August 1892
Address Lira 575, Valparaiso
Founded 1892
Colours green shirts, white shorts
Stadium Estadio Playa Ancha (18,000)
Champions 1968

Season	Opponents	Playoff Home	Result	Away	Round
1969	Universidad Catolica, Chile	3-1		2-3	1
	Sporting Cristal, Peru	2-0	1-1	1-2	1
	Juan Aurich de Chiclana, Peru	4-1	1-0	1-3	1
	Nacional, Uruguay	1-1		0-2	qf
	Deportivo Cali, Colombia	3-3		1-5	qf

CLUB PALESTINO (SANTIAGO del CHILE)

Founded 8th August 1920
Address Avenuda Presidente Kennedy 9351, Santiago
Colours green, red and white broad striped shirts with black trim, black shorts
Stadium La Cisterna (20,000) or Estadio Nacional (74,159)
Champions 1955, 1978

Season	Opponents	Home	Result	Away	Round
1976	Union Espanola, Chile	0-1		0-1	1
	Nacional, Uruguay	2-1		1-1	1
	Penarol, Uruguay	1-0		1-2	1
1978	Union Espanola, Chile	2-3		0-0	1
	Sao Paulo FC, Brazil	0-1		2-1	1
	Atletico Mineiro Belo Horizonte, Brazil	4-5		0-2	1
1979	Galicia Caracas, Venezuela	5-0		1-1	1
	Portuguesa Acariga, Venezuela	6-0		2-0	1
	O'Higgins Rancagua, Chile	1-0		1-1	1
	Guarani, Paraguay	0-0		2-2	sf
	Olimpia, Paraguay	0-2		0-3	sf

CLUB de DEPORTES COBRELOA (CALAMA)

Founded 7th January 1977
Address Atacama 1482, Castilla 156, Calama
Colours all orange with white trim
Stadium Municipal de Calama (20,000)
Champions 1980, 1982, 1985, 1988
Libertadores Cup Finalists 1981, 1982

Season	Opponents	Home	Playoff Result	Away	Round
1981	Sporting Cristal, Peru	6-1		0-0	1
	Atletico Torino Talara, Peru	6-1		1-1	1
	Universidad de Chile, Chile	1-0		0-0	1
	Nacional, Uruguay	2-1		2-1	sf
	Penarol, Uruguay	4-2		1-0	sf
	Flamengo Rio de Janeiro, Brazil	1-0	0-2	1-2	FINAL
1982	Colo Colo, Chile	2-0		0-0	1
	Barcelona Sporting Guayaquil, Ecuador	3-0		1-1	1
	Liga Deportivo Universitaria Quito, Ecuador	3-1		0-0	1
	Tolima Ibague, Colombia	3-0		0-1	sf
	Olimpia, Paraguay	1-0		1-1	sf
	Penarol, Uruguay	0-1		0-0	FINAL
1983	Colo Colo, Chile	2-0		1-2	1
	Estudiantes La Plata, Argentina	3-0		0-2	1
	FC Oeste, Argentina	2-1		0-1	1
1987	Colo Colo, Chile	1-0		0-0	1
	Guarani Campinas, Brazil	3-1		0-0	1
	Sao Paulo FC, Brazil	3-1		1-2	1
	America de Cali, Colombia	2-2		1-1	sf
	Barcelona Sporting Guayaquil, Ecuador	3-0		2-0	sf
1989	Colo Colo, Chile	2-0		2-2	1
	Sol de America, Paraguay	1-0		0-0	1
	Olimpia, Paraguay	2-0		0-2	1
	Deportivo Quito, Ecuador	1-0		0-0	2
	Danubio, Uruguay	0-2		1-2	qf

CHILE

DEPORTES HAUCHIPATO (TALCAHUANO)

Founded 6th June 1947
Address Parque Aravcaria, Talcahuano
Colours black and mid blue broad striped shirts, mid blue shorts
Stadium Estadio Las Higueras (12,000)
Champions 1974

Season	Opponents	Home	Result	Away	Round
1975	Union Espanola, Chile	0-0		2-7	1
	Jorge Wilsterman Cochabamba, Bolivia	4-0		0-0	1
	The Strongest, Bolivia	4-2		0-1	1

O'HIGGINS (RANCAGUA)

Founded 7th April 1955
Address Deportes O'Higgins, Avenida Brasil 1079, Rancagua
Colours all sky blue with black trim
Stadium Estadio El Teniente (20,000)

Season	Opponents	Home	Result	Away	Round
1979	Portuguesa Acarigua, Venezuela	1-1		1-1	1
	Galicia Caracas, Venezuela	6-0		1-0	1
	Palestino, Chile	1-1		0-1	1
1980	Colo Colo, Chile	3-1		1-1	1
	Sol de America, Paraguay	2-0		4-1	1
	Cerro Porteno, Paraguay	0-0		0-1	1
	Nacional, Uruguay	0-1		0-2	sf
	Olimpia, Paraguay	0-1		0-2	sf
1984	Universidad Catolica, Chile	0-2		0-2	1
	Bolivar, Bolivia	0-0		1-5	1
	Blooming Santa Cruz, Bolivia	3-4		0-3	1

UNION (SAN FELIPE)

Founded 16th October 1956
Address Prat 320, San Felipe
Colours all white with red trim
Stadium Estadio Municipal (12,000)
Champions 1971

Season	Opponents	Home	Result	Away	Round
1972	Universitario Lima, Peru	1-3		0-0	1
	Alianza Lima, Peru	0-0		0-1	1
	Universidad de Chile, Chile	3-2		1-2	1

EVERTON (VINA DEL MAR)

Founded 24th June 1909
Address Everton, Viana 161, Vina del Mar
Colours blue and yellow striped shirts, blue shorts
Stadium Estadio Sausalito (25,000)
Champions 1950, 1952, 1976

Season	Opponents	Home	Result	Away	Round
1977	Universitario Lima, Peru	0-0		0-1	1
	Libertad, Paraguay	1-3		1-2	1
	Olimpia, Paraguay	1-0		2-2	1

RANGERS (TALCA)

Founded 2nd November 1902
Address Rangers Talca, Estadio Fiscal, Talca
Colours red and black hooped shirts, white shorts
Stadium Estadio Fiscal (10,000)

Season	Opponents	Home	Result	Away	Round
1970	Guarani, Paraguay	0-1		0-2	1
	Olimpia, Paraguay	4-4		1-5	1
	America de Cali, Colombia	2-0		0-1	1
	Deportivo Cali, Colombia	0-2		2-3	1
	Universidad de Chile, Chile	1-2		1-7	1

MAGALLANES (SAN BERNADO)

Founded 27th October 1897
Address
Colours sky blue and white striped shirts, black shorts
Stadium Estadio Vulco (15,000) or Santa Laura Santiago (35,000)
Champions 1933, 1934, 1935, 1938

Season	Opponents	Home	Result	Away	Round
1985	Colo Colo, Chile	1-3		1-2	1
	Penarol, Uruguay	1-1		0-1	1
	Bella Vista, Uruguay	2-1		1-0	1

COBRESAL (EL SALVADOR)

Founded 9th March 1979
Colours white shirts with thin orange stripes, orange shorts
Stadium Estadio El Cobre (10,000)

Season	Opponents	Home	Result	Away	Round
1986	America de Cali, Colombia	2-2		0-0	1
	Deportivo Cali, Colombia	1-1		1-1	1
	Universidad Catolica, Chile	1-1		1-0	1

COLOMBIA

Founded 1924
Federacion Colombiana de Fulbol, Avenida 32n.16-22, Apartado Aereo 17602, Bogota ☎ 010 57-1 245 5370/285
5220 Telex 45598 Colfu co Fax (57-1) 285 43 40
Language Spanish, English
National colours white shirts with blue, yellow and red stripes, blue shorts
Season March to December

LEAGUE CHAMPIONS

1948 Independiente Santa Fe	1960 Independiente Santa Fe	1970 Deportivo Cali	1980 Junior Barranquilla
1949 Millonarios Bogota	1961 Millonarios Bogota	1971 Independiente Santa Fe	1981 Nacional Medellin
	1962 Millonarios Bogota	1972 Millonarios Bogota	1982 America de Cali
1950 Once Caldes	1963 Millonarios Bogota	1973 Nacional Medellin	1983 America de Cali
1951 Millonarios Bogota	1964 Millonarios Bogota	1974 Deportivo Cali	1984 America de Cali
1952 Millonarios Bogota	1965 Deportivo Cali	1975 Independiente Santa Fe	1985 America de Cali
1953 Millonarios Bogota	1966 Independiente Santa Fe	1976 Nacional Medellin	1986 America de Cali
1954 Nacional Medellin	1967 Deportivo Cali	1977 Junior Barranquilla	1987 Millonarios Bogota
1955 Independiente Medellin	1968 Union Magdalena	1978 Millonarios Bogota	1988 Millonarios Bogota
1956 Atletico Quindio Armenia	1969 Deportivo Cali	1979 America de Cali	1989 not held
1957 Independiente Medellin			
1958 Independiente Santa Fe			
1959 Millonarios Bogota			

FEATURED CLUBS IN COPA LIBERTADORES DE AMERICA

Nacional Medellin	Independiente Santa Fe	Millonarios Bogota	Deportivo Cali
Tolima Ibague	Junior Barranquilla	Deportivo Independiente Medellin	
America de Cali	Union Magdelina		

CLUB DEPORTIVO ATLETICO NACIONAL (MEDELLIN)

Founded 15th February 1936
Address Carrera 76 No 48-11, Medellin
Colours green and white striped shirts, white shorts
Stadium Atanasio Girardot (36,000)
Champions 1954, 1973, 1976, 1981
Libertadores Cup Winners 1989

Season	Opponent	Home	Playoff Result	Away	Rnd
1972	Independiente Santa Fe, Colombia	0-1		1-1	1
	Independiente, Argentina	1-1		0-2	1
	Rosario Central, Argentina	1-0		1-3	1
1974	Millonarios Bogota, Colombia	1-2		0-3	1
	Valencia FC Acarigua, Venezuela	2-1		2-1	1
	Portuguesa Acarigua, Venezuela	3-0		0-0	1
1975	Deportivo Cali, Colombia	2-1		0-0	1
	Vasco da Gama Rio de Janeiro, Brazil	1-1		0-2	1
	Cruzeiro Belo Horizonte, Brazil	1-2		3-2	1

1977	Deportivo Cali, Colombia	0-3		1-3	1
	Bolivar, Bolivia	1-0		0-3	1
	Oriente Petrolero Santa Cruz, Bolivia	3-1		0-4	1
1982	Tolima Ibague, Colombia	0-3		0-0	1
	Tachira San Cristobal, Venezuela	1-0		0-0	1
	Estudiantes de Merida, Venezuela	2-0		3-1	1
1989	Millonarios Bogota, Colombia	0-2		1-1	1
	Emelec Guayaquil, Ecuador	3-1		1-1	1
	Deportivo Quito, Ecuador	2-1		1-1	1
	Racing Club Avellaneda, Argentina	2-0		1-2	2
	Millonarios Bogota, Colombia	1-0		1-1	qf
	Danubio, Uruguay	6-0		0-0	sf
	Olimpia, Paraguay	2-0aet	5-4p	0-2	FINAL
1990	bye				1
	Cerro Porteno, Paraguay	1-0		0-0	2
	Olimpia, Paraguay	1-2*	1-2p in Santiago	3-2 aet	sf

* As the Colombian League was suspended, no league games were played to qualifiy for the Libertadores Cup.

CLUB INDEPENDIENTE SANTA FE (BOGOTA)

Founded 28th February 1941
Address Avenida 39 No 15-22, Bogota
Colours red shirts with white sleeves and trim, white shorts
Stadium El Campin, District Nemesio Campo (52,000)
Champions 1948, 1958, 1960, 1966, 1971, 1975

Season	Opponent	Home	Result	Away	Round
1961	Barcelona Sporting Guayaquil, Ecuador	1-0		2-2	1
	Jorge Wilsterman Cochabamba, Bolivia	1-0	wag	2-3	2
	Palmeiras Sao Paulo, Brazil	2-2		1-4	sf
1967	Independiente Medellin, Colombia	2-0		0-4	1
	Racing Club Avellaneda, Argentina	1-2		1-4	1
	River Plate, Argentina	2-2		0-4	1
	Bolivar, Bolivia	1-2		2-2	1
	31st de Octubre, Bolivia	2-0		2-6	1
1972	Nacional Medellin, Colombia	1-1		0-1	1
	Independiente, Argentina	4-2		0-2	1
	Rosario Central, Argentina	0-0		0-2	1
1976	Alfonso Ugarte Puno, Peru	2-2		1-2	1
	Alianza Lima, Peru	2-3		0-3	1
	Millonarios Bogota, Colombia	1-1		1-0	1
1980	America de Cali, Colombia	1-1		0-1	1
	Universidad Catolica, Chile	1-0		0-1	1
	Emelec Guayaquil, Ecuador	1-2		2-0	1

DEPORTIVO CLUB LOS MILLONARIOS (BOGOTA)

Founded 1938 as Deportivo Municipal, 22nd May 1946 Millonarios
Address Calle 67 No 7-82, Bogota
Colours blue shirts, white shorts
Stadium El Campin, District Nemesio Campo (52,000)
Champions 1949, 1951, 1952, 1953, 1959, 1961, 1962, 1963, 1964, 1972, 1978, 1987, 1988

Season	Opponent	Home	Result	Away	Rnd
1960	Universidad de Chile, Chile	1-0		6-0	1
	Olimpia, Paraguay	0-0		1-5	sf
1962	Emelec Guayaquil, Ecuador	3-1		2-4	1
	Universidad Catolica, Chile	1-1		1-4	1
1963	Alianza Lima, Peru	0-0		0-1	1
	Botafogo Rio de Janeiro, Brazil	0-2		0-2	1
1964	Independiente, Argentina	disqualified		1-5	1
	Alianza Lima, Peru	3-2		2-1	1
1968	Independiente, Argentina	1-2		1-3	1
	Deportivo Cali, Colombia	4-2		0-1	1
	Estudiantes La Plata, Argentina	0-1		0-0	1
1973	Deportivo Cali, Colombia	6-2		0-0	1
	San Lorenzo, Argentina	0-0		0-2	sf
	Independiente, Argentina	1-0		0-2	sf

COLOMBIA

1974	Nacional Medellin, Colombia	3-0		2-1	1
	Portuguesa Acarigua, Venezuela	2-1		0-2	1
	Valencia FC Acarigua, Venezuela	2-1		1-1	1
	Sao Paulo FC, Brazil	0-0		0-4	sf
	Defensor Lima, Peru	1-0		4-1	sf
1976	Alianza Lima, Peru	1-0		1-2	1
	Alfonso Ugarte Puno, Peru	4-0		1-1	1
	Independiente Santa Fe, Colombia	0-1		1-1	1
1979	Deportivo Cali, Colombia	1-1		0-2	1
	Independiente, Argentina	3-3		1-4	1
	Quilmes, Argentina	1-0		2-1	1
1985	America de Cali, Colombia	0-0		0-0	1
	Guarani, Paraguay	5-1		0-2	1
	Cerro Porteno, Paraguay	0-2		0-0	1
1988	Nacional, Uruguay	6-1		1-4	1
	Wanderers, Uruguay	3-0		1-2	1
	America de Cali, Colombia	2-3		1-2	1
1989	Nacional Medellin, Colombia	1-1		2-0	1
	Emelec Guayaquil, Ecuador	4-1		2-0	1
	Deportivo Quito, Ecuador	3-1		0-0	1
	Bolivar, Bolivia	3-2aet	4-3p	0-1	2
	Nacional Medellin, Colombia	1-1		0-1	qf

ASOCIACION DEPORTIVO CALI

Founded 5th August 1918 as Cali Futbol Club, 1947 as Deportivo
Address Calle 34 No 2 bis-75, Apartado 4593, Cali
Colours green shirts with white trim, white shorts
Stadium Pascual Guerrero (61,000)
Champions 1965, 1967, 1969, 1970, 1974
Libertadores Finalists 1978

Season	Opponent	Home	Playoff Result	Away	Round
1968	Independiente, Argentina	1-0	2-3	1-1	1
	Millonarios Bogota, Colombia	1-0		2-4	1
	Estudiantes La Plata, Argentina	1-2		0-3	1
1969	Union Magdelena, Colombia	3-1		2-2	1
	Union Deportivo Canarias Caracas, Venezuela	2-0		1-1	1
	Italia Caracas, Venezuela	3-0		1-2	1
	Nacional, Uruguay	1-5		0-2	qf
	Santiago Wanderers, Chile	5-1		3-3	qf
1970	Universidad de Chile, Chile	2-0		1-3	1
	Rangers Talca, Chile	3-2		2-0	1
	America de Cali, Colombia	4-2		4-2	1
	Guarani, Paraguay	1-1	1-4	0-0	1
	Olimpia, Paraguay	1-5		0-1	1
1971	Juniors Barranquilla, Colombia	2-0		1-2	1
	Emelec Guayaquil, Ecuador	1-0		1-3	1
	Barcelona Sporting Guayaquil, Ecuador	3-0		0-1	1
1973	Millonarios Bogota, Colombia	0-0		2-6	1
1975	Naconal Medellin, Colombia	0-0		1-2	1
	Cruzeiro Belo Horizonte, Brazil	1-0		1-2	1
	Vasco da Gama Rio de Janeiro, Brazil	2-1		0-0	1
1977	Nacional Medellin, Colombia	3-1		3-0	1
	Bolivar, Bolivia	3-0		0-3	1
	Oriente Petrolero Santa Cruz, Bolivia	3-0		0-1	1
	Boca Juniors, Argentina	1-1		1-1	sf
	Libertad, Paraguay	0-0		1-2	sf
1978	Juniors Barranquilla, Colombia	0-0		0-0	1
	Danubio, Uruguay	2-0		1-3	1
	Penarol, Uruguay	1-0		2-0	1
	Alianza Lima, Peru	3-2		4-1	sf
	Cerro Porteno, Paraguay	1-1		4-0	sf
	Boca Juniors, Argentina	0-0		0-4	FINAL

1979	Quilmes, Argentina	3-2		1-3	1
	Independiente, Argentina	1-0		0-1	1
	Millonarios Bogota, Colombia	2-0		1-1	1
1981	River Plate, Argentina	2-1		2-1	1
	Rosario Central, Argentina	1-0		1-2	1
	Juniors Barranquilla, Colombia	4-1		0-1	1
	Flamengo Rio de Janeiro, Brazil	0-1		0-3	sf
	Jorge Wilsterman Cochabamba, Bolivia	1-0		1-1	sf
1986	America de Cali, Colombia	0-1		0-0	1
	Cobresal El Salvador, Chile	1-1		1-1	1
	Universidad Catolica, Chile	3-1		3-1	1

CORPORACION DEPORTES TOLIMA (IBAGUE)

Founded 25th October 1954
Address Calle 12 No 3-43, Oficina 411, Ibague
Colours yellow shirts with white sleeves, red shorts
Stadium Estadio Manuel Murillo Toro (20,000)

Season	Opponent	Home	Result	Away	Round
1982	Nacional Medellin, Colombia	0-0		3-0	1
	Tachira San Cristobal, Venezuela	2-2		2-0	1
	Estudiantes de Merida, Venezuela	1-0		1-1	1
	Cobreloa Calama, Chile	1-0		0-3	sf
	Olimpia, Paraguay	1-1		0-2	sf
1983	America de Cali, Colombia	0-2		1-1	1
	Universitario Lima, Peru	1-1		2-2	1
	Alianza Lima, Peru	0-0		1-0	1

CLUB ATLETICO JUNIOR (BARRANQUILLA)

Founded 7th August 1948
Address Carrera 57 No 72-56, Barranquilla
Colours red and white striped shirts, blue shorts
Champions 1977, 1980
Stadium Estadio Romelio Martinez (20,000) or Metropolitano (60,000)

Season	Opponent	Home	Result	Away	Round
1971	Deportivo Cali, Colombia	2-1		0-2	1
	Barcelona Sporting Guayaquil, Ecuador	0-2		1-3	1
	Emelec Guayaquil, Ecuador	0-0		1-1	1
1978	Deportivo Cali, Colombia	0-0		0-0	1
	Penarol, Uruguay	1-0		0-1	1
	Danubio, Uruguay	0-0		0-0	1
1981	River Plate, Argentina	0-0		0-3	1
	Rosario Central, Argentina	1-2		0-5	1
	Deportivo Cali, Colombia	1-0		1-4	1
1984	Flamengo Rio de Janeiro, Brazil	1-2		1-3	1
	Santos FC Sao Paulo, Brazil	0-3		3-1	1
	America de Cali, Colombia	4-1		0-2	1

COLOMBIA

CLUB DEPORTIVO INDEPENDIENTE (MEDELLIN)

Founded 25th January 1914
Address Carrera 76 No 48-22, Medellin
Colours red shirts, blue shorts
Stadium Estadio Atanasio Girardot (36,000)
Champions 1955, 1957

Season	Opponent	Home	Result	Away	Round
1967	Independiente Santa Fe, Colombia	4-0		0-2	1
	Racing Club Avellaneda, Argentina	0-2		2-5	1
	River Plate, Argentina	0-1		2-6	1
	Bolivar, Bolivia	2-0		2-2	1
	31st de Octubre, Bolivia	2-1		2-1	1

CLUB DEPORTIVO AMERICA (CALI)

America de Cali
Founded 15th February 1924
Address Calle 24 Norte, 5BN-22, Apartado 1383, Cali
Colours all red with white trim
Stadium Pascual Guerrero (61,000)
Champions 1979, 1982, 1983, 1984, 1985, 1986
Libertadores Finalists 1985, 1986, 1987

Season	Opponent	Home	Playoff Result	Away	Round
1970	Universidad de Chile, Chile	1-2		2-2	1
	Rangers Talca, Chile	1-0		0-2	1
	Deportivo Cali, Colombia	2-4		2-4	1
	Olimpia, Paraguay	1-1		0-1	1
	Guarani, Paraguay	1-4		2-2	1
1980	Independiente Santa Fe, Colombia	1-0		1-1	1
	Universidad Catolica, Chile	1-0		2-4	1
	Emelec Guayaquil, Ecuador	4-1		2-1	1
	Velez Sarsfield, Argentina	0-0		0-0	sf
	Internacional Porto Alegre, Brazil	0-0		0-0	sf
1983	Tolima Ibague, Colombia	1-1		2-0	1
	Alianza Lima, Peru	2-0		2-1	1
	Universitario Lima, Peru	2-0		1-1	1
	Estudiantes La Plata, Argentina	0-0		0-2	sf
	Gremio Porto Alegre, Brazil	1-0		1-2	sf
1984	Flamengo Rio de Janeiro, Brazil	1-1		2-4	1
	Santos FC Sao Paulo, Brazil	1-0		1-0	1
	Junior Barranquilla, Colombia	2-0		1-4	1
1985	Millonarios Bogota, Colombia	0-0		0-0	1
	Cerro Porteno, Paraguay	2-0		0-0	1
	Guarani, Paraguay	2-1		1-1	1
	Penarol, Uruguay	4-0		1-1	sf
	Nacional Quito, Ecuador	5-0		0-2	sf
	Argentinos Juniors, Argentina	1-0	1-1 in Asuncion	0-1 4-5 pen	FINAL
1986	Deportivo Cali, Colombia	0-0		1-0	1
	Cobresal El Salvador, Chile	0-0		2-2	1
	Universidad Catolica, Chile	2-1		3-1	1
	Olimpia, Paraguay	1-0		1-1	sf
	Bolivar, Bolivia	2-1		0-2	sf
	River Plate, Agentina	1-2		0-1	FINAL
1987	Deportivo Cali, Colombia	1-0	0-0 4-2p	1-2	1
	The Strongest, Bolivia	6-0		1-1	1
	Oriente Petrolero Santa Cruz, Bolivia	3-1		1-1	1
	Cobreloa Calama, Chile	1-1		2-2	sf

	Opponent	Home	Result	Away	Round
	Barcelona Sporting Guayaquil, Ecuador	4-0		2-0	sf
	Penarol, Uruguay	2-0	0-1 in Santiago	1-2	FINAL
1988	Millonarios Bogota, Colombia	2-1		3-2	1
	Wanderers, Uruguay	1-0		2-1	1
	Nacional, Uruguay	0-0		0-2	1
	Universitario Lima, Peru	1-0		2-2	2
	Oriente Petrolero Santa Cruz, Bolivia	2-0		1-1	qf
	Nacional, Uruguay	1-1		0-1	sf

ASOCIACION DEPORTIVA UNION MAGDELINA (SANTA MARTA)

Founded 20th October 1950
Address Calle 16 No 3-101, Oficina No 4, Santa Marta
Colours blue and red broad striped shirts, blue shorts
Stadium Estadio Eduarda Santos (28,000)
Champions 1968

Season	Opponent	Home	Result	Away	Round
1969	Union Deportivo Canaries Caracas, Venezuela	1-0		0-1	1
	Italia Caracas, Venezuela	3-0		0-2	1
	Deportivo Cali, Colombia	2-2		1-3	1

1976 **Cruzeiro** (Brazil)

ECUADOR

Founded 1925
Federacion Ecuatoriana de Futbol, Calle Jose Mascotell 1.103, Piso 2, y Luque, Casilla 7447, Guayaquil
☎ **010 593-4 371674 Telex 42970 feec fu ed Fax (593-4) 37 3320.**
Language Spanish
National colours yellow shirts with blue band, dark blue shorts

CHAMPIONSHIP

1922 Racing Club	**1924** Racing Club	**1926** Sporting Packard	**1928** Club Sport General
1923 Clube Sport Oriente	**1925** Club Sport General Cordova	**1927** Club Sport General Cordova	Cordova

LEAGUE CHAMPIONS

1957 Emelec Guayaquil	**1965** Emelec Guayaquil	**1972** Emelec Guayaquil	**1980** Barcelona Guayaquil
1958 not held	**1966** Barcelona Guayaquil	**1973** Nacional Quito	**1981** Barcelona Guayaquil
1959 not held	**1967** Nacional Quito	**1974** Liga Deportiva Universitaria Quito	**1982** Nacional Quito
	1968 Deportivo Quito		**1983** Nacional Quito
1960 Barcelona Guayaquil	**1969** Liga Deportiva Universitaria Quito	**1975** Liga Deportiva Universitaria Quito	**1984** Nacional Quito
1961 Emelec Guayaquil			**1985** Barcelona Guayaquil
1962 Everest Guayaquil		**1976** Nacional Quito	**1986** Nacional Quito
1963 Barcelona Guayaquil	**1970** Barcelona Guayaquil	**1977** Nacional Quito	**1987** Barcelona Guayaquil
1964 Deportivo Quito	**1971** Barcelona Guayaquil	**1978** Nacional Quito	**1988** Emelec Guayaquil
		1979 Emelec Guayaquil	**1989** Barcelona Guayaquil

1966 **Penarol** (Uruguay)

Emelec Guayaquil	Deportivo Cuenca	America Quito	Nueve de Octubre Guayaquil
Deportico Quito	Universidad Catolica Quito	Nacional Quito	
Liga Deportiva Universitaria Quito		Technico Universitario de Ambato	
Barcelona Sporting Guayaquil		Everest Guayaquil	

CLUB SPORT EMELEC (GUAYAQUIL)

Founded 28th April 1929
Address Velez 1109, Guayaquil
Colours all blue with grey sash, grey shorts
Stadium Estadio Modelo (48,772)
Champions 1957, 1961, 1965, 1972, 1979, 1988

Season	Opponent	Home	Playoff Result	Away	Rnd
1962	Universidad Catolica, Chile	7-2		0-3	1
	Millonarios Bogota, Colombia	4-2		1-3	1
1966	Penarol, Uruguay	1-2		1-4	1
	Nacional, Uruguay	0-2		0-1	1
	Jorge Wilsterman Cochabamba, Bolivia	3-1		1-2	1
	Municipal La Paz, Bolivia	2-1		1-4	1
	Nueve de Octubre Guayaquil, Ecuador	1-1		5-0	1
1967	Barcelona Sporting Guayaquil, Ecuador	3-0		1-2	1
	Nacional, Uruguay	1-4		0-3	1
	Cerro Porteno, Paraguay	2-1		1-1	1
	Guarani, Paraguay	0-2		0-3	1
	Colo Colo, Chile	4-3		2-3	1
	Universidad Catolica, Chile	2-1		2-5	1
1968	Nacional Quito, Ecuador	0-0		1-0	1
	Universidad Catolica, Chile	1-2		1-1	1
	Universidad de Chile, Chile	2-1		0-0	1
	Penarol, Uruguay	0-1		0-2	qf
	Portuguesa Acarigua, Venezuela	2-0		0-2	qf
	Sporting Cristal, Peru	0-2		1-0	qf
1971	Barcelona Sporting Guayaquil, Ecuador	1-0	0-3	1-1	1
	Deportivo Cali, Colombia	3-1		0-1	1
	Junior Barranquilla, Colombia	1-1		0-0	1
1973	Colo Colo, Chile	1-0		1-5	1
	Union Espanola, Chile	1-0		1-1	1
	Nacional Quito, Ecuador	2-0		0-1	1
1980	Independiente Santa Fe, Colombia	0-2		2-1	1
	America de Cali, Colombia	1-2		1-4	1
	Universidad Catolica Quito, Ecuador	1-0		0-5	1
1989	Deportivo Quito, Ecuador	1-0		0-1	1
	Nacional Medellin, Colombia	1-1		1-3	1
	Millonarios Bogota, Colombia	0-2		1-4	1
1990	Barcelona Guayaquil, Ecuador	3-1		0-0	1
	The Strongest, Bolivia	1-0		3-4	1
	Oriente Petrolero, Bolivia	2-2		0-1	1
	Union Huraral, Peru	2-0		0-1	2
	Barcelona Guayaquil, Ecuador	0-0		0-1	3

CLUB DEPORTIVO CUENCA

Founded 4th March 1971
Colours red shirts with yellow trim, black shorts
Stadium Estadio Serrano Aquilar (15,000)

Season	Opponent	Home	Playoff Result	Away	Round
1976	Liga Deportiva Universitaria Quito, Ecuador	0-0	1-2	1-1	1
	Guabira Santa Cruz, Bolivia	1-0		2-0	1
	Bolivar, Bolivia	3-1		2-4	1

ECUADOR

1977	Nacional Quito, Ecuador	0-2		0-0	1
	Internacional Porto Alegre, Brazil	0-2		1-3	1
	Corinthians Sao Paulo, Brazil	2-1		0-4	1

CLUB DEPORTIVO AMERICA (QUITO)

Founded 25th November 1939 Address Estadio Olimpico Atahualpa, Quito
Colours green shirts with white trim, white shorts
Stadium Olimpico Atahualpa (40,000) or Olimpico de Batan (25,000)

Season	Opponent	Home	Result	Away	Round
1970	Defensor Arica, Peru	1-1		1-0	1
	Universitario Lima, Peru	0-3		0-3	1
	Liga Deportiva Universitaria Quito, Ecuador	1-3		1-4	1
1972	Barcelona Sporting Guayaquil, Ecuador	0-0		1-3	1
	Oriente Petrolero Santa Cruz, Bolivia	3-0		2-4	1
	Chaco Petrolero, Bolivia	1-0		2-1	1

ASOCIACION DEPORTIVO NUEVE DE OCTUBRE (GUAYAQUIL)

Founded 16th April 1926
Address Estadio Los Chirijos de Milagro, Guayaquil
Colours red shirts with white trim, white shorts
Stadium Estradio Los Chirjos (10,000)

Season	Opponent	Home	Result	Away	Round
1966	Penarol, Uruguay	1-2		0-2	1
	Nacional, Uruguay	2-3		1-3	1
	Jorge Wilsterman Cochabamba, Bolivia	3-2		1-4	1
	Deportivo Municipal La Paz, Bolivia	3-4		1-5	1
	Emelec Guayaquil, Ecuador	1-1		0-5	1
1984	Nacional Quito, Ecuador	2-2		1-3	1
	Danubio, Uruguay	2-2		1-5	1
	Nacional, Uruguay	1-3		0-6	1
1985	Universitario Lima, Peru	1-0		not played	1
	Sport Boys Callao, Peru	4-0		not played	1
	Nacional Quito, Ecuador	0-1		1-3	1

SOCIEDAD DEPORTIVO QUITO

Founded 18th June 1955
Address Veintimilla 325, Quito
Colours blue and red broad striped shirts, white shorts
Stadium Olimpico Atahualpa (40,000)
Champions 1964, 1968

Season	Opponent	Home	Result	Away	Round
1965	The Strongest, Bolivia	0-1		2-2	1
	Boca Juniors, Argentina	1-2		0-4	1
1969	Barcelona Sporting Guayaquil, Ecuador	1-0		0-0	1
	Nacional, Uruguay	0-0		0-4	1
	Penarol, Uruguay	1-1		2-5	1
1986	Barcelona Sporting Guayaquil, Ecuador	0-0		3-3	1
	Coritiba Curitiba, Brazil	2-1		1-3	1
	Bangu Rio de Janeiro, Brazil	3-1		3-3	1
1989	Emelec Guayaquil, Ecuador	1-0		0-1	1
	Nacional Medellin, Colombia	1-1		1-2	1
	Millonarios Bogota, Colombia	0-0		1-3	1
	Cobreloa Calama, Chile	0-0		0-1	2

UNIVERSIDAD CATOLICA CLUB DEPORTIVO (QUITO)

Founded 14th October 1965
Address CD Universidad Catolica, Avenida 12 de Octubre y Ladron de Guevara, Quito
Colours sky blue shirts with white trim and U on chest, dark blue shorts
Stadium Olimpico Atahualpa (40,000)

Season	Opponent	Home	Result	Away	Round
1974	Nacional Quito, Ecuador	0-0		0-0	1
	Defensor Lima, Peru	1-0		0-1	1
	Sporting Cristal, Peru	0-0		1-2	1
1980	Independiente Santa Fe, Colombia	1-0		0-1	1
	America de Cali, Colombia	4-2		0-1	1
	Emelec Guayaquil, Ecuador	5-0		0-1	1

CLUB DEPORTIVO EL NACIONAL (QUITO)

Founded 14th March 1963 as Mariscal Sucre, 11th November 1964 as Nacional
Address Avenida 10 de Agosto 645, Quito
Colours light grey shirts with red, dark blue and sky blue sash, red shorts
Stadium Olimpico Atahualpa (40,000)
Champions 1967, 1973, 1976, 1977, 1978, 1982, 1983, 1984, 1986

Season	Opponent	Home	Result	Away	Round
1968	Emelec Guayaquil, Ecuador	0-1		0-0	1
	Universidad Catolica, Chile	2-1		0-2	1
	Universidad de Chile, Chile	3-1		0-1	1
1973	Colo Colo, Chile	1-1		1-5	1
	Union Espanola, Chile	1-0		1-2	1
	Emelec Guayaquil, Ecuador	1-0		0-2	1
1974	Universidad Catolica Quito, Ecuador	0-0		0-0	1
	Defensor Lima, Peru	0-0		1-2	1
	Sporting Cristal, Peru	3-0		3-1	1
1975	Liga Deportiva Universitaria Quito, Ecuador	1-1		1-3	1
	Galicia Caracas, Venezuela	0-0		0-4	1
	Portuguesa Acarigua, Venezuela	5-1		0-1	1
1977	Deportivo Cuenca, Ecuador	0-0		2-0	1
	Corinthians Sao Paulo, Brazil	2-1		0-3	1
	Internacional Porto Alegre, Brazil	2-0		0-2	1
1978	Liga Deportivo Universitaria Quito, Ecuador	2-0		2-3	1
	River Plate, Argentina	1-1		0-2	1
	Independiente, Argentina	1-2		0-2	1
1979	Tecnico Universitario Ambato, Ecuador	2-1		2-2	1
	Nacional, Uruguay	1-0		0-3	1
	Penarol, Uruguay	0-2		1-2	1
1983	Barcelona Sporting Guayaquil, Ecuador	3-1		0-2	1
	Tachira San Cristobal, Venezuela	3-0		0-0	1
	San Cristobal, Venezuela	1-0		0-1	1
1984	Nueve de Octubre Guayaquil, Ecuador	3-1		2-2	1
	Nacional, Uruguay	3-1		1-1	1
	Danubio, Uruguay	3-0		0-1	1
1985	Nueve de Octubre Guayaquil, Ecuador	3-1		1-0	1
	Universitario Lima, Peru	4-1		not played	1
	Sport Boys Callao, Peru	2-0		2-1	1
	America de Cali, Colombia	2-0		0-5	sf
	Penarol, Uruguay	2-0		0-2	sf
1987	Barcelona Sporting Guayaquil, Ecuador	2-0		1-2	1
	Sol de America, Paraguay	4-1		1-2	1
	Olimpia, Paraguay	4-0		0-2	1

ECUADOR

LIGA DEPORTIVO UNIVERSITARIA (LDU) (QUITO)

Founded 18th March 1930
Address Madrid 868, Quito
Colours all white with red trim and U on chest
Stadium Olimpico Atahualpa (40,000)
Champions 1969, 1974, 1975

Season	Opponent	Home	Playoff Result	Away	Round
1970	Universitario Lima, Peru	2-0		0-2	1
	Defensor Arica, Peru	1-2		0-0	1
	America Quito, Ecuador	4-1		3-1	1
	Penarol, Uruguay	1-3		1-2	qf
	Guarani, Paraguay	1-0		1-1	qf
1975	Nacional Quito, Ecuador	3-1		2-2	1
	Galicia Caracas, Venezuela	4-2		1-0	1
	Portuguesa Acarigua, Venezuela	1-1		1-1	1
	Universitario Lima, Peru	0-0		1-2	sf
	Union Espanola, Chile	4-2		0-2	sf
1976	Deportivo Cuenca, Ecuador	1-1	2-1	0-0	1
	Guabira Santa Cruz, Bolivia	4-0		1-0	1
	Bolivar, Bolivia	2-1		2-3	1
	Alianza Lima, Peru	2-1		0-2	sf
	Cruzeiro Belo Horizonte, Brazil	1-3		0-4	sf
1978	Nacional Quito, Ecuador	3-2		0-2	1
	River Plate, Argentina	0-0		0-4	1
	Independiente, Argentina	1-0		0-2	1
1982	Barcelona Sporting Guayaquil, Ecuador	4-2		1-4	1
	Colo Colo, Chile	2-2		0-1	1
	Cobreloa Calama, Chile	0-0		1-3	1

TECNICO UNIVERSITARIO (AMBATO)

Founded 18th September 1971
Address Centro Comercial BL 2, Ambato
Colours all red shirts with white sleeves and trim, red shorts
Stadium Estadio Bellavista (20,000)

Season	Opponent	Home	Result	Away	Round
1979	Nacional Quito, Ecuador	2-2		1-2	1
	Penarol, Uruguay	0-1		0-4	1
	Nacional, Uruguay	1-1		0-2	1
1981	Barcelona Sporting Guayaquil, Ecuador	4-1		1-2	1
	Jorge Wilsterman Cochabamba, Bolivia	1-2		1-3	1
	The Strongest, Bolivia	2-3		2-4	1

EVEREST (GUAYAQUIL)

Founded 1925
Colours all white
Stadium Estadio Modelo (48,772)
Champions 1962

Season	Opponent	Home	Result	Away	Round
1963	Penarol, Uruguay	0-5		1-9	1

118

DEPORTIVO FILANBANCO (GUAYAQUIL)

Founded 29th January 1979
Address Chimborazo y Garcia Goyena, Guayaquil
Colours orange shirts with dark brown trim and shorts
Stadium Estadio Modelo (48,772)

Season	Opponent	Home	Result	Away	Round
1988	Barcelona Sporting Guayaquil, Ecuador	1-2		2-4	1
	Newell's Old Boys Rosario, Argentina	1-1		0-1	1
	San Lorenzo, Argentina	1-2		0-2	1

BARCELONA SPORTING CLUB (GUAYAQUIL)

Founded 1st May 1925
Address Maldonado 508, Guayaquil
Colours yellow shirts with red trim, black shorts
Stadium Estadio Modelo (48,772)
Champions 1960, 1963, 1966, 1970, 1971, 1980, 1981, 1985, 1987, 1989
Libertadores Finalists 1990

Season	Opponent	Home	Playoff Result	Away	Round
1961	Independiente Santa Fe, Colombia	2-2		0-1	1
1964	Colo Colo, Chile	2-3		4-0	1
	Italia Caracas, Venezuela	1-0		0-3	1
1967	Emelec Guayaquil, Ecuador	2-1		0-3	1
	Nacional, Uruguay	2-1		0-2	1
	Cerro Porteno, Paraguay	1-2		2-1	1
	Guarani, Paraguay	2-1		1-4	1
	Colo Colo, Chile	1-1		2-3	1
	Universidad Catolica, Chile	0-2		1-3	1
1969	Deportivo Quito, Ecuador	0-0		0-1	1
	Penarol, Uruguay	0-2		0-5	1
	Nacional, Uruguay	1-1		0-2	1
1971	Emelec Guayanquil, Ecuador	1-1	3-0	0-1	1
	Juniors Barranquilla, Colombia	3-1		2-0	1
	Deportivo Cali, Colombia	1-0		1-3	1
	Estudiantes La Plata, Argentina	0-1		1-0	sf
	Union Espanola, Chile	1-0		1-3	sf
1972	Oriente Petrolero Santa Cruz, Bolivia	1-1		0-0	1
	Chaco Petrolero, Bolivia	3-0		2-1	1
	America Quito, Ecuador	3-1		0-0	1
	Independiente, Argentina	1-1		0-1	sf
	Sao Paulo FC, Brazil	0-0		1-1	sf
1981	Tecnico Universitario Ambato, Ecuador	2-1		1-4	1
	Jorge Wilsterman Cochabamba, Bolivia	3-0		0-1	1
	The Strongest, Bolivia	2-1		0-1	1
1982	Liga Deportiva Universitaria Quito, Ecuador	4-1		2-4	1
	Cobreloa Calama, Chile	1-1		0-3	1
	Colo Colo, Chile	1-3		0-2	1
1983	Nacional Quito, Ecuador	2-0		1-3	1
	San Cristobal, Venezuela	3-3		0-2	1
	Tachira San Cristobal, Venezuela	not played		1-1	1
1986	Deportivo Quito, Ecuador	3-3		0-0	1
	Coritiba Curitiba, Brazil	1-1		0-0	1
	Bangu Rio de Janeiro, Brazil	1-0		2-1	1
	River Plate, Argentina	0-3		1-4	sf
	Argentinos Juniors, Argentina	1-0		0-1	sf
1987	Nacional Quito, Ecuador	2-1		2-2	1
	Olimpia, Paraguay	3-2		0-1	1
	Sol de America, Paraguay	1-0		2-1	1

119

ECUADOR

	Cobreloa Calama, Chile	0-2		0-3	sf
	America de Cali, Colombia	0-2		0-4	sf
1988	Filanbanco Guayaquil, Ecuador	4-2		2-1	1
	Newell's Old Boys Rosario, Argentina	0-0		0-3	1
	San Lorenzo, Argentina	2-0		1-2	1
1990	Emelec, Ecuador	0-0		1-3	1
	Oriente Petrolero, Bolivia	2-1		1-1	1
	The Strongest, Bolivia	1-0		1-2	1
	Oriente Petrolero, Bolivia	3-1	wag	2-3	1 po
	Progreso, Uruguay	2-0		2-2	2
	Emelec, Ecuador	1-0		0-0	3
	River Plate, Argentina	1-0	4-3p	0-1	sf
	Olimpia, Paraguay	1-1		0-2	FINAL

1972 **Independiente** (Argentina)

PARAGUAY

Founded 1906
Liga Paraguaya de Football, Calles Mayor Martinezy Alejo Garcia, Asuncion ☎ 010 595-21 81 743 Telex 627 py Futbol
Fax (595-21) 81.743
Colours red and white striped shirts, blue shorts
Language Spanish

LEAGUE CHAMPIONS

1906 Guarani	**1927** Olimpia	**1950** Cerro Porteno	**1970** Cerro Porteno
1907 Guarani	**1928** Olimpia	**1951** Sportivo Luqueno	**1971** Olimpia
1908 not held	**1929** Olimpia	**1952** Presidenti Hayes	**1972** Cerro Porteno
1909 Nacional		**1953** Sportivo Luqueno	**1973** Cerro Porteno
	1930 Libertad	**1954** Cerro Porteno	**1974** Cerro Porteno
1910 Libertad	**1931** Olimpia	**1955** Libertad	**1975** Olimpia
1911 Nacional	**1932/33/34 not held**	**1956** Olimpia	**1976** Libertad
1912 Olimpia	**1935** Cerro Porteno	**1957** Olimpia	**1977** Cerro Porteno
1913 Cerro Porteno	**1936** Olimpia	**1958** Olimpia	**1978** Olimpia
1914 Olimpia	**1937** Olimpia	**1959** Olimpia	**1979** Olimpia
1915 Cerro Porteno	**1938** Olimpia		
1916 Olimpia	**1939** Cerro Porteno	**1960** Olimpia	**1980** Olimpia
1917 Libertad		**1961** Cerro Porteno	**1981** Olimpia
1918 Cerro Porteno	**1940** Cerro Porteno	**1962** Olimpia	**1982** Olimpia
1919 Cerro Porteno	**1941** Cerro Porteno	**1963** Cerro Porteno	**1983** Olimpia
	1942 Nacional	**1964** Guarani	**1984** Guarani
1920 Libertad	**1943** Libertad	**1965** Olimpia	**1985** Olimpia
1921 Guarani	**1944** Cerro Porteno	**1966** Cerro Porteno	**1986** Sol de America
1922 not held	**1945** Libertad	**1967** Guarani	**1987** Cerro Porteno
1923 Guarani	**1946** Nacional	**1968** Olimpia	**1988** Olimpia
1924 Nacional	**1947** Olimpia	**1969** Olimpia	**1989** Olimpia
1925 Olimpia	**1948** Olimpia		
1926 Nacional	**1949** Guarani		**1990** Atletico Colegiales

FEATURED CLUBS IN COPA LIBERTADORES DE AMERICA

Olimpia Asuncion   **Cerro Porteno, Asuncion**   **Guarani, Asuncion**   **Libertad, Asuncion**
Sol de America,Asuncion   **Sportivo Luqueno, Luque**   **Nacional, Asuncion**

CLUB OLIMPIA (ASUNCION)

Founded 25th July 1902
Address Avenida Mariscal Lopez 1499, Asuncion
Colours all white with black hoop on the shirt
Stadium Estadio Manuel Ferreira (40,000) or Defensores del Chaco (60,000)
Champions 1912, 1914, 1916, 1925, 1927, 1928, 1929, 1931, 1936, 1937, 1938, 1947, 1948, 1956, 1957, 1958, 1959,
1960, 1962, 1965, 1968, 1969, 1971, 1975, 1978, 1979, 1980, 1981, 1982, 1983, 1985, 1988, 1989
Libertadores Winners 1979, 1990 Finalists 1960, 1989
World Club Champions 1979
Inter America Cup Winners 1980

PARAGUAY

Season	Opponents	Home	Playoff Result	Away	Round
1960	Universitario Lima, Peru	wo		wo	1
	Millonarios Bogota, Colombia	0-0		5-1	sf
	Penarol, Uruguay	1-1		0-1	FINAL
1961	Colo Colo, Chile	5-2		1-2	2
	Penarol, Uruguay	1-2		1-3	sf
1963	Boca Juniors, Argentina	1-0		3-5	1
	Universidad de Chile, Chile	2-1		1-4	1
1966	Universidad Catolica, Chile	0-4		0-0	1
	Guarani, Paraguay	3-3	1-2	0-2	1
	Universidad de Chile, Chile	2-0		2-1	1
1969	Cerro Porteno, Paraguay	1-2		1-4	1
	Litoral, Bolivia	2-0		3-0	1
	Bolivar, Bolivia	4-0	2-1	1-1	1
	Penarol, Uruguay	0-1		1-1	qf
1970	Guarani, Paraguay	0-0		0-1	1
	Rangers Talca, Chile	5-1		4-4	1
	Universidad de Chile, Chile	1-1		1-2	1
	Deportivo Cali, Colombia	1-0		5-1	1
	America de Cali, Colombia	1-0		1-1	1
1972	Sao Paulo FC, Brazil	0-1		1-3	1
	Atletico Mineiro Belo Horizonte, Brazil	2-2		0-0	1
	Cerro Porteno, Paraguay	3-1		1-1	1
1973	Cerro Porteno, Paraguay	2-1		2-4	1
	Sporting Cristal, Peru	1-0		0-1	1
	Universitario Lima, Peru	1-0		1-2	1
1974	Cerro Porteno, Paraguay	1-1		0-1	1
	Nacional, Uruguay	2-0		1-1	1
	Penarol, Uruguay	0-2		0-0	1
1975	Cerro Porteno, Paraguay	2-1		0-0	1
	Newell's Old Boys Rosario, Argentina	2-0		2-3	1
	Rosario Central, Argentina	0-0		1-1	1
1976	Sportivo Luqueno Luque, Paraguay	2-3		1-0	1
	Internacional Porto Alegre, Brazil	1-1		0-1	1
	Cruzeiro Belo Horizonte, Brazil	2-2		1-4	1
1977	Libertad, Paraguay	0-0		2-2	1
	Universidad de Chile, Chile	1-0		0-1	1
	Everton Vina del Mar, Chile	2-2		0-1	1
1979	Sol de America, Paraguay	1-0		1-0	1
	Jorge Wilsterman Cochabamba, Bolivia	4-2		2-0	1
	Bolivar, Bolivia	3-0		1-2	1
	Guarani Campinas, Brazil	2-1		1-1	sf
	Palestino, Chile	3-0		2-0	sf
	Boca Juniors, Argentina	2-0		0-0	FINAL
1980	O'Higgins Rancagua, Chile	2-0		1-0	sf
	Nacional, Uruguay	0-1		1-1	sf
1981	Cerro Porteno, Paraguay	3-0		0-0	1
	Flamengo Rio de Janeiro, Brazil	0-0		1-1	1
	Atletico Mineiro Belo Horizonte, Brazil	0-0		0-1	1
1982	Sol de America, Paraguay	1-1		1-1	1
	Deportivo Municipal Lima, Peru	1-0		2-1	1
	Mariano Melgar FC Arequipa, Peru	4-0		3-0	1
	Tolima Ibague, Colombia	2-0		1-1	sf
	Cobreloa Calama, Chile	1-1		0-1	sf
1983	Nacional Asuncion, Paraguay	0-0		1-2	1
	Nacional, Uruguay	0-1		0-3	1
	Wanderers, Uruguay	2-3		0-1	1
1984	Independiente, Argentina	1-0		2-3	1
	Estudiantes La Plata, Argentina	2-1		1-0	1
	Sportivo Luqueno Luque, Paraguay	0-0		2-1	1
1986	Nacional Asuncion, Paraguay	3-1		2-1	1
	America de Cali, Colombia	1-1		0-1	sf
	Bolivar, Bolivia	3-1		1-1	sf
1987	Sol de America, Paraguay	2-2		2-1	1
	Barcelona Sporting Guayaquil, Ecuador	1-0		2-3	1
	Nacional Quito, Ecuador	2-0		0-4	1

1988	Oriente Petrolero Santa Cruz, Bolivia	1-2		0-1	1
	Bolivar, Bolivia	4-2		0-2	1
	Cerro Porteno, Paraguay	1-0		0-0	1
1989	Sol de America, Paraguay	0-0		4-5	1
	Colo Colo, Chile	2-0		0-2	1
	Cobreloa Calama, Chile	2-0		0-2	1
	Boca Juniors, Argentina	2-0	7-6p	3-5	2
	Sol de America, Paraguay	2-0		4-4	qf
	Internacional Porto Alegre, Brazil	0-1	5-3p	3-2 aet	sf
	Nacional Medellin, Colombia	2-0	4-5p	0-2 aet	FINAL
1990	Cerro Porteno, Paraguay	2-1		2-3	1
	Gremio Porto Alegre, Brazil	1-0		2-2	1
	Vasco de Gama Rio, Brazil	2-1		0-1	1
	bye				2
	Universidad Catolica, Chile	2-0		4-4	3
	Nacional Medellin, Colombia	2-3 aet	2-1p	2-1 in Santiago	sf
	Barcelona Guayaquile, Ecuador	2-0		1-1	FINAL

CLUB CERRO PORTENO (ASUNCION)

Founded 1st October 1912
Colours red and blue broad striped shirts, white shorts
Stadium Dr Adriano Irala (30,000)
Address Aveneda de las Americas 828, Asuncion
Champions 1913, 1915, 1918, 1919, 1935, 1939, 1940, 1941, 1944, 1950, 1954, 1961, 1963, 1966, 1970, 1972, 1973, 1974, 1977, 1987

Season	Opponents	Home	Playoff Result	Away	Round
1962	Deportivo Municipal La Paz, Bolivia	3-2		2-1	1
	Santos FC Sao Paulo, Brazil	1-1		1-9	1
1964	Aurora Cochabamba, Bolivia	7-0		2-2	1
1967	Barcelona Sporting Guayaquil, Ecuador	1-2		2-1	1
	Nacional, Uruguay	1-4		2-6	1
	Emelec Guayaquil, Ecuador	1-1		1-2	1
	Guarani, Paraguay	1-0		2-1	1
	Colo Colo, Chile	0-1		1-5	1
	Universidad Catolica, Chile	1-0		1-3	1
1969	Olimpia, Paraguay	4-1		2-1	1
	Bolivar, Bolivia	1-1	2-1	1-2	1
	Litoral, Bolivia	6-0		1-0	1
	Italia Caracas, Venezuela	1-0		0-0	qf
	Universidad Catolica, Chile	0-0		0-1	qf
1971	Guarani, Paraguay	1-1		2-2	1
	Colo Colo, Chile	0-0		0-1	1
	Union Espanola, Chile	2-1		0-0	1
1972	Sao Paulo FC, Brazil	3-2		0-4	1
	Atletico Mineiro Belo Horizonte, Brazil	1-0		1-1	1
	Olimpia, Paraguay	1-1		1-3	1
1973	Olimpia, Paraguay	4-2		1-2	1
	Sporting Cristal, Peru	5-0		1-1	1
	Universitario Lima, Peru	1-0		2-0	1
	Colo Colo, Chile	5-1		0-4	sf
	Botafogo Rio de Janeiro, Brazil	3-2		0-2	sf
1974	Olimpia, Paraguay	1-0		1-1	1
	Nacional, Uruguay	2-2		2-1	1
	Penarol, Uruguay	1-1		0-1	1
1975	Olimpia, Paraguay	0-0		1-2	1
	Rosario Central, Argentina	1-3		1-2	1
	Newell's Old Boys Rosario, Argentina	0-1		2-3	1
1978	Libertad, Paraguay	1-0		0-0	1
	Portuguesa Galicia, Venezuela	1-0		1-1	1
	Estudiantes Merida, Venezuela	1-1		3-2	1
	Alianza Lima, Peru	3-1		0-3	sf

PARAGUAY

	Opponent	Home	Away	Round
	Deportivo Cali, Colombia	0-4	1-1	sf
1980	Colo Colo, Chile	5-3	1-2	1
	O'Higgins Rancagua, Chile	1-0	0-0	1
	Sol de America, Paraguay	0-0	1-2	1
1981	Olimpia, Paraguay	0-0	0-3	1
	Flamengo Rio de Janeiro, Brazil	2-4	2-5	1
	Atletico Mineiro Belo Horizonte, Brazil	2-2	0-1	1
1985	Guarani, Paraguay	3-1	0-0	1
	Millonarios Bogota, Colombia	0-0	2-0	1
	America de Cali, Colombia	0-0	0-2	1
1988	Olimpia, Paraguay	0-0	0-1	1
	Bolivar, Bolivia	3-2	0-2	1
	Oriente Petrolero Santa Cruz, Bolivia	1-0	2-2	1
1990	Olimpia, Paraguay	3-2	1-2	1
	Gremio Porto Alegre, Brazil	3-1	0-0	1
	Vasco da Gama, Brazil	1-1	0-2	2
	Nacional Medellin, Colombia	0-0	0-1	2

CLUB GUARANI (ASUNCION)

Founded 12th October 1903
Colours black and yellow striped shirts, black shorts
Stadium Lorenzo Livieres (20,000)
Champions 1906, 1907, 1921, 1923, 1949, 1964, 1967, 1984

Season	Opponents	Home	Playoff Result	Away	Round
1965	Galicia Caracas, Venezuela	2-0		2-1	1
	Penarol, Uruguay	2-1		0-2	1
1966	Universidad Catolica, Chile	3-1		0-2	1
	Universidad de Chile, Chile	1-1		0-2	1
	Olimpia, Paraguay	2-0	2-1	3-3	1
	Boca Juniors, Argentina	1-3		1-1	sf
	River Plate, Argentina	1-3		1-3	sf
	Independiente, Argentina	0-2		1-2	sf
1967	Emelec Guayaquil, Ecuador	3-0		2-0	1
	Barcelona Sporting Guayaquil, Ecuador	4-1		1-2	1
	Nacional, Uruguay	0-1		1-3	1
	Cerro Porteno, Paraguay	1-2		0-1	1
	Colo Colo, Chile	4-2		0-1	1
	Universidad Catolica, Chile	1-1		1-1	1
1968	Libertad, Paraguay	1-1		2-0	1
	Penarol, Uruguay	1-1		0-2	1
	Nacional, Uruguay	2-1		2-2	1
	Palmeiras Sao Paulo, Brazil	2-0		1-2	sf
	Universidad Catolica, Chile	2-1		2-4	sf
1970	Olimpia, Paraguay	1-0		0-0	1
	Rangers Talca, Chile	2-0		1-0	1
	Universidad de Chile, Chile	1-0		0-0	1
	Deportivo Cali, Colombia	0-0	4-1	1-1	1
	America de Cali, Colombia	2-2		4-1	1
	Penarol, Uruguay	2-0		0-1	qf
	Liga Deportiva Universitaria Quito, Ecuador	1-1		0-1	qf
1971	Cerro Porteno, Paraguay	2-2		1-1	1
	Union Espanola, Chile	1-1		1-2	1
	Colo Colo, Chile	2-0		2-3	1
1985	Cerro Porteno, Paraguay	0-0		1-3	1
	Millonarios Bogota, Colombia	2-0		1-5	1
	America de Cali, Colombia	1-1		1-2	1

PARAGUAY

CLUB LIBERTAD (ASUNCION)

Founded 30th June 1905
Colours black and white striped shirts, black shorts
Stadium Alfredo Stroessner (45,000)
Address Aveneda Artigas y Cusmanich, Asuncion
Champions 1910, 1917, 1920, 1930, 1943, 1945, 1955, 1976

Season	Opponents	Home	Result	Away	Round
1968	Guarani, Paraguay	0-2		1-1	1
	Penarol, Uruguay	1-0		0-4	1
	Nacional, Uruguay	0-2		0-4	1
1977	Olimpia, Paraguay	2-2		0-0	1
	Universidad de Chile, Chile	3-0		0-1	1
	Everton Vina del Mar, Chile	2-1		3-1	1
	Boca Juniors, Argentina	0-1		0-1	sf
	Deportivo Cali, Colombia	2-1		0-0	sf
1978	Cerro Porteno, Paraguay	0-0		0-1	1
	Portuguesa Acarigua, Venezuela	1-2		0-1	1
	Estudiantes Merida, Venezuela	2-1		1-1	1

CLUB SOL DE AMERICA (ASUNCION)

Founded 1909
Colours blue shirts with white trim, white shorts
Stadium Estadio Luis A Giagni "Villa Elisa" (10,000)
Address Aveneda A de Figueroa y Tacuary, Asuncion
Champions 1986, 1989

Season	Opponents	Home	Result	Away	Round
1979	Olimpia, Paraguay	0-1		0-1	1
	Bolivar, Bolivia	2-2		1-4	1
	Jorge Wilsterman Cochabamba, Bolivia	2-1		3-2	1
1980	Colo Colo, Chile	2-1		1-1	1
	O'Higgins Rancagua, Chile	1-4		0-2	1
	Cerro Porteno, Paraguay	2-1		0-0	1
1982	Olimpia, Paraguay	1-1		1-1	1
	Deportivo Municipal, Peru	2-1		3-0	1
	Mariano Melgar FC Arequipa, Peru	0-2		2-3	1
1987	Olimpia, Paraguay	1-2		2-2	1
	Nacional Quito, Ecuador	2-1		1-4	1
	Barcelona Sporting Guayaquil, Ecuador	1-2		0-1	1
1989	Olimpia, Paraguay	5-4		0-0	1
	Colo Colo, Chile	1-0		1-3	1
	Cobreloa Calama, Chile	0-0		0-1	1
	Tachira San Cristobal, Venezuela	3-0	3-2p	0-3	2
	Olimpia, Paraguay	4-4		0-2	qf

PARAGUAY

CLUB SPORTIVO LUQUENO (LUQUE)

Founded 1921
Colours blue and yellow striped shirts, blue shorts
Stadium Feliciano Caceres (38,000)
Address Calle Rodriguez de Francis, Luque
Champions 1951, 1953

Season	Opponents	Home	Result	Away	Round
1976	Olimpia, Paraguay	0-1		3-2	1
	Cruzeiro Belo Horizionte, Brazil	1-3		1-4	1
	Internacional Porto Alegre, Brazil	0-1		0-3	1
1984	Independiente, Argentina	0-1		0-2	1
	Estudiantes La Plata, Argentina	0-0		1-1	1
	Olimpia, Paraguay	1-2		0-0	1

CLUB NACIONAL (ASUNCION)

Founded 5th June 1904
Colours white shirts with blue and red trim, blue shorts
Address Caballero y Cerro Leon, Asuncion
Stadium Arsenio Erico (10,000) or Defensores del Chaco (60,000) Champions 1909, 1911, 1924, 1926, 1942, 1946

Season	Opponents	Home	Result	Away	Round
1983	Olimpia, Paraguay	2-1		0-0	1
	Wanderers, Uruguay	1-1		1-3	1
	Nacional, Uruguay	0-3		2-4	1

1971 **Nacional** (Uruguay)

PERU

Founded 1922
Federacion Peruana de Football, Estadio Nacional, Calle Jose Diaz, Puerta 4, Lima ☎ 010 51-14 32 05 17
Telex 20066 Feputuf Fax (51-14) 320646
Language Spanish, French, English
Season March to November
National colours white shirts with red diagonal stripe, white shorts, grey socks with red striped turnover

LEAGUE CHAMPIONS

1926	CS Progreso	1942	Sport Boys	1960	Universitario Lima	1977	Alianza Lima
1927	Alianza Lima	1943	Deportivo Municipal	1961	Sporting Cristal	1978	Alianza Lima
1928	Alianza Lima	1944	Mariscal Sucre	1962	Alianza Lima	1979	Sporting Cristal
1929	Universitario Lima	1945	Universitario Lima	1963	Alianza Lima		
		1946	Universitario Lima	1964	Universitario Lima	1980	Sporting Cristal
1930	Atletico Chalaco	1947	Atletico Chalaco	1965	Alianza Lima	1981	Melgar Arequipa
1931	Alianza Lima	1948	Alianza Lima	1966	Universitario Lima	1982	Universitario Lima
1932	Alianza Lima	1949	Universitario Lima	1967	Universitario Lima	1983	Sporting Cristal
1933	Alianza Lima			1968	Sporting Cristal	1984	Sports Boys Callao, Lima
1934	Alianza Lima	1950	Deportivo Municipal	1969	Universitario Lima		
1935	Sport Boys	1951	Sport Boys			1985	Universidad Tecnica Calamarja
1936	not held	1952	Alianza Lima	1970	Sporting Cristal		
1937	Sport Boys	1953	Mariscal Sucre	1971	Universitario Lima	1986	Alianza Lima
1938	Deportivo Municipal	1954	Alianza Lima	1972	Sporting Cristal	1987	Colegio San Agustin Lima
1939	Universitario Lima	1955	Alianza Lima	1973	Sporting Cristal		
		1956	Sporting Cristal	1974	Defensor Lima	1988	Universitario
1940	Deportivo Municipal	1957	Alianza Lima	1975	Universitario Lima	1989	Sporting Cristal v Universitario 2-1 aet
1941	Universitario Lima	1958	Sport Boys	1976	Union Huaral		
		1959	Universitario Lima				

COPA PERU

Non League Cup - from 1973 the winners of this Cup gain entry to the National League

1967	Alfonso Ugarte	1974	not held	1980	Leon de Huanuco	1984	Espartanos, Pacasmayo
1968	Carlos Mannucci	1975	Torino	1981	Universidad Tecnica de Cajamurca		
1969	Carlos Mannucci	1976	Bolognesi			1985	Hungaritas
		1977	Torino	1982	Torino	1986	Deportivo Canana
1970	Torino	1978	Juventud La Palma, Huado	1983	Sport Pilsen, Guadalupe	1987	
1971	Melgar					1988	
1972	Atletico Grau Piura	1979	Asociacon Deportiva, Tarma				
1973	Sport Huracan, Arequipa						

FEATURED CLUBS IN COPA LIBERTADORES DE AMERICA

Universitario Lima	**Sport Boys Callao Lima**	**Alianza Lima**	**Defensor Lima**
Juan Aurich de Chiclana	**Sporting Cristal Lima**	**Atletico Chalaco Lima**	**Defensor Arica**
Union Huaral Lima	**Alfonso Ugarte Puno**	**Atletico Torino Talaca**	**Mariano Melgar FC Arequipa**
Deportivo Municipal Lima	**Universidad Tecnica Cajamarca**		**Colegio San Agustin Lima**

127

PERU

CLUB UNIVERSITARIO DE DEPORTES (CLUB)

Founded 7th August 1924 as Federacion Universitaria, 1933 Universitaria de Deportes
Colours all cream
Stadium Estadio Teodoro Lolo Fernandez (20,000)
Address 04 J.Chavez, Lima
Champions 1929, 1939, 1941, 1945, 1946, 1949, 1959, 1960, 1964, 1966, 1967, 1969, 1971, 1974, 1982, 1988
Libertadores Cup Finalists 1972

Season	Opponent	Home	Playoff Result	Away	Rnd
1960	Olimpia, Paraguay	withdrew			1
1961	Penarol, Uruguay	2-0		0-5	2
1965	Santos FC Sao Paulo, Brazil	1-2		1-2	1
	Universidad de Chile, Chile	1-0		2-5	1
1966	River Plate, Argentina	1-1		0-5	1
	Boca Juniors, Argentina	2-1		0-2	1
	Italia Caracas, Venezuela	1-2		2-2	1
	Alianza Lima, Peru	2-0		1-1	1
	Lara Basquimento, Venezuela	1-0		0-0	1
1967	Italia Caracas, Venezuela	3-0		1-0 in Lima	1
	Galicia Caracas, Venezuela	2-0		0-2	1
	Cruzeiro Belo Horizonte, Brazil	1-4		2-2	1
	Sport Boys Callao, Peru	1-0		1-0	1
	Racing Club Avellaneda, Argentina	1-2		2-1	sf
	Colo Colo, Chile	3-0		1-0	sf
	River Plate, Argentina	2-2	1-2	1-0	sf
1968	Sporting Cristal, Peru	1-1		2-2	1
	Jorge Wilsterman Cochabamba, Bolivia	5-1		0-0	1
	Always Ready, Bolivia	6-0		3-0	1
	Independiente, Argentina	0-3		0-3	qf
	Estudiantes La Plata, Argentina	1-0		0-1	qf
1970	Liga Deportivo Universitaria Quito, Ecuador	2-0		0-2	1
	America Quito, Ecuador	3-0		3-0	1
	Defensor Arica, Peru	2-1		1-1	1
	Boca Juniors, Argentina	1-3		0-1	qf
	River Plate, Argentina	1-2		3-5	qf
1971	Sporting Cristal, Peru	0-0		3-0	1
	Rosario Central, Argentina	3-2		2-2	1
	Boca Juniors, Argentina	0-0		walk over	1
	Nacional, Uruguay	0-0		0-3	sf
	Palmeiras Sao Paulo, Brazil	1-2		0-3	sf
1972	Union San Felipe, Chile	0-0		3-1	1
	Alianza Lima, Peru	2-1		2-2	1
	Universidad de Chile, Chile	2-1		0-1	1
	Penarol, Uruguay	2-3		1-1	sf
	Nacional, Uruguay	3-0		3-3	sf
	Independiente, Argentina	0-0		1-2	FINAL
1973	Cerro Porteno, Paraguay	0-2		0-1	1
	Olimpia, Paraguay	2-1		0-1	1
	Sporting Cristal, Peru	2-2		0-1	1
1975	Union Huaral Lima, Peru	1-1		2-2	1
	Wanderers, Uruguay	1-1		2-2	1
	Penarol, Uruguay	3-2		1-0	1
	Liga Deportivo Universitaria Quito, Ecuador	2-1		0-0	sf
	Union Espanola, Chile	1-1		1-2	sf
1979	Alianza Lima, Peru	1-0		6-3	1
	Guarani Campinas, Brazil	3-0		1-6	1
	Palmeiras Sao Paulo, Brazil	2-5		2-1	1
1983	Alianza Lima, Peru	0-0		1-2	1
	Tolima Ibague, Colombia	2-2		1-1	1
	America de Cali, Colombia	1-1		0-2	1
1985	Sport Boys Callao, Peru	4-0		2-0	1
	Nueve de Octubre Guayaquil, Ecuador	not played		0-1	1
	Nacional Quito, Ecuador	not played		1-4	1

1986	Universidad Tecnica Cajarmarca, Peru	2-0		3-1	1
	Bolivar, Bolivia	3-0		0-4	1
	Jorge Wilsterman Cochabamba, Bolivia	1-2		0-4	1
1988	Alianza Lima, Peru	2-0		0-0	1
	Guarani Campinas, Brazil	2-1		0-1	1
	Sport Recife, Brazil	1-0		1-1	1
	America de Cali, Colombia	2-2		0-1	2
1989	Sporting Cristal, Peru	4-0		0-1	1
	Boca Juniors, Argentina	1-0		0-2	1
	Racing Club Avellaneda, Argentina	2-1		0-2	1
	Esporte Clube Bahia Salvador, Brazil	1-1		1-2	2

SPORT BOYS ASOCIACION

Founded 28th July 1927
Colours pink shirts with black trim, black shorts
Stadium Telmo Carbajo Callao (15,000)
Champions 1935, 1937, 1942, 1951, 1958, 1984

Season	Opponent	Home	Result	Away	Round
1967	Italia Caracas, Venezuela	5-2		0-0	1
	Galicia Caracas, Venezuela	1-2		2-0	1
	Cruzeiro Belo Horizonte, Brazil	1-2		1-3	1
	Universitario Lima, Peru	0-1		0-1	1
1977	Union Huaral, Peru	0-0		0-1	1
	Estudiantes de Merida, Venezuela	1-3		0-1	1
	Portuguesa Acarigua, Venezuela	1-2		0-0	1
1985	Universitario Lima, Peru	0-2		0-4	1
	Nacional Quito, Ecuador	1-2		0-2	1
	Nueve de Octubre Guayaquil, Ecuador	not played		0-4	1

CLUB ALIANZA

Founded 1901
Colours blue and white striped shirts, blue shorts
Stadium Alejandro Villanueva (38,000)
Address Puerta 4, Estadio Alianza, Alejandro Villanueva, Lima
Champions 1927, 1928, 1931, 1932, 1933, 1934, 1948, 1952, 1954, 1955, 1957, 1962, 1963, 1965, 1975, 1977, 1978, 1986

Season	Opponent	Home	Result	Away	Round
1963	Millonarios Bogota, Colombia	0-0		1-0	1
	Botafogo Rio de Janeiro, Brazil	1-2		0-1	1
1964	Independiente, Argentina	2-2		0-4	1
	Millonarios Bogota, Colombia	1-2		2-3	1
1966	River Plate, Argentina	0-2		2-3	1
	Boca Juniors, Argentina	0-1		1-0	1
	Italia Caracas, Venezuela	1-2		1-3	1
	Universitario Lima, Peru	1-1		0-2	1
	Lara Basquimento, Venezuela	3-0		1-2	1
1972	Union San Felipe, Chile	0-0		0-1	1
	Universitario Lima, Peru	2-2		1-2	1
	Universidad de Chile, Chile	3-4		3-2	1
1976	Millonarios Bogota, Colombia	2-1		0-1	1
	Independiente Santa Fe, Colombia	3-0		3-2	1
	Alfonso Ugarte Puno, Peru	0-0		0-0	1
	Liga Deportivo Universitaria Quito, Ecuador	2-0		1-2	sf
	Cruzeiro Belo Horizonte, Brazil	0-4		1-7	sf
1978	Sporting Cristal, Peru	4-1		2-2	1
	Oriente Petrolero Santa Cruz, Bolivia	5-1		4-0	1
	The Strongest, Bolivia	2-0		2-1	1
	Deportivo Cali, Colombia	1-4		2-3	sf

129

1979	Cerro Porteno, Paraguay	3-0		1-3	sf
	Universitario Lima, Peru	3-6		0-1	1
	Guarani Campinas, Brazil	0-3		1-2	1
	Palmeiras Sao Paulo, Brazil	2-4		0-4	1
1983	Universitario Lima, Peru	2-1		0-0	1
	Tolima Ibague, Colombia	0-1		0-0	1
	America de Cali, Colombia	1-2		0-2	1
1987	Colegio San Agustin Lima, Peru	0-0		2-1	1
	Progreso, Uruguay	0-0		0-0	1
	Penarol, Uruguay	0-1		0-2	1
1988	Universitario Lima, Peru	0-0		0-2	1
	Guarani Campinas, Brazil	2-1		0-1	1
	Sport Recife, Brazil	0-1		0-5	1

CLUB ATLETICO DEFENSOR LIMA

Founded
Colours maroon shirts with white trim, white shorts
Stadium Estadio San Martin de Porres

Season	Opponent	Home	Result	Away	Round
1974	Sporting Cristal, Peru	2-0		2-0	1
	Universidad Catolica Quito, Ecuador	1-0		0-1	1
	Nacional Quito, Ecuador	2-1		0-0	1
	Sao Paulo FC, Brazil	0-1		0-4	sf
	Millonarios Bogota, Colombia	1-4		0-1	sf

JUAN AURICH DE CHICLANA

Founded 21st February 1922
Colours red shirts, white shorts
Stadium Estadio Elias Aguirre (21,240)

Season	Opponent	Home	Playoff Result	Away	Round
1969	Sporting Cristal, Peru	2-2		3-3	1
	Universidad Catolica, Chile	2-4	1-4	2-1	1
	Santiago Wanderers, Chile	3-1	0-1	1-4	1

CLUB SPORTING CRISTAL-BACKUS

Founded 1922 as Sporting Tabaca, 1955 Club Sporting Cristal-Backus
Colours sky blue shirts, white shorts
Stadium Alejandro Villanueva (38,000)
Address Puerta 4, Estadio Alianza, Alejandro Villanueva, Lima
Champions 1956, 1961, 1968, 1970, 1972, 1979, 1980, 1983, 1989

Season	Opponent	Home	Playoff Result	Away	Round
1962	Racing Club Avellaneda, Argentina	2-1		1-2	1
	Nacional, Uruguay	0-1		1-2	1
1968	Jorge Wilsterman Cochabamba, Bolivia	2-0		1-0	1
	Always Ready, Bolivia	1-1		4-1	1
	Universitario Lima, Peru	2-2		1-1	1
	Penarol, Uruguay	0-0		1-1	qf
	Portuguesa Acarigua, Venezuela	2-0		1-1	qf
1969	Santiago Wanderers, Chile	2-1	1-1	0-2	1
	Juan Aurich de Chiclana, Peru	3-3		2-2	1
	Universidad Catolica, Chile	2-0	1-2	2-3	1

1971	Universitario Lima, Peru	0-3		0-0	1
	Rosario Central, Argentina	1-2		0-4	1
	Boca Juniors, Argentina	2-0		2-2	1
1973	Cerro Porteno, Paraguay	1-1		0-5	1
	Olimpia, Paraguay	1-0		0-1	1
	Universitario Lima, Peru	1-0		2-2	1
1974	Defensor Lima, Peru	0-2		0-2	1
	Universidad Catolica Quito, Ecuador	2-1		0-0	1
	Nacioanal Quito, Ecuador	1-3		0-3	1
1978	The Strongest, Bolivia	2-0		1-3	1
	Oriente Petrolero Santa Cruz, Bolivia	1-0		1-0	1
	Alianza Lima, Peru	1-2		0-2	1
1980	Atletico Chalcao Callao, Peru	0-0		2-0	1
	Velez Sarsfield, Argentina	0-1		0-2	1
	River Plate, Argentina	1-2		2-3	1
1981	Atletico Torino Talara, Peru	2-1		2-0	1
	Cobreloa Calama, Chile	0-0		1-6	1
	Universidad de Chile, Chile	2-2		1-1	1
1984	Mariano Melgar FC Arequipa, Peru	3-2		0-2	1
	Universidad de Los Andes (ULA) Merida, Venezuela	2-0		1-0	1
	Portuguesa Acarigua, Venezuela	2-1		0-1	1
1989	Universitario Lima, Peru	1-0		0-4	1
	Boca Juniors, Argentina	1-0		3-4	1
	Racing Club Avellaneda, Argentina	1-2		0-2	1
1990	Union Huaral, Peru	0-0		3-0	1
	Universidad Catolica, Chile	0-0		0-2	1
	Colo Colo, Chile	1-2		0-2	1

ATLETICO CHALACO (CALLAO)

Founded 1902
Colours red and white striped shirts, white shorts
Stadium Telmo Carbajo (15,000)
Address 585 V Fajarda, Callo
Champions 1930, 1947

Season	Opponent	Home	Result	Away	Round
1980	Sporting Cristal, Peru	0-2		0-0	1
	Velez Sarsfield, Argentina	0-2		2-5	1
	River Plate, Argentina	0-2		0-3	1

DEFENSOR ARICA

Arica is now situated in Chile
Founded
Colours sky blue shirts, white shorts
Stadium

Season	Opponent	Home	Result	Away	Round
1970	Liga Deportivo Universitaria Quito, Ecuador	0-0		2-1	1
	America Quito , Ecuador	0-1		1-1	1
	Universitario Lima, Peru	1-1		1-2	1

UNION HUARAL

Founded 20th September 1947
Colours red and white striped shirts, dark blue shorts
Address Estadio Huaras, Huaral, Lima
Champions 1976 Stadium Julio Lores Colan (10,140)

Season	Opponent	Home	Result	Away	Round
1975	Universitario Lima, Peru	2-2		1-1	1
	Penarol, Uruguay	0-3		2-5	1
	Wanderers, Uruguay	2-2		0-4	1
1977	Sport Boys Callao, Peru	1-0		0-0	1
	Portuguesa Acarigua, Venezuela	1-1		0-2	1
	Estudiantes de Merida, Venezuela	2-1		0-1	1
1990	Sporting Cristal, Peru	0-3		0-0	1
	Universidad Catolica, Chile	1-0		2-2	1
	Colo Colo, Chile	1-1		1-3	1
	Emelec, Ecuador	1-0		0-2	2

ALFONSO UGARTE (PUNO)

Founded 1929
Colours white with red sash, white shorts
Stadium Estadio Torres Belon de Puno (18,500)
Address Club Alfonso Ugarte Puno, Province de Puno

Season	Opponent	Home	Result	Away	Round
1976	Independiente Santa Fe, Colombia	2-1		2-2	1
	Millonarios Bogota, Colombia	1-1		0-4	1
	Alianza Lima, Peru	0-0		0-0	1

ATLETICO TORINO (TALARA)

Founded 1952
Colours all maroon with two white stripes on the right side, white shorts
Stadium Campeonisimo (10,000)

Season	Opponent	Home	Result	Away	Round
1981	Sporting Cristal, Peru	0-2		1-2	1
	Cobreloa Calama, Chile	1-1		1-6	1
	Universidad de Chile, Chile	1-2		0-3	1

MARIANO MELGAR FC

Founded 1915
Colours red and black halved shirts, black shorts
Stadium Mariano Melgar (15,000) formerly IV Centenario
Address Santo Domingo 313, Arequipa
Champions 1981

Season	Opponent	Home	Result	Away	Round
1982	Deportivo Municipal Lima, Peru	2-1		2-0	1
	Olimpia, Paraguay	0-3		0-4	1
	Sol de America, Paraguay	3-2		2-0	1
1984	Sporting Cristal, Peru	2-0		2-3	1
	Union de Los Andes (ULA) Merida, Venezuela	0-1		0-1	1
	Portuguesa Acarigua, Venezuela	1-2		0-4	1

CLUB DEPORTIVO MUNICIPAL

Founded 1935
Colours white shirts with red sash, blue shorts
Address Puerta No 4, Calle Jose Diaz, Lima
Stadium Estadio Nacional (45,000)
Champions 1938, 1940, 1943, 1950

Season	Opponent	Home	Result	Away	Round
1982	Mariano Melgar FC Arequipa, Peru	0-2		1-2	1
	Olimpia, Paraguay	1-2		0-1	1
	Sol de America, Paraguay	0-3		1-2	1

UNIVERSIDAD TECNICA de CAJARMARCA

Founded 14th July 1964
Colours all cream with maroon trim
Stadium Estadio Municipal "Heroes de San Ramon"
Champions 1985

Season	Opponent	Home	Result	Away	Round
1986	Universitario Lima, Peru	1-3		0-2	1
	Bolivar, Bolivia	2-2		1-2	1
	Jorge Wilsterman Cochabamba, Bolivia	3-2		0-2	1

DEPORTIVO COLEGIO SAN AGUSTIN SAN ISIDRO

Founded 1982 as Huracan
Colours yellow shirts with red trim, red shorts
Stadium Estadio Matute (8,000)
Champions 1986

Season	Opponent	Home	Result	Away	Round
1987	Alianza Lima, Peru	1-2		0-0	1
	Progreso, Uruguay	3-1		0-3	1
	Penarol, Uruguay	1-1		0-2	1

1964 **Independiente** (Argentina)

133

URUGUAY

Founded 1900
Asociacion Uruguaya De Football, Guayabo 1531, Montevideo ☎ 010 598-2 407101 Telex 22607 auf uy
Fax (598-2) 407873
National colours sky blue shirts, black shorts, black socks with sky blue band
Season February to December
Language Spanish, English, French

LEAGUE CHAMPIONS

CURCC=Central Uruguay Railways Cricket Club

1900	Penarol (CURCC)	**1924**	Nacional	**1946**	Nacional	**1970**	Nacional
1901	Penarol (CURCC)	**1925**	not held	**1947**	Nacional	**1971**	Nacional
1902	Nacional	**1926**	Penarol	**1948**	not finished	**1972**	Nacional
1903	Nacional	**1927**	Rampla Juniors	**1949**	Penarol	**1973**	Penarol
1904	not held	**1928**	Penarol			**1974**	Penarol
1905	Penarol (CURCC)	**1929**	Penarol	**1950**	Nacional	**1975**	Penarol
1906	Wanderers			**1951**	Penarol	**1976**	Defensor
1907	Penarol (CURCC)	**1930**	not finished	**1952**	Nacional	**1977**	Nacional
1908	River Plate	**1931**	Wanderers	**1953**	Penarol	**1978**	Penarol
1909	Wanderers	**PROFESSIONAL**		**1954**	Penarol	**1979**	Penarol
		1932	Penarol	**1955**	Nacional		
1910	River Plate	**1933**	Nacional	**1956**	Nacional	**1980**	Nacional
1911	Penarol (CURCC)	**1934**	Nacional	**1957**	Nacional	**1981**	Penarol
1912	Nacional	**1935**	Penarol	**1958**	Penarol	**1982**	Penarol
1913	River Plate	**1936**	Penarol	**1959**	Penarol	**1983**	Nacional
1914	River Plate	**1937**	Penarol			**1984**	Central Espanol
1915	Nacional	**1938**	Penarol	**1960**	Penarol	**1985**	Penarol
1916	Nacional	**1939**	Nacional	**1961**	Penarol	**1986**	Penarol
1917	Nacional			**1962**	Penarol	**1987**	Defensor
1918	Penarol	**1940**	Nacional	**1963**	Nacional	**1988**	Danubio
1919	Nacional	**1941**	Nacional	**1964**	Penarol	**1989**	Progreso
1920	Nacional	**1942**	Nacional	**1965**	Penarol		
1921	Penarol	**1943**	Nacional	**1966**	Nacional	**1990**	Bella Vista
1922	Nacional	**1944**	Penarol	**1967**	Penarol		
1923	Naconal	**1945**	Penarol	**1968**	Penarol		
				1969	Nacional		

FEATURED CLUBS IN COPA LIBERTADORES DE AMERICA

All the clubs are from Montevideo

Penarol	Nacional	Wanderers	Danubio
Defensor	Bella Vista	Progreso	

ATLETICO PENAROL

Founded 28th September 1891 as Central Uruguay Railways Cricket Club (CURCC)
Colours black and yellow striped shirts, black shorts
Address Magallanes 1721, Palacio Contador Gaston Guelfi, Montevideo
Stadium Las Acacias (15,000) or Centenario (73,609)
Champions 1900, 1901, 1905, 1907, 1911, 1918, 1921, 1926, 1928, 1929, 1932, 1935, 1936, 1937, 1938, 1944, 1945, 1949, 1951, 1953, 1954, 1958, 1959, 1960, 1967, 1968, 1973, 1974, 1975, 1978, 1979, 1981, 1982, 1985, 1986
Libertadores Cup Winners 1960, 1961, 1966, 1982, 1987 Finalists 1962, 1965, 1970, 1983
Inter America Cup Winners 1969
World Club Champions 1961, 1966, 1982 Finalists 1987

Season	Opponent	Home	Playoff Result	Away	Rnd
1960	Jorge Wilsterman Cochabamba, Bolivia	7-1		1-1	1
	San Lorenzo, Argentina	0-0	2-1	1-1	sf
	Olimpia, Paraguay	1-0		1-1	FINAL
1961	Universitaria Lima, Peru	5-0		0-2	2
	Olimpia, Paraguay	3-1		2-1	sf
	Palmeiras Sao Paulo, Brazil	1-0		1-1	FINAL
1962	Nacional, Uruguay	3-1	1-1*	1-2	sf
			* won on goal difference		
	Santos FC Sao Paulo, Brazil	3-2	0-3*	1-2	FINAL
			* in Buenos Aires		
1963	Everest Guayaquil, Ecuador	9-1		5-0	1
	Boca Juniors, Argentina	1-2		0-1	sf
1965	Guarani, Paraguay	2-0		1-2	1
	Galicia Caracas, Venezuela	2-0		0-0	1
	Santos FC Sao Paulo, Brazil	4-5	3-2	2-1	sf
	Independiente, Argentina	3-1	1-4*	0-1	FINAL
			* in Santiago		
1966	Nacional, Uruguay	3-0		0-4	1
	Jorge Wilsterman Cochabamba, Bolivia	2-0		0-1	1
	Municipal La Paz, Bolivia	3-1		2-1	1
	Emelec Guayaquil, Ecuador	4-1		2-1	1
	Nueve de Octubre Guayaquil, Ecuador	2-0		2-1	1
	Universidad Catolica, Chile	2-0		0-1	sf
	Nacional, Uruguay	3-0		1-0	sf
	River Plate, Argentina	2-0	4-2*	0-3	FINAL
			* Santiago		
1967	Nacional, Uruguay	0-1		2-2	sf
	Cruzeiro Belo Horizonte, Brazil	3-2		0-1	sf
1968	Libertad, Paraguay	4-0		0-1	1
	Guarani, Paraguay	2-0		1-1	1
	Nacional, Uruguay	1-0		0-0	1
	Portugues Caracas, Venezuela	4-0		3-0	qf
	Sporting Cristal, Peru	1-1		0-0	qf
	Emelec Guayaquil, Ecuador	2-0		1-0	qf
	Palmeiras Sao Paulo, Brazil	1-1		0-1	sf
1969	Nacional, Uruguay	1-1		2-2	1
	Barcelona Sporting Guayaquil, Ecuador	5-2		2-0	1
	Deportivo Quito, Ecuador	5-2		1-1	1
	Olimpia, Paraguay	1-1		1-0	qf
	Nacional, Uruguay	0-2		0-0	sf
1970	Nacional, Uruguay	0-0		1-1	1
	Valencia FC Acarigua, Venezuela	11-2		0-0	1
	Galicia Caracas, Venezuela	4-1		1-0	1
	Liga Deportivo Universitaria Quito, Ecuador	2-1		3-1	sf
	Guarani, Paraguay	1-0		0-2	sf
	Universidad de Chile, Chile	2-0	2-2* aet	0-1	sf
			* gd Buenos Aires		
	Estudiantes La Plata, Argentina	0-0		0-1	FINAL

URUGUAY

1971	Nacional, Uruguay	0-2	1-2	1
	Chaco Petrolero, Bolivia	1-0	1-1	1
	The Strongest, Bolivia	9-0	2-1	1
1972	Italia Caracas, Venezuela	5-1	1-0	1
	Valencia FC Acarigua, Venezuela	4-1	2-1	1
	Nacional, Uruguay	0-3	1-1	sf
	Universitario Lima, Peru	1-1	3-2	sf
1973	Palmeiras Sao Paulo, Brazil	0-2	0-1	1
	Botafogo Rio de Janeiro, Brazil	2-2	1-4	1
	Nacional, Uruguay	1-2	1-1	1
1974	Nacional, Uruguay	1-0	0-2	1
	Olimpia, Paraguay	0-0	2-0	1
	Cerro Porteno, Paraguay	1-0	1-1	1
	Huracan, Argentina	1-1	3-0	sf
	Independiente, Argentina	1-1	2-3	sf
1975	Wanderers, Uruguay	1-0	2-1	1
	Union Huaral Lima, Peru	5-3	3-0	1
	Universitario Lima, Peru	0-1	2-3	1
1976	Nacional, Uruguay	1-1	2-1	1
	Union Espanola, Chile	2-0	0-0	1
	Palestino, Chile	2-1	0-1	1
	Independiente, Argentina	0-1	0-1	sf
	River Plate, Argentina	1-0	0-3	sf
1977	Defensor Sporting, Uruguay	0-2	4-2	1
	River Plate, Argentina	2-2	1-2	1
	Boca Juniors, Argentina	0-1	0-1	1
1978	Danubio, Uruguay	4-2	1-2	1
	Junior Barranquilla, Colombia	1-0	0-1	1
	Deportivo Cali, Colombia	0-2	0-1	1
1979	Nacional, Uruguay	1-1	0-0	1
	Tecnico Universitario de Ambato, Ecuador	4-0	1-0	1
	Nacional Quito, Ecuador	2-1	2-0	1
	Independiente, Argentina	0-0	0-1	sf
	Boca Juniors, Argentina	0-0	0-1	sf
1981	Bella Vista, Uruguay	3-1	0-0	1
	Portuguesa Acarigua, Venezuela	3-0	1-0	1
	Estudiantes Merida, Venezuela	4-2	2-0	1
	Nacional, Uruguay	1-1	1-1	sf
	Cobreloa Calama, Chile	0-1	2-4	sf
1982	Defensor Sporting, Uruguay	0-0	3-0	1
	Sao Paulo FC, Brazil	1-0	1-0	1
	Gremio Porto Alegre, Brazil	1-0	1-3	1
	Flamengo Rio de Janeiro, Brazil	1-0	1-0	sf
	River Plate, Argentina	2-1	4-2	sf
	Cobreloa Calama, Chile	0-0	1-0	FINAL
1983	San Cristobal, Venezuela	1-0	0-0	sf
	Nacional, Uruguay	2-0	2-1	sf
	Gremio Porto Alegre, Brazil	1-1	1-2	FINAL
1985	Bella Vista, Uruguay	1-0	2-0	1
	Magallanes San Bernardo, Chile	1-0	1-1	1
	Colo Colo, Chile	3-1	2-1	1
	America de Cali, Colombia	1-1	0-4	sf
	Nacional Quito, Ecuador	2-0	0-2	sf
1986	Boca Juniors, Argentina	1-2	1-1	1
	River Plate, Argentina	0-2	1-3	1
	Wanderers, Uruguay	1-3	0-1	1
1987	Progreso, Uruguay	3-2	1-1	1
	Colegio San Agustin Lima, Peru	2-0	1-1	1
	Alianza Lima, Peru	2-0	1-0	1
	Independiente, Argentina	3-0	4-2	sf
	River Plate, Argentina	0-0	0-1	sf
	America de Cali, Colombia	2-1	1-0* 0-2	FINAL
			* Santiago	
1988	San Lorenzo, Argentina	0-0	0-1	qf
1989	The Strongest, Bolivia	1-1	2-1	1
	Bolivar, Bolivia	5-0	0-3	1
	Danubio, Uruguay	2-0	1-4	1
136	Internacional Porto Alegre, Brazil	1-2	2-6	2

CLUB NACIONAL de FUTBOL

Founded 14th May 1899
Colours white shirts with blue and red striped collar and sleeves, blue shorts
Address Avenida 8 de Octubre 2847, Montevideo
Stadium Parque Central (20,000) or Centenario (73,609)
Champions 1902, 1903, 1912, 1915, 1916, 1917, 1919, 1920, 1922, 1923, 1924, 1933, 1934, 1939, 1940, 1941, 1942,
1943, 1946, 1947, 1950, 1952, 1955, 1956, 1957, 1966, 1969, 1970, 1971, 1972, 1977, 1980, 1983
Inter America Cup Winners 1971, 1972
South American Super Cup Winners 1989
Libertadores Cup Winners 1971, 1980 Finalists 1964, 1967, 1969
World Club Champions 1971, 1980

Season	Opponents	Home	Playoff Result	Away	Round
1962	Sporting Cristal, Peru	2-1		1-0	1
	Racing Club Avellaneda, Argentina	3-2		2-2	1
	Penarol, Uruguay	2-1	1-1*	1-3	sf
			won on goal difference		
1964	Aurora Cochabamba, Bolivia	2-0		3-0	1
	Cerro Porteno, Paraguay	2-0		2-2	1
	Colo Colo, Chile	4-2		4-2	sf
	Independiente, Argentina	0-0		0-1	FINAL
1966	Penarol, Uruguay	4-0		0-3	1
	Jorge Wilsterman Cochabamba, Bolivia	3-0		0-0	1
	Deportivo Municipal La Paz, Bolivia	4-1		2-3	1
	Emelec Guayaquil, Ecuador	1-0		2-0	1
	Nueve de Octubre Guayaquil, Ecuador	3-1		3-2	1
	Penarol, Uruguay	0-1		0-3	sf
	Universidad Catolica, Chile	3-2		0-1	sf
1967	Emelec Guayaquil, Ecuador	3-0		4-1	1
	Barcelona Sporting Guayaquil, Ecuador	2-0		1-2	1
	Cerro Porteno, Paraguay	6-2		4-1	1
	Guarani, Paraguay	3-1		1-0	1
	Colo Colo, Chile	5-2		2-3	1
	Universidad Catolica, Chile	0-0		3-0	1
	Penarol, Uruguay	2-2		1-0	sf
	Cruzeiro Belo Horizonte, Brazil	2-0		1-2	sf
	Racing Club Avellaneda, Argentina	0-0	1-2*	0-0	FINAL
			* in Santiago		
1968	Libertad, Paraguay	4-0		2-0	1
	Guarani, Paraguay	2-2		1-2	1
	Penarol, Uruguay	0-0		0-1	1
1969	Penarol, Uruguay	2-2		1-1	1
	Deportivo Quito, Ecuador	4-0		0-0	1
	Barcelona Sporting Guayaquil, Ecuador	2-0		1-1	1
	Deportivo Cali, Colombia	2-0		5-1	qf
	Santiago Wanderers, Chile	2-0		1-1	qf
	Penarol, Uruguay	0-0		2-0	sf
	Estudiantes La Plata, Argentina	0-1		0-2	FINAL
1970	Penarol, Uruguay	1-1		0-0	1
	Galicia Caracas, Venezuela	2-0		4-0	1
	Valencia FC Acarigua, Venezuela	1-0		5-2	1
	Universidad de Chile, Chile	2-0	1-2*	0-3	qf
			* Porto Alegre		
1971	Penarol, Uruguay	2-1		2-0	1
	Chaco Petrolero, Bolivia	3-0		1-0	1
	The Strongest, Bolivia	5-0		1-1	1
	Universitario Lima, Peru	3-0		0-0	sf
	Palmeiras Sao Paulo, Brazil	3-1		3-0	sf
	Estudiantes La Plata, Argentina	1-0	2-0*	0-1	FINAL
			* in Lima		
1972	Penarol, Uruguay	1-1		3-0	sf
	Universitario Lima, Peru	3-3		0-3	sf
1973	Penarol, Uruguay	1-1		2-1	1
	Palmeiras Sao Paulo, Brazil	1-2		1-1	1

URUGUAY

	Opponents	Home	Result	Away	Round
	Botafogo Rio de Janeiro, Brazil	1-2		2-3	1
1974	Penarol, Uruguay	2-0		0-1	1
	Olimpia, Paraguay	1-1		0-2	1
	Cerro Porteno, Paraguay	1-2		2-2	1
1976	Penarol, Uruguay	1-2		1-1	1
	Palestino, Chile	1-1		1-2	1
	Union Espanola, Chile	1-1		0-2	1
1979	Penarol, Uruguay	0-0		1-1	1
	Tecnico Universitario de Ambato, Ecuador	2-0		1-1	1
	Nacional Quito, Ecuador	3-0		0-1	1
1980	Oriente Petrolero Santa Cruz, Bolivia	5-0		3-1	1
	The Strongest, Bolivia	2-0		0-3	1
	Defensor Sporting, Uruguay	1-0		3-0	1
	O'Higgins Rancagua, Chile	2-0		1-0	sf
	Olimpia, Paraguay	1-1		1-0	sf
	Internacional Porto Alegre, Brazil	1-0		0-0	FINAL
1981	Penarol, Uruguay	1-1		1-1	sf
	Cobreloa Calama, Chile	1-2		1-2	sf
1983	Wanderers, Uruguay	0-1	2-0	1-1	1
	Olimpia, Paraguay	3-0		1-0	1
	Nacional Asuncion, Paraguay	4-2		3-0	1
	San Cristobal, Venezuela	5-1		2-1	sf
	Penarol, Uruguay	1-2		0-2	sf
1984	Danubio, Uruguay	1-0		1-0	1
	Nacional Quito, Ecuador	1-1		1-3	1
	Nueve de Octubre Guayaquil, Ecuador	6-0		3-1	1
	Independiente, Argentina	1-1		0-1	sf
	Universidad Catolica, Chile	2-0		not played	sf
1988	Wanderers, Uruguay	1-0		0-0	1
	America de Cali, Colombia	2-0		0-0	1
	Millonarios Bogota, Colombia	4-1		1-6	1
	Universidad Catolica, Chile	0-0	wag	1-1	2
	Newell's Old Boys Rosario, Argentina	2-1		1-1	
	America de Cali, Colombia	1-0		1-1	sf
	Newell's Old Boys Rosario, Argentina	3-0 aet		0-1	FINAL
1989	Danubio, Uruguay	1-3		0-0	2

MONTEVIDEO WANDERERS FC

Founded 15th August 1902
Colours black and white striped shirts, black shorts
Address Avenida Agraciada 2871, Montevideo
Stadium Parque Alfredo V Viera (12,500)
Champions 1906, 1909, 1931

Season	Opponents	Home	Result	Away	Round
1975	Penarol, Uruguay	1-2		0-1	1
	Union Huaral Lima, Peru	4-0		2-2	1
	Universitario Lima, Peru	0-2		1-3	1
1983	Nacional, Uruguay	1-1	0-2	1-0	1
	Nacional Asuncion, Paraguay	3-1		1-1	1
	Olimpia, Paraguay	0-0		3-2	1
1986	Boca Juniors, Argentina	2-0		2-3	1
	River Plate, Argentina	0-2		2-4	1
	Penarol, Uruguay	1-0		3-1	1
1988	Nacional, Uruguay	0-0		0-1	1
	America de Cali, Colombia	1-2		0-1	1
	Millonarios Bogota, Colombia	2-1		0-3	1

DANUBIO FUTBOL CLUB

Founded 1st March 1932
Colours all white with black sash
Address Avenida 8 de Octubre 4584, Montevideo
Stadium Jardins del Hipodromo (18,000)
Champions 1988

Season	Opponents	Home	Result	Away	Round
1978	Penarol, Uruguay	2-1		2-4	1
	Junior Barranquilla, Colombia	0-0		0-0	1
	Deportivo Cali, Colombia	3-1		0-2	1
1984	Nacional, Uruguay	0-1		0-1	1
	Nueve de Octubre Guayaquil, Ecuador	5-1		2-2	1
	Nacional Quito, Ecuador	1-0		0-3	1
1989	The Strongest, Bolivia	1-0		0-1	1
	Bolivar, Bolivia	1-0		1-3	1
	Penarol, Uruguay	4-1		0-2	1
	Nacional, Uruguay	0-0		3-1	2
	Cobreloa Calama, Chile	2-1		2-0	qf
	Nacional Medellin, Colombia	0-0		0-6	sf

CLUB ATLETICO DEFENSOR SPORTING

Founded 15th March 1913
Colours violet shirts with white trim, white shorts
Address Jaine Zudanez 2537, Montevideo
Stadium Luis Frazzini (15,000)
Champions 1976, 1987

Season	Opponents	Home	Playoff Result	Away	Round
1977	Penarol, Uruguay	2-4		2-0	1
	Boca Juniors, Argentina	0-0		0-2	1
	River Plate, Argentina	0-0		1-1	1
1980	Oriente Petrolero Santa Cruz, Bolivia	1-1		1-0	1
	The Strongest, Bolivia	1-1		0-2	1
	Nacional, Uruguay	0-3		0-1	1
1982	Penarol, Uruguay	0-3		0-0	1
	Sao Paulo FC, Brazil	1-3		1-2	1
	Gremio Porto Alegre, Brazil	0-0		not played	1
1990	Progreso, Uruguay	0-0	4-0	1-1	1
	Mineros De Guyana, Venezuela	3-1		0-0	1
	Pepeganga Margarita, Venezuela	1-0		0-1	1
	River Plate Argentina	1-2		1-2	2

CLUB ATLETICO BELLA VISTA

Founded 4th October 1920
Colours gold and white halved shirts, blue shorts
Address Lucas Obes 849 y Felix Olmedo, Montevideo
Stadium Parque Jose Nasazzi (20,000)
Champions 1990

Season	Opponents	Home	Result	Away	Round
1981	Estudiantes Merida, Venezuela	3-1		4-1	1
	Penarol, Uruguay	0-0		1-3	1
	Portuguesa Acarigua, Venezuela	4-0		4-0	1
1985	Penarol, Uruguay	0-2		0-1	1
	Colo Colo, Chile	2-1		0-2	1
	Magallanes San Bernado, Chile	0-1		1-2	1

139

CLUB ATLETICO PROGRESO

Founded 30th April 1917
Colours yellow and red broad striped shirts, red shorts
Address Carlos Manuel Ramirez 758, Montevideo
Stadium Parque Abraham Paladino (10,000)
Champions 1989

Season	Opponent	Home	Result	Away	Round
1987	Penarol, Uruguay	1-1		2-3	1
	Colegio San Agustin Lima, Peru	3-0		1-3	1
	Alianza Lima, Peru	0-0		0-0	1
1990	Defenser Sporting, Uruguay	1-1	0-4	0-0	1
	Mineros De Guyana, Venezuela	1-1		3-1	1
	Pepeganga Margarita, Venezuela	2-0		0-1	1
	Barcelona Guayaquil, Ecuador	2-2		0-2	2

1962 **Santos** (Brazil)

VENEZUELA

Founded 1926
Federacion Venezolana de Futbol, Avenida da Este Estadio Nacional-El Paraiso, Apartado Postal 14160 Candelaria,
Caracas ☎ 010 58-2 461 8010 Telex 26140 Fufcs vc Fax (58-2) 461 8010
Language Spanish, French, English
National colours dark red shirts, black shorts
Season February to December

LEAGUE CHAMPIONS

AMATEUR

1921 America	**1940** Union SC		
1922 Centro Atletico	**1941** Litoral FC		
1923 America	**1942** Dos Caminos SC		
1924 Centro Atletico	**1943** Loyola Sport Club		
1925 Loyola Sport Club	**1944** Loyola Sport Club		
1926 Centro Atletico	**1945** Dos Caminos SC		
1927 Venzoleo FC	**1946** Deportivo Espanol		
1928 Deportivo Venezuela	**1947** Union SC		
1929 Centro Atletico &	**1948** Loyola Sport Club		
Deportico Venezuela	**1949** Dos Caminos SC		
1930 Centro Atletico	**1950** Union Sport Club		
1931 Deportivo Venezuela	**1951** Universidad Central		
1932 Union SC	**1952** Le Salle		
1933 Deportivo Venezuela	**1953** Universidad Central		
1934 Union SC	**1954** Deportivo Vasco		
1935 Union SC	**1955** Le Salle		
1936 Dos Calamos SC			
1937 Dos Calamas SC			
1938 Dos Caminos SC			
1939 Union SC			

PROFESSIONAL

1956 Banco Obrero	**1970** Galicia Caracas
1957 Universidad Central	**1971** Valencia FC Acarigua
1958 Deportivo Portugues	**1972** Italia Caracas
Caracas	**1973** Portuguesa Acarigua
1959 Celta Deportivo	**1974** Galicia Caracas
	1975 Portuguesa Acarigua
1960 Deportivo Portugues	**1976** Portuguesa Acarigua
Caracas	**1977** Portuguesa Acarigua
1961 Italia Caracas	**1978** Portuguesa Acarigua
1962 Deportivo Portugues	**1979** Tachira San Cristobal
Caracas	
1963 Italia Caracas	**1980** Estudiantes Merida
1964 Galicia Caracas	**1981** Tachira San Cristobal
1965 Lara Basquimento	**1982** San Cristobal
1966 Italia Caracas	**1983** Universidad Los Andes
1967 Deportivo Portugues	(ULA), Merida
Caracas	**1984** Deportivo Tachira
1968 Union Deportiva	**1985** Estudiantes Merida
Canarias Caracas	**1987** Sport Maritimo Caracas
1969 Galicia Caracas	**1988** Sport Maritimo Caracas
	1989 Mineros Guyana
	Puerto Ordaz

FEATURED CLUBS IN COPA LIBERTADORES DE AMERICA

Portuguesa Acarigua	Union Deportivo Canaries Caracas		Valencia FC Acarigua
Lara Basquimento	Galicia Caracas	Italia Caracas	Tachira San Cristobal
Estudiantes Merida	San Cristobal	Univeridad Los Andes (ULA) Merida	
Sport Maritimo Caracas	Portuguse Caracas	Mineros de Guyana	Pepeganga Margarita

PORTUGUESA ACARIGUA

Founded 1926
Colours white shirts with red sleeves 1 green 1 red hoop, white shorts
Stadium General Jose Antonio Paez, Acarigua (11,000)
Champions 1973, 1975, 1976, 1977, 1978

Season	Opponent	Home	Result	Away	Rnd
1974	Valencia FC Acarigua, Venezuela	0-0		1-0	1
	Millonarios Bogota, Colombia	2-0		1-2	1
	Nacional Medellin, Colombia	0-0		0-3	1

141

VENEZUELA

1975	Nacional Quito, Ecuador	1-0		1-5	1
	Liga Deportivo Universitaria Quito, Ecuador	1-1		1-1	1
	Galicia Caracas, Venezuela	1-1		0-0	1
1976	Galicia Caracas, Venezuela	3-1		2-1	1
	Estudiantes La Plata, Argentina	2-2		0-3	1
	River Plate, Argentina	0-2		1-2	1
1977	Estudiantes Merida, Venezuela	3-0		2-0	1
	Union Huaral Lima, Peru	2-0		1-1	1
	Sport Boys Callao, Peru	0-0		2-1	1
	Internacional Porto Alegre, Brazil	3-0		1-2	sf
	Cruzeiro Belo Horizonte, Brazil	0-4		1-2	sf
1978	Estudiantes Merida, Venezuela	0-0		1-2	1
	Cerro Porteno, Paraguay	1-1		0-1	1
	Libertad, Paraguay	1-0		2-1	1
1979	Galicia Caracas, Venezuela	1-1		1-1	1
	O'Higgins Rancagua, Chile	1-1		1-1	1
	Palestino, Chile	0-2		0-6	1
1981	Estudiantes Merida, Venezuela	0-0		1-1	1
	Penarol, Uruguay	0-1		0-3	1
	Bella Vista, Uruguay	0-4		0-4	1
1984	Sporting Cristal, Peru	1-0		1-2	1
	Mariano Melgar, Peru	4-0		2-1	1
	Universidad Los Andes (ULA), Venezuela	1-2		0-2	1

CLUB DEPORTIVO PORTUGUES

Founded
Colours red and green striped shirts, white shorts
Stadium Olimpico Ciudad universitaria, Caracas (25,000)
Champions 1958, 1960, 1962, 1967

Season	Opponent	Home	Result	Away	Round
1968	Palmeiras Sao Paulo, Brazil	1-2		0-3	1
	Nautico Capiberibe Recife, Brazil	1-1		2-3	1
	Penarol, Uruguay	0-3		0-4	qf
	Sporting Cristal, Peru	1-1		0-2	qf
	Emelec Guayaquil, Ecuador	2-0		0-2	qf

UNION DEPORTIVO CANARIES

Founded
Colours
Stadium, Caracas
Champions 1968

Season	Opponent	Home	Result	Away	Round
1969	Italia Caracas, Venezuela	1-1		0-2	1
	Deportivo Cali, Colombia	1-1		0-2	1
	Union Magdelina Santa Marta, Colombia	1-0		0-1	1

VALENCIA FC ACARIGUA

Founded 1926
Colours green shirts with white trim and shorts
Stadium General Jose Antonio Paez (11,000)
Champions 1971

Season	Opponent	Home	Result	Away	Round
1970	Galicia Caracas, Venezuela	2-0		3-1	1
	Penarol, Uruguay	0-0		2-11	1
	Nacional, Uruguay	2-5		0-1	1
1972	Penarol, Uruguay	1-2		1-4	1
	Italia Caracas, Venezuela	1-1		0-2	1
1974	Portuguesa Acarigua, Venezuela	0-1		0-0	1
	Nacional Medellin, Colombia	1-2		1-2	1
	Millonarios Bogota, Colombia	1-1		1-2	1

DEPORTIVO LARA BASQUIMENTO

Founded 1951
Colours all red with white trim
Stadium Estadio Farid Richa (10,000)
Champions 1965

Season	Opponent	Home	Result	Away	Round
1966	River Plate, Argentina	0-3		1-2	1
	Boca Juniors, Argentina	0-3		1-2	1
	Italia Caracas, Venezuela	1-1		0-1	1
	Universitario Lima, Peru	0-0		0-1	1
	Alianza Lima, Peru	2-1		0-3	1

DEPORTIVO GALICIA

Founded 1926
Colours all white with sky blue sash and trim
Stadium main matches at Estadio Olimpico (25,000)
Stadium Olimpico Cuidad Universitaria, Caracas (25,000)
Champions 1964, 1969, 1970, 1974

Season	Opponent	Home	Result	Away	Round
1965	Guarani, Paraguay	1-2		0-2	1
	Penarol, Uruguay	0-0		0-2	1
1967	Italia Caracas, Venezuela	0-0		0-1	1
	Cruzeiro Belo Horizonte, Brazil	0-1		1-3	1
	Universitario Lima, Peru	2-0		0-2	1
	Sport Boys Callao, Peru	0-2	both played in Peru	2-1	1
1968	Palmeiras Sao Paulo, Brazil	1-2		0-2	1
	Nautico Capiberibe Recife, Brazil	2-1		0-1	1
	Portuguesa Acarigua, Venezuela	2-0		0-1	1
1970	Valencia FC Acarigua, Venezuela	1-3		0-2	1
	Nacional, Uruguay	0-4		0-2	1
	Penarol, Uruguay	0-1		1-4	1
1971	Italia Caracas, Venezuela	0-0		5-6	1
	Palmeiras Sao Paulo, Brazil	2-3		0-3	1
	Fluminense Rio de Janeiro, Brazil	1-4		1-3	1
1975	Liga Deportivo Universitaria Quito, Ecuador	0-1		2-4	1
	Nacional Quito, Ecuador	4-0		0-0	1
	Portuguesa Acarigua, Venezuela	0-0		1-1	1
1976	Portuguesa Acarigua, Venezuela	1-2		1-3	1
	River Plate, Argentina	0-1		1-4	1
	Estudiantes La Plata, Argentina	0-1		0-4	1
1979	Portuguesa Acarigua, Venezuela	1-1		1-1	1
	Palestino, Chile	1-1		0-5	1
	O'Higgins Rancagua, Chile	0-1		0-6	1
1980	Tachira San Cristobal, Venezuela	1-0		1-0	1
	Internacional Porto Alegre, Brazil	2-1		0-2	1
	Vasco da Gama Rio de Janiero, Brazil	0-0		0-4	1

VENEZUELA

TACHIRA SAN CRISTOBAL

Formerly Deportivo Tachira
Founded 1978
Colours red and black broad striped shirts, black shorts
Stadium Estadio Tachira (12,000)
Champions 1979, 1981, 1984

Season	Opponent	Home	Result	Away	Round
1980	Galicia Caracas, Venezuela	0-1		0-1	1
	Internacioal Porto Alegre, Brazil	0-1		0-4	1
	Vasco da Gama Rio de Janeiro, Brazil	0-1		0-1	1
1982	Estudiantes Merida, Venezuela	0-0		0-1	1
	Tolima Ibague, Colombia	0-2		2-2	1
	Nacional Medellin, Colombia	0-0		0-1	1
1983	San Cristobal, Venezuela	0-0		0-2	1
	Barcelona Sporting Guayaquil, Ecuador	1-1		not played	1
	Nacional Quito, Ecuador	0-0		0-3	1
1985	Italia Caracas, Venezuela	0-0		3-1	1
	Oriente Petrolero Santa Cruz, Bolivia	1-1		2-3	1
	Blooming Santa Cruz, Bolivia	0-1		1-6	1
1987	Estudiantes Merida, Venezuela	3-2		3-0	1
	Independiente, Argentina	3-2		0-5	1
	Rosario Central, Argentina	0-0		2-3	1
1988	Sport Maritimo Caracas, Venezuela	0-0		1-1	1
	Colo Colo, Chile	0-1		0-2	1
	Universidad Catolica, Chile	0-1		1-3	1
1989	Sport Maritimo Caracas, Venezuela	2-0		1-0	1
	Internacional Porto Alegre, Brazil	1-0		1-3	1
	Esporte Clube Bahia Salvador, Brazil	1-1		1-4	1
	Sol de America, Paraguay	3-0	2-3p	0-3	2

DEPORTIVO ITALIA

Founded 1952
Colours blue shirts with white trim, white shorts
Stadium Olimpico Ciudad Universitaria (25,000)
Address Centro Profesional, Flor-Los Chris, Caracas
Champions 1961, 1963, 1966, 1972.

Season	Opponent	Home	Result	Away	Round
1964	Esporte Clube Bahia Salvador, Brazil	0-0		2-1	prelimin
	Colo Colo, Chile	1-2		0-4	1
	Barcelona Sporting Guayaquil, Ecuador	3-0		0-1	1
1966	River Plate, Argentina	0-3		1-2	1
	Boca Juniors, Argentina	1-2		2-5	1
	Universitario Lima, Peru	2-2		2-1	1
	Alianza Lima, Peru	3-1		2-1	1
	Lara Basquimento, Venezuela	1-0		1-1	1
1967	Galicia Caracas, Venezuela	1-0		0-0	1
	Cruzeiro Belo Horizonte, Brazil	0-3		0-4	1
	Universitario Lima, Peru	0-1*	* in Lima	0-3	1
	Sport Boys Callao, Peru	0-0*	* in Lima	2-5	1
1969	Union Deportivo Canaries Caracas, Venezuela	2-0		1-1	1
	Deportivo Cali, Colombia	2-1		0-3	1
	Union Magdelina Santa Marta, Colombia	2-0		0-3	1
	Cerro Porteno, Paraguay	0-0		0-1	1
	Universidad Catolica, Chile	3-2		0-4	1
1971	Galicia Caracas, Venezuela	6-5		0-0	1
	Palmeiras Sao Paulo, Brazil	0-3		0-1	1
	Fluminense Rio de Janeiro, Brazil	1-0		0-6	1

1972	Penarol, Uruguay	0-1		1-5	1
	Valencia FC Acarigua, Venezuela	2-0		1-1	1
1985	Blooming Santa Cruz, Bolivia	0-3		0-8	1
	Oriente Petrolero Santa Cruz, Bolivia	0-3		1-3	1
	Tachira San Cristobal, Venezuela	1-3		0-0	1

ESTUDIANTES MERIDA

Founded 1952
Colours red and white striped shirts, red shorts
Stadium Guillermo Rosa Soto (10,000)
Champions 1980, 1985

Season	Opponent	Home	Result	Away	Round
1977	Portuguesa Acarigua, Venezuela	0-2		0-3	1
	Union Huaral Lima, Peru	1-0		1-2	1
	Sport Boys Callao, Peru	1-0		3-1	1
1978	Portuguesa Acarigua, Venezuela	2-1		0-0	1
	Cerro Porteno, Paraguay	2-3		1-1	1
	Libertad, Paraguay	1-1		1-2	1
1981	Portuguesa Acarigua, Venezuela	1-1		0-0	1
	Bella Vista, Uruguay	1-4		1-3	1
	Penarol, Uruguay	0-2		2-4	1
1982	Tachira San Cristobal, Venezuela	1-0		0-0	1
	Nacional Medellin, Colombia	1-3		0-2	1
	Tolima Ibague, Colombia	1-1		0-1	1
1987	Tachira San Cristobal, Venezuela	0-3		2-3	1
	Rosario Central, Argentina	0-3		2-5	1
	Independiente, Argentina	0-1		0-2	1

DEPORTIVO SAN CRISTOBAL

Club no longer exists
Founded 1981
Colours green and white striped shirts, white shorts
Stadium Estadio San Cristobal (20,000)
Champions 1982

Season	Opponent	Home	Result	Away	Round
1983	Tachira San Cristobal, Venezuela	2-0		0-0	1
	Barcelona Sporting Guayaquil, Ecuador	2-0		3-3	1
	Nacional Quito, Ecuador	1-0		0-1	1
	Penarol, Uruguay	0-0		0-1	sf
	Nacional, Uruguay	1-2		1-5	sf

UNIVERSIDAD DE LOS ANDES (ULA)

Founded 1977
Colours all white with blue trim
Stadium Guillermo Rosa Soto, Merida (10,000)
Champions 1983

Season	Opponent	Home	Playoff Result	Away	Round
1984	Sporting Cristal, Peru	0-1	1-2 in Cali	0-2	1
	Mariano Melgar FC Arequipa, Peru	1-0		1-0	1
	Portuguesa Acarigua, Venezuela	2-0		2-1	1
	Flamengo Rio de Janeiro, Brazil	0-3		1-2	sf
	Gremio Porto Alegre, Brazil	0-2		1-6	sf

145

VENEZUELA

SPORT MARITIMO

Founded
Colours all blue with white trim
Stadium Olimpico Cuidad Universiaria, Caracas (25,000)
Champions 1987, 1988

Season	Opponent	Home	Result	Away	Round
1988	Tachira San Cristobal, Venezuela	1-1		0-0	1
	Universidad Catolica, Chile	0-0		1-2	1
	Colo Colo, Chile	0-1		0-1	1
1989	Tachira San Cristobal, Venezuela	0-1		0-2	1
	Internacional Porto Alegre, Brazil	1-1*		0-3	1
		* behind closed doors			
	Esporte Clube Bahia Salvador, Brazil	0-0*		2-3	1
		* political dispute			

MINEROS DE GUYANA CIUDAD BOLIVAR

Founded 1981 as professionals
Colours sky blue and white striped shirts, black shorts
Stadium Olimpico de Ciudad Bolivar (10,000)

Season	Opponent	Home	Result	Away	Round
1990	Pepeganga Margarita, Venezuela	1-0		1-2	1
	Progreso, Uruguay	1-3		1-1	1
	Defensor Sporting, Uruguay	0-0		1-3	1

PEPEGANGA MARGARITA

Founded 1987 as professionals
Colours yellow and blue shirts, black shorts
Stadium

Season	Opponent	Home	Result	Away	Round
1990	Mineros de Guyana, Venezuela	2-1		0-1	1
	Progreso, Uruguay	1-0		0-2	1
	Defensor Sporting, Uruguay	1-0		0-1	1
	Independiente, Argentina	0-6		0-3	2

SOUTH AMERICAN CHAMPIONSHIPS

1910 UNOFFICIAL (EXTRAORDINARIOS)

Champions ARGENTINA, in Argentina

				H/T	F/T	Venue	Attend
29.05.10	URUGUAY	v CHILE		(1-0)	3-0	Buenos Aires	5,000
	J Piendibene, J Brachi, R S Buck						
05-06-10	ARGENTINA	v CHILE			5-1	Buenos Aires	
	E Brown 2, M Susan 2, E R Brown	C Campbell					
12.06.10	ARGENTINA	v URUGUAY		(2-0)	4-1	Buenos Aires	22,000
	J Viali, H Hayes, A Watson-Hutton,	J Piendibene					
	M Susan						

Argentina	2	2	0	0	9-2	5
Uruguay	2	1	0	1	4-4	2
Chile	2	0	0	2	1-8	0

1916 UNOFFICIAL (EXTRAORDINARIOS)

Champions ARGENTINA, in Argentina

				H/T	F/T	Venue	Attend
02.07.16	URUGUAY	v CHILE		(1-0)	4-0	Buenos Aires	30,000
	J Piendibene 3, I Gradin						
06.07.16	ARGENTINA	v CHILE			6-1	Buenos Aires	15,000
	A Marcovecchio 2, J D Brown 2,	T.Baez					
	A Ohaco 2						
08.07.16	CHILE	v BRAZIL			1-1	Buenos Aires	15,000
	E Salazar	Sylas					
10.07.16	ARGENTINA	v BRAZIL			1-1	Buenos Aires	20,000
	J Laguna	Alencar					
12.07.16	URUGUAY	v BRAZIL		(0-1)	2-1	Buenos Aires	15,000
	I Gradin, J Tognola	A Friedenreich					
17.07.16	ARGENTINA	v URUGUAY			0-0	Buenos Aires	30,000

Uruguay	3	2	1	0	6-1	5
Argentina	3	1	2	0	7-2	4
Brazil	3	0	2	1	3-4	2
Chile	3	0	1	2	2-11	1

147

SOUTH AMERICAN CHAMPIONSHIPS

1917 (OFFICIAL)

Champions URUGUAY, in Uruguay

				H/T	F/T	Venue	Attend
30.09.17	URUGUAY	v	CHILE	(2-0)	4-0	Parque Pereira, Montevideo	22,000
	C Scarone 2, A Romano 2						
03.10.17	ARGENTINA	v	BRAZIL	(2-0)	4-2	Parque Pereira	20,000
	A Ohaco 3, P Calomino, A Blanco		Sylvio Lagreca, Neco				
06.10.17	ARGENTINA	v	CHILE		1-0	Parque Pereira	12,000
	L A Garcia own goal						
07.10.17	URUGUAY	v	BRAZIL	(2-0)	4-0	Parque Pereira	21,000
	A Romano 2, H Scarone, C Scarone						
12.10.17	BRAZIL	v	CHILE		5-0	Parque Pereira	10,000
	Haroldo 2, Cectano, Almicar, Neco						
14.10.17	URUGUAY	v	ARGENTINA	(0-0)	1-0	Parque Pereira	40,000
	H Scarone						

Uruguay	3	3	0	0	9-0	6
Argentina	3	2	0	1	5-3	4
Brazil	3	1	0	2	7-8	2
Chile	3	0	0	3	0-10	0

1919 (OFFICIAL)

Champions BRAZIL, in Brazil

				H/T	F/T	Venue	Attend
11.05.19	BRAZIL	v	CHILE		6-0	Fluminense, Rio de Janeiro	25,000
	A Friedenreich 3, Neco 2, Haroldo						
13.05.19	ARGENTINA	v	URUGUAY	(1-2)	2-3	Fluminense	25,000
	C Izaguirre, P Calomino		I Gradin, C Scarone, H Scarone				
17.05.19	URUGUAY		CHILE	(2-0)	2-0	Fluminese	7,000
	C Scarone, J Perez						
18.05.19	BRAZIL	v	ARGENTINA		3-1	Fluminese	28,000
	Amilcar, Millon, Heitor Domingues		C Izaguirre				
22.05.19	ARGENTINA	v	CHILE		4-1	Fluminese	5,000
	E Clarke 3, C Izaguirre		A France				
15.05.19	BRAZIL	v	URUGUAY	(1-2)	2-2	Fluminese	25,000
	Neco 2		I Gradin, H Scarone				
29.05.19	BRAZIL	v	URUGUAY	(0-0)	0-0 1-0aet	Fluminese	28,000
	A. Friedenreich					Championship play off	

Brazil	3	2	1	0	11-3	5
Uruguay	3	2	1	0	7-4	5
Argentina	3	1	0	2	7-7	2
Chile	3	0	0	3	1-12	0

1920 (OFFICIAL)

Champions URUGUAY, in Chile

				H/T	F/T	Venue	Attend
11.09.20	CHILE	v	BRAZIL		0-1	Vina del Mar	15,000
	Alvariza						
12.09.20	ARGENTINA	v	URUGUAY	(0-1)	1-1	Vina del Mar	20,000
	R Echeverria		J Piendibene				
17.09.20	CHILE	v	ARGENTINA		1-1	Vina del Mar	16,000
	A Dominquez		M Dellavalle				

18.09.20	URUGUAY A Campolo, S Perez 2, A Romano 2 L Urdinaran penalty	v BRAZIL	(3-0)	6-0	Vina del Mar	16,000
25.09.20	BRAZIL R Echeverria, J Libonetti	v ARGENTINA		0-2	Vina del Mar	12,000
03.10.20	CHILE I D Bolados	v URUGUAY A Romano, J Perez	(0-1)	1-2	Vina del Mar	10,000

Uruguay	3	2	1	0	9-2	5
Argentina	3	1	2	0	4-2	4
Brazil	3	1	0	2	1-8	2
Chile	3	0	1	2	2-4	1

1921 (OFFICIAL)

Champions ARGENTINA, in Argentina

			H/T	F/T	Venue	Attend
02.10.21	ARGENTINA J Libonetti	v BRAZIL		1-0	Sportivo Barracas Buenos Aires	20,000
09.10.21	URUGUAY J Piendibene	v PARAGUAY G Rivas, E Lopez		1-2	Sportivo Barracas	18,000
12.10.21	PARAGUAY	v BRAZIL Machado 2, Candiota		0-3	Sportivo Barracas	25,000
16.10.21	ARGENTINA J Libonetti, B Saruppo R Etcheverria	v PARAGUAY		3-0	Sportivo Barracas	25,000
23.10.21	URUGUAY A Romano 2	v BRAZIL I Zeze		2-1	Sportivo Barracas	18,000
30.10.21	ARGENTINA J Libonetti	v URUGUAY		1-0	Sportivo Barracas	35,000

Argentina	3	3	0	0	5-0	6
Brazil	3	1	0	2	4-3	2
Uruguay	3	1	0	2	3-4	2
Paraguay	3	1	0	2	2-7	2

SOUTH AMERICAN CHAMPIONSHIPS

1922 (OFFICIAL)

Champions BRAZIL, in Brazil

				H/T	F/T	Venue	Attend
17.09.22	BRAZIL	v	CHILE		1-1	Laranjeiras Std	30,000
	Tatu		M Bravo			Rio de Janeiro	
24.09.22	URUGUAY	v	CHILE		2-0	Laranjeiras Std	6,000
	J C Heguy, L Urdinaran penalty						
24.09.22	BRAZIL	v	PARAGUAY		1-1	Laranjeira Std	25,000
	Amilcar		G Rivas				
28.09.22	ARGENTINA	v	CHILE		4-0	Laranjeira Std	6,000
	J Gaslini, J Francia 2, A Chiessia						
01.10.22	BRAZIL	v	URUGUAY		0-0	Laranjeira Std	30,000
05.10.22	CHILE	v	PARAGUAY		0-3	Laranjeira Std	1,000
			C Ramirez, E Lopez, A Fretes				
09.10.22	URUGUAY	v	ARGENTINA		1-0	Laranjeira Std	7,000
	M Buffoni						
12.10.22	URUGUAY	v	PARAGUAY		0-1	Laranjeira Std	3,000
			C Elizeche Benitez				
15.10.22	BRAZIL	v	ARGENTINA		2-0	Laranjeira Std	25,000
	Amilcar, Neco						
18.10.22	ARGENTINA	v	PARAGUAY		2-0	Laranjeira Std	8,000
	J Francia 2						
22.10.22	BRAZIL	v	PARAGUAY		3-1	Laranjeira Std	20,000
	Formiga 2, Neco		G Rivas			Championship play off	

Brazil	4	1	3	0	4-2	5
Paraguay	4	2	1	1	5-3	5
Uruguay	4	2	1	1	3-1	5
Argentina	4	2	0	2	6-3	4
Chile	4	0	1	3	1-10	1

1923 (OFFICIAL)

Champions URUGUAY, in Uruguay

				H/T	F/T	Venue	Attend
28.10.23	ARGENTINA	v	PARAGUAY		4-3	Parque Central	20,000
	V Aguirre 3, B Saruppo		G Rivas, Zelada, Fretes			Montevideo	
04.11.23	URUGUAY	v	PARAGUAY		2-0	Parque Central	20,000
	H Scarone, P Petrone						
11.11.23	PARAGUAY	v	BRAZIL		1-0	Parque Central	15,000
	I Lopez						
18.11.23	ARGENTINA	v	BRAZIL		2-1	Parque Central	15,000
	C Onzari 2, B Saruppo		Nilo				
25.11.23	URUGUAY	v	BRAZIL		2-1	Parque Central	20,000
	P Petrone, P Cea		Nilo				
02.12.23	URUGUAY	v	ARGENTINA		2-0	Parque Central	22,000
	P Petrone, P Somma						

Uruguay	3	3	0	0	6-1	6
Argentina	3	2	0	1	6-6	4
Paraguay	3	1	0	2	4-6	2
Brazil	3	0	0	3	2-5	0

SOUTH AMERICAN CHAMPIONSHIPS

1924 (OFFICIAL)

Champions URUGUAY, in Uruguay

				H/T	F/T	Venue	Attend
12.10.24	PARAGUAY	v ARGENTINA			0-0	Parque Central Montevideo	8,000
19.10.24	URUGUAY	v CHILE			5-0	Parque Central	15,000
	A Romano 2, P Petrone 3, Zingone						
25.10.24	ARGENTINA	v CHILE			2-0	Parque Central	4,000
	Loyarte, G Sosa						
26.10.24	URUGUAY	v PARAGUAY			3-1	Parque Central	14,000
	P Petrone, P Cea, A Romano	P Urbieta Sosa					
01.11.24	PARAGUAY	v CHILE			3-1	Parque Central	1,000
	G Rivas, I Lopez 2	D.Arellano					
02.11.24	URUGUAY	v ARGENTINA			0-0	Parque Central	20,000

Uruguay	3	2	1	0	8-1	5
Argentina	3	1	2	0	2-0	4
Paraguay	3	1	1	1	4-4	3
Chile	3	0	0	3	1-10	0

1925 (OFFICIAL)

Champions ARGENTINA, in Argentina

				H/T	F/T	Venue	Attend
29.11.25	ARGENTINA	v PARAGUAY			2-0	Baracas Stadium Buenos Aires	18,000
	M Seoanne, M Sanchez						
06.12.25	BRAZIL	v PARAGUAY			5-2	Baracas	12,000
	Lagarto 2, Nilo, A Friendenrich, Moderato	G Rivas 2					
13.12.25	ARGENTINA	v BRAZIL			4-1	Baracas	25,000
	M Seoane 3, A Garasini,	Nilo					
17.12.25	BRAZIL	v PARAGUAY			3-1	Baracas	14,000
	Lagarto 2, Nilo	I Fretes					
20.12.25	ARGENTINA	v PARAGUAY			3-1	Baracas	25,000
	D Tarascone, M Seoane, J Irurieta	Fleitas Solich					
25.12.25	ARGENTINA	v BRAZIL			2-2	Baracas	18,000
	A Cerrotti, M Seoane	Friendenrich, Nilo					

Argentina	4	3	1	0	11-4	7
Brazil	4	2	1	1	11-9	5
Paraguay	4	0	0	4	4-13	0

1926 (OFFICIAL)

Champions URUGUAY, in Chile

				H/T	F/T	Venue	Attend
12.10.26	CHILE	v BOLIVIA			7-1	Sport de Nunoa Santiago	12,000
	M Ramarex, H Moreno, D Arellano 3, G Subiabre 2	Aguilar					
16.10.26	ARGENTINA	v BOLIVIA			5-0	Sport de Nunoa	8,000
	R Cherro 2, A de Miguel, G Sosa, B Delgado						
17.10.26	CHILE	v URUGUAY			1-3	Sport de Nunoa	13,000
	G Subiabre penalty	R Borjas, H Castro, H Scarone					

20.10.26	ARGENTINA G Sosa 4, B Delgado 2, R Cherro, A de Miguel	PARAGUAY	8-0	Sport de Nunoa	3,000
23.10.26	PARAGUAY C Ramirez 2, Julio Ramirez 3, I Lopez	v BOLIVIA	6-1	Sport de Nunoa	2,000
24.10.26	URUGUAY H Castro, Borjas	v ARGENTINA	2-0	Sport de Nunoa	15,000
28.10.26	URUGUAY H Scarone 5, A Romano	v BOLIVIA	6-0	Sport de Nunoa	8,000
31.10.26	CHILE G Saavedra	v ARGENTINA B Tarasconi	1-1	Sport de Nunoa	8,000
01.11.26	URUGUAY H Castro 4, Saldombide 2	v PARAGUAY I Fretes	6-1	Sport de Nunoa	12,000
03.11.26	CHILE D Arellano 2, G Subiabre 3	v PARAGUAY Vargas	5-1	Sport de Nunoa	6,000

Uruguay	4	4	0	0	17-2	8
Argentina	4	2	1	1	14-3	5
Chile	4	2	1	1	14-6	5
Paraguay	4	1	0	3	8-20	2
Bolivia	4	0	0	4	2-24	0

1927 (OFFICIAL)

Champions ARGENTINA, in Peru

			H/T	F/T	Venue	Attend
30.10.27	ARGENTINA M Luna 2, A Carricaberry 2, H Recannatine,, M Seonae 2	v BOLIVIA Algorta		7-1	Estadio Nacional Lima	15,000
01.11.27	PERU	v URUGUAY H Castro 2, H Scarone, Figueroa	(0-0)	0-4	Estadio Nacional	22,000
06.11.27	URUGUAY P Petrone, R Figueroa 3, Arremon H Castro, H Scarone	v BOLIVIA		9-0	Estadio Nacional	6,000
13.11.27	PERU J Sarmiento, D Neira, A Montallanes	v BOLIVIA Buitamente 2	(3-2)	3-2	Estadio Nacional	15,000
20.11.27	ARGENTINA H Recanattini, M Luna, Cavavessi own goal	v URUGUAY H Scarone 2		3-2	Estadio Nacional	26,000
27.11.27	PERU A Villanueva	v ARGENTINA J Maglio 2, M Ferreira, Orsi H Carricaberry		1-5	Lima	

Argentina	3	3	0	0	15-4	6
Uruguay	3	2	0	1	15-3	4
Peru	3	1	0	2	4-11	2
Bolivia	3	0	0	3	3-19	0

1929

Champions ARGENTINA, in Argentina

			H/T	F/T	Venue	Atten
01.11.29	PARAGUAY Sosa Lago, A Gonzalez 2	v URUGUAY		3-0	River Plate Std Buenos Aires	40,00

03.11.29	ARGENTINA	v PERU		3-0	San Lorenzo Std	20,000
	C Peucelle, A Zumelzu					
10.11.29	ARGENTINA	v PARAGUAY		4-1	San Lorenzo Std	20,000
	M Ferreyra 2, M Evaristo, R Cherro	D Dominguez				
11.11.29	URUGUAY	v PERU		4-1	River Plate Std	22,000
	L Fernandez, J L Andrade	Bulnes				
16.11.29	PERU	v PARAGUAY		0-5	Independiente	8,000
		L Nessi, A Gonzalez 3,				
		D Dominguez				
17.11.29	ARGENTINA	v URUGUAY		2-0	San Lorenzo Std	60,000
	M Ferreyra, M Evaristo					

Argentina	3	3	0	0	9-1	6
Paraguay	3	2	0	1	9-4	4
Uruguay	3	1	0	2	4-6	2
Peru	3	0	0	3	1-12	0

1935 (UNOFFICIAL-EXTRAORDINARIOS)

Champions URUGUAY, in Peru

			H/T	F/T	Venue	Attend
06.01.35	ARGENTINA	v CHILE		4-1	Estadio Nacional	25,000
	L Arrieta, M Lauri, H Masantonio,	A Carmona			Lima	
	D Garcia					
13.01.35	URUGUAY	v PERU	1-0	1-0	Estadio Nacional	28,000
	H Castro					
18.01.35	URUGUAY	v CHILE		2-1	Estadio Nacional	13,000
	A Ciocca 2	C Giudice				
20.01.35	ARGENTINA	v PERU	1-1	4-1	Estadio Nacional	28,000
	D Garcia 2, H Masantonio 3	T Fernandez				
26.01.35	PERU	v CHILE	1-0	1-0	Estadio Nacional	12,000
	A Montellanes					
27.01.35	URUGUAY	v ARGENTINA		3-0	Estadio Nacional	25,000
	A Cicoca, Taboada, H Castro					

Uruguay	3	3	0	0	6-1	6
Argentina	3	2	0	1	8-5	4
Peru	3	1	0	2	2-5	2
Chile	3	0	0	3	2-7	0

1937 (OFFICIAL)

Champions ARGENTINA, in Argentina

			H/T	F/T	Venue	Attend
27.12.36	BRAZIL	v PERU	3-2	3-2	Buenos Aires	
	Afonsinho, I Roberto, Nignho	T Fernandez, A Villanueve				
30.12.36	ARGENTINA	v CHILE		2-1	Buenos Aires	
	F Varallo 2	R Toro				
02.01.37	PARAGUAY	v URUGUAY		4-2	Buenos Aires	
	Cambai Ortega 2, A Erico,	S. Varela 2				
	A Gonzalez					
03.01.37	BRAZIL	v CHILE		6-4	Buenos Aires	
	Luiz M Oliveira 2, Patesko 2,	R Toro 2, J Avendano, G Rivaros				
	Carvalho Leite, I Roberto					
06.01.37	URUGUAY	v PERU	2-2	4-2	Buenos Aires	
	Chanaiti 2, S Varela 2	T Fernandez, A Magallanes				

SOUTH AMERICAN CHAMPIONSHIPS

09.01.37	ARGENTINA	v PARAGUAY		6-1	Buenos Aires
	A Zozaya 3, A Scopelli 2,	A. Gonzalez			
	E Garcia				
09.01.37	URUGUAY	v CHILE		0-3	Buenos Aires
	R Toro 2, M Arancibia				
13.01.37	BRAZIL	v PARAGUAY		5-0	Buenos Aires
	Luiz M Oliveira 2, Tim 2,				
	Carvalho Leite				
16.01.37	ARGENTINA	v PERU	1-0	1-0	Buenos Aires
	F Varello				
17.01.37	PARAGUAY	v CHILE		3-2	Buenos Aires
	Amarilla, Nunez Velloso, M Flor	R Toro 2			
19.01.37	BRAZIL	v URUGUAY		3-2	Buenos Aires
	Bahia, Carvalho Leite, Niginho	Roselli, Piriz			
21.01.37	CHILE	v PERU	1-2	2-2	Buenos Aires
	G Torres, M Arancibia	J Alcalde 2			
23.01.37	ARGENTINA	v URUGUAY		2-3	Buenos Aires
	A Zozaya, F Varello	Iturbide, Piriz, S Varela			
24.01.37	PARAGUAY	v PERU	0-1	0-1	Buenos Aires
	A Magallanes				
30.01.37	ARGENTINA	v BRAZIL		1-0	Buenos Aires
	E Garcia				
01.02.37	ARGENTINA	v BRAZIL		2-0	Buenos Aires
	V de la Mata, B Ferreira				Championship play off

Argentina	5	4	0	1	12-5	8
Brazil	5	4	0	1	17-9	8
Paraguay	5	2	0	3	10-16	4
Uruguay	5	2	0	3	11-14	4
Chile	5	1	1	3	12-13	3
Peru	5	1	1	3	7-10	3

1939 (OFFICIAL)

Champions PERU, in Peru

			H/T	F/T	Venue	Attend
15.01.39	PERU	v ECUADOR		3-0	5-2	Lima
	T Fernandez 2, J Alcade 2,	E Herrera, A Suarez				
	P Ibanez					
15.01.39	PARAGUAY	v CHILE			5-1	Lima
	E Mingo, T Godoy 2, M Barrios,	E Sorrel penalty				
	Aquino					
22.01.39	PERU	v CHILE	0-0	3-1	Lima
	T Fernandez 3 (1 penalty)	A Dominguez				
22.01.39	URUGUAY	v ECUADOR			6-0	Lima
	S Varela 2, A Ciocca, Chirimino	R Porta, Chamaiti				
29.01.39	PERU	v PARAGUAY	2-0	3-0	Lima
	J Fernandez 2, J Alcalde					
29.01.39	URUGUAY	v CHILE			3-2	Lima
	S Varela 2, R Porta	R Munoz, R Luco				
05.02.39	CHILE	v ECUADOR			4-1	Lima
	R Toro, J Avendano 2, E Sorrel pen					
05.02.39	PARAGUAY	v URUGUAY			1-3	Lima
	M Barrios	A Ciocca, R Porta, S Varela				
12.02.39	PERU	v URUGUAY	1-0	2-1	Lima
	J Alcade, V Bielich	Ciocca				
12.02.39	PARAGUAY	v ECUADOR			3-1	Lima
	T Godoy, Bareiro 2					

Peru	4	4	0	0	13-4	8
Uruguay	4	3	0	1	13-5	6
Paraguay	4	2	0	2	9-8	4
Chile	4	1	0	3	8-12	2
Ecuador	4	0	0	4	4-18	0

SOUTH AMERICAN CHAMPIONSHIPS

1941 (UNOFFICIAL-EXTRAORDINARIOS)

Champions ARGENTINA, in PERU

			H/T	F/T	Venue	Attend
02.02.41	CHILE R Toro, E Sorrel 2, M Arancibia, A Contreres	v ECUADOR		5-0	SANTIAGO	
02.02.41	URUGUAY R Porta 3, Rivaro, Riepoff	v ECUADOR		6-0	Santiago	
09.02.41	CHILE R Perez	v PERU	(1-0)	1-0	Santiago	
12.02.41	ARGENTINA J Marvezzi 2	v PERU C Socarraz	(1-0)	2-1	Santiago	
16.02.41	CHILE	v URUGUAY Magliano, Rivero		0-2	Santiago	
16.02.41	ARGENTINA J Marvezzi 2, E Garcia 2, J M Moreno 2	v ECUADOR		6-1	Santiago	
23.02.41	PERU T Fernandez 3, M Vallejas	v ECUADOR	(3-0)	4-0	Santiago	
23.02.41	ARGENTINA A Pedernera	v URUGUAY		1-0	Santiago	
26.02.41	URUGUAY Magliano, R Porta	v PERU	(1-0)	2-0	Santiago	
04.03.41	CHILE	v ARGENTINA J Marvezzi		0-1	Santiago	

Argentina	4	4	0	0	10-2	8
Uruguay	4	3	0	1	10-1	6
Chile	4	2	0	2	6-3	4
Peru	4	1	0	3	5-5	2
Ecuador	4	0	0	4	1-21	0

1942 (OFFICIAL)

Champions URUGUAY, in Uruguay

		H/T	F/T	Venue	Attend
10.01.42	URUGUAY Le Castro 2, O Varela, A Ciocca, Zapirain, R Porta	v CHILE A Contreras	(4-1)	6-1	Montevideo
11.01.42	ARGENTINA E Sandoval, H Massantonio 2, A Perucca	v PARAGUAY Aveiro, Sanchez, M Barrios		4-3	Montevideo
14.01.42	BRAZIL Pirilo 3, Claudio C Pinho, Patesko 2	v CHILE A Dominguez	(2-1)	6-1	Montevideo
17.01.42	URUGUAY S Varela 3, R Porta 2, Zapirain, Cambatta	v ECUADOR	(6-0)	7-0	Montevideo
18.01.42	ARGENTINA L Rossini, H Massantonio	v BRAZIL Servilio I		2-1	Montevideo
18.01.42	PARAGUAY M Barrios	v PERU A Magallanes	(1-1)	1-1	Montevideo
21.01.42	BRAZIL Pedro Amorim 2	v PERU T Fernandez	(1-0)	2-1	Montevideo
22.01.42	ARGENTINA J M Moreno 5, H Massantonio 3, E.Garcia, A Pedernera 2, A R Laferrara	v ECUADOR		12-0	Montevideo
22.01.42	PARAGUAY M Barrios, Baudo Franco	v CHILE	(2-0)	2-0	Montevideo

155

SOUTH AMERICAN CHAMPIONSHIPS

24.01.42	URUGUAY S Varela	v BRAZIL		1-0	Montevideo
25.01.42	ARGENTINA J C Heredia, J M Moreno 2	v PERU T Fernandez	(1-1)	3-1	Montevideo
27.01.42	URUGUAY S Varela, A Ciocca, R Porta	v PARAGUAY M Barrios		3-1	Montevideo
28.01.42	PERU L Quinonez, L Guzman	v ECUADOR Alcivar	(1-0)	2-1	Montevideo
31.01.42	ARGENTINA	v CHILE		0-0	Montevideo
31.01.42	PARAGUAY Baudo Franco, E Mingo, Ibarrola	v ECUADOR		3-1	Montevideo
01.02.42	BRAZIL Pirilo 3, Tim, Zizinho	v ECUADOR Alvarez penalty		5-1	Montevideo
01.02.42	URUGUAY S Varela, A Ciocca, Le Castro	v PERU	(2-0)	3-0	Montevideo
05.02.42	CHILE A Dominguez, G Casanova	v ECUADOR	(0-0)	2-1	Montevideo
05.02.42	BRAZIL Zizinho	v PARAGUAY Baudo Franco		1-1	Montevideo
07.02.42	CHILE	v PERU		0-0	Montevideo
07.02.42	URUGUAY Zapirain	v ARGENTINA	(1-0)	1-0	Montevideo

Uruguay	6	6	0	0	21-2	12
Argentina	6	4	1	1	21-6	9
Brazil	6	3	1	2	15-7	7
Paraguay	6	2	2	2	11-10	6
Peru	6	1	2	3	5-10	4
Chile	6	1	2	3	4-15	4
Ecuador	6	0	0	6	4-31	0

1945 (UNOFFICIAL-EXTRAORDINARIOS)

Champions ARGENTINA, in CHILE

			H/T	F/T	Venue	Attend
14.01.45	CHILE J Alcantara 3, E Vera, F Hormazabal, G Clavero	v ECUADOR Raymondi, Jimenez, Mendoza		6-3	Santiago	
18.01.45	ARGENTINA N Mendez 2, F Pontoni 2	v BOLIVIA		4-0	Santiago	
18.01.45	URUGUAY A Garcia 2, R Porta, L Castro, J Garcia	ECUADOR		5-1	Santiago	
21.01.45	BRAZIL Heleno de Freitas, Jaime, Jorginho I	v COLOMBIA		3-0	Santiago	
21.01.45	URUGUAY A Garcia 2	v BOLIVIA		2-0	Santiago	
24.01.45	CHILE G Clavaro 2, J Alcantara 2, D Medina	v BOLIVIA		5-0	Santiago	
28.01.45	URUGUAY A Garcia 2, J Garcia, L Castro Riepoff, R Porta, Zapirain	v COLOMBIA	(2-0)	7-0	Santiago	
28.01.45	BRAZIL Tesourinha, Ademir Menezes	v BOLIVIA		2-0	Santiago	
31.01.45	CHILE D Medina, M Pinero	v COLOMBIA		2-0	Santiago	
31.01.45	ARGENTINA F Pontoni 2, R Martino 2	v ECUADOR Raymondi, Mendoza		4-2	Santiago	
??.02.45	COLOMBIA	v BOLIVIA		3-3	Santiago	
??.02.45	COLOMBIA	v ECUADOR		3-1	Santiago	

156

07.02.45	ARGENTINA F Pontoni, N Mendez 3, J Ferraro, R Martino 2, J Munoz, A Perucca	v COLOMBIA Mendoza	(6-0)	9-1	Santiago
07.02.45	BRAZIL Heleno de Freitas 2, Rui	v URUGUAY		3-0	Santiago
11.01.45	BOLIVIA	v ECUADOR		0-0	Santiago
11.02.45	CHILE D Medina	v ARGENTINA F Pontoni		1-1	Santiago
14.02.45	ARGENTINA N Mendez 3	v BRAZIL Ademir Menezes		3-1	Santiago
18.02.45	CHILE D Medina	v URUGUAY		1-0	Santiago
21.02.45	BRAZIL Ademir Menezes 3, Jair R Pinto 2, Heleno de Freitas 2, Zizinho 2	v ECUADOR		9-0	Santiago
25.02.45	ARGENTINA R Martino	v URUGUAY		1-0	Santiago
28.02.45	CHILE	v BRAZIL Heleno de Freitas		0-1	Santiago

Argentina	6	5	1	0	22-5	11
Brazil	6	5	0	1	19-3	10
Chile	6	4	1	1	15-4	9
Uruguay	6	3	0	3	14-6	6
Colombia	6	1	1	4	7-25	3
Bolivia	6	0	2	4	3-16	2
Ecuador	6	0	1	5	7-27	1

1946 (UNOFFICIAL-EXTRAORDINARIOS)

Champions ARGENTINA, in ARGENTINA

			H/T	F/T	Venue	Attend
12.01.46	ARGENTINA N Mendez 2	v PARAGUAY		2-0	Buenos Aires	
16.01.46	BRAZIL Heleno de Freitas 2, Zizinho	v BOLIVIA		3-0	Buenos Aires	
16.01.46	CHILE	v URUGUAY D Medina		0-1	Buenos Aires	
19.01.46	CHILE J Araya, V Mancilla penalty	v PARAGUAY P Rolon		2-1	Buenos Aires	
19.01.46	ARGENTINA J Salvini 2, A Labruna 2, V de la Mata, A Pedernera, F Loustau	v BOLIVIA Peredo		7-1	Buenos Aires	
23.01.46	BRAZIL Jair R Pinto 2, Heleno de Freitas, Chico	v URUGUAY D Medina 2, Vasquez		4-3	Buenos Aires	
26.01.46	PARAGUAY JB Villalba 2, B Caceres, R Genes	v BOLIVIA Coronel own goal, Ortega		4-2	Buenos Aires	
26.01.46	ARGENTINA A Labruna 2, R Martino	v CHILE J Alcantara		3-1	Buenos Aires	
29.01.46	BRAZIL Norival	v PARAGUAY J B Villalba		1-1	Buenos Aires	
29.01.46	URUGUAY J Schiaffino 2, Medina, Riepoff, L Castro	v BOLIVIA		5-0	Buenos Aires	
02.02.46	ARGENTINA M Boye, A Labruna, N Mendez	v URUGUAY Zapirain		3-1	Buenos Aires	
03.02.46	BRAZIL Zizinho 4, Chico	v CHILE S.Salfate penalty		5-1	Buenos Aires	
08.02.46	CHILE O Saez 2, A Cremaschi, D Medina	v BOLIVIA		4-1	Buenos Aires	

08.02.46	PARAGUAY *J B Villalba, A Rodriquez*	v URUGUAY *J.Schiaffino*		2-1	Buenos Aires
10.02.46	ARGENTINA *N Mendez 2*	BRAZIL		2-0	Buenos Aires

Argentina	5	5	0	0	17-3	10
Brazil	5	3	1	1	13-7	7
Paraguay	5	2	1	2	8-8	5
Uruguay	5	2	0	3	11-9	4
Chile	5	2	0	3	8-11	4
Bolivia	5	0	0	5	4-23	0

1947 (OFFICIAL)

Champions ARGENTINA, in ECUADOR

02.12.47	ECUADOR	v BOLIVIA		2-2	Guayaquil
02.12.47	ARGENTINA *F Loustou 2, F Pontoni 2, N Mendez, M Boye*	v PARAGUAY		6-0	Guayaquil
02.12.47	URUGUAY *Falero, J Garcia*	v COLOMBIA	(1-0)	2-0	Guayaquil
04.12.47	ECUADOR	v COLOMBIA		0-0	Guayaquil
04.12.47	ARGENTINA *A Di Stefano 3, N Mendez, M Boye, F.Pontoni, F.Loustou*	v BOLIVIA		7-0	Guayaquil
06.12.47	BOLIVIA	v COLOMBIA		0-0	Guayaquil
06.12.47	PARAGUAY *J B Villalba, R Genes*	v PERU *F Castillo, M.Mosquera*	(1-1)	2-2	Guayaquil
06.12.47	URUGUAY *Magliano 2, J.Garcia 2, Sarro, Brittos*	v CHILE		6-0	Guayaquil
08.12.47	ECUADOR	v PARAGUAY *L Marin 3, R Genes*		0-4	Guayaquil
09.12.47	CHILE *C Varala, O Saez*	v PERU *V Lopez*	(2-0)	2-1	Guayaquil
10.12.47	PARAGUAY *L Marin, R Genes, E Avalos*	v BOLIVIA		3-1	Guayaquil
10.12.47	URUGUAY *Falero, Sarro, Riepoff*	v BOLIVIA		3-0	Guauaquil
11.12.47	PARAGUAY *J B Villalba 2*	v COLOMBIA		3-0	Guayaquil
11.12.47	ECUADOR	v CHILE *P Lopez, J Penaloza 2*		0-3	Guayaquil
11.12.47	ARGENTINA *M Boye, F Pontoni, J M Moreno*	v PERU *C Gomez, V Lopez*	(1-1)	3-2	Guayaquil
13.12.47	PARAGUAY *R Genes, L Marin 2, J B illalba*	v URUGUAY *Brittos, Falero*		4-2	Guayaquil
16.12.47	ARGENTINA *F Pontoni*	v CHILE *F Riera*		1-1	Guayaquil
18.12.47	ARGENTINA *F Loustou 2, M Boye 2, A Di Stefano, N Mendez*	v COLOMBIA	(3-0)	6-0	Guayaquil
18.12.47	ECUADOR	v URUGUAY *Falero 2, J Garcia 2, Sarro, Magliano*		1-6	Guayaquil
20.12.47	ECUADOR	v PERU		0-0	Guayaquil
23.12.47	PERU *C Gomez 2, M Mosquera, L Guzman 2*	v COLOMBIA *Arango*	(1-0)	5-1	Guayaquil
23.12.47	CHILE	v PARAGUAY *J B Villalba*		0-1	Guayaquil
25.12.47	ECUADOR	v ARGENTINA *A Di Stefano, F Loustou*		0-2	Guayaquil

25.12.47	URUGUAY	v PERU		(0-0)	1-0	Guayaquil
	Falero					
27.12.47	PERU	v BOLIVIA		(2-0)	2-0	Guayaquil
	L Guzman, F Castillo					
27.12.47	CHILE	v COLOMBIA			4-1	Guayaquil
	A Prieto, O Saez 2, F Riera					
28.12.47	ARGENTINA	v URUGUAY			3-1	Guayaquil
	F Pontoni, N Mendez,	*J.Garcia*				
	A Di Stefano					
30.12.47	CHILE	v BOLIVIA			4-3	Guayaquil
	R Infante 2, O Sacz, P Lopez					

Argentina	7	6	1	0	28-4	13
Paraguay	7	5	1	1	16-11	11
Uruguay	7	5	0	2	21-8	10
Chile	7	4	1	2	14-13	9
Peru	7	2	2	3	12-9	6
Ecuador	7	0	3	4	3-17	3
Bolivia	7	0	2	5	6-21	2
Colombia	7	0	2	5	2-19	2

1949 (OFFICIAL)

Champions BRAZIL, in BRAZIL

			H/T	F/T	Venue	Attend
02.04.49	BRAZIL	v ECUADOR		9-1	Rio de Janeiro	
	Jair R Pinto 2, Simao 2,					
	Tesourinha 2, Ademir Menezes,					
	Otavio, Zizin					
06.04.49	BOLIVIA	v CHILE		3-2	Sao Paulo	
		F Riera, M.Salamanca				
08.05.49	BOLIVIA	v ECUADOR		2-0	Rio de Janeiro	
06.04.49	PARAGUAY	v COLOMBIA		3-0	Sao Paulo	
	D Benitez, Lopez Fretes 2					
10.04.49	PARAGUAY	v ECUADOR		1-0	Rio de Janeiro	
	M Barrios					
10.04.49	PERU	v COLOMBIA	(1-0)	4-0	Rio de Janeiro	
	V Pedroza 2, R Drago, F Castillo					
10.04.49	BRAZIL	v BOLIVIA		10-1	Sao Paulo	
	Nininho 3, Claudio C Pinho 2,					
	Zizinho 2, Simao 2, Jair R Pinto					
13.04.49	PARAGUAY	v PERU	(1-0)	3-1	Rio de Janeiro	
	M Barrios, D Arce, Lopez Fretes	*G.Colunga*				
13.04.49	BRAZIL	v CHILE		2-1	Sao Paulo	
	Claudio C Pinho, Zizinho	*P.Lopez*				
13.04.49	URUGUAY	v ECUADOR	(2-2)	3-2	Rio de Janeiro	
	R Castro 2, Moreno					
17.04.49	CHILE	v ECUADOR		1-0	Rio de Janeiro	
	C R Rojas					
17.04.49	BRAZIL	v COLOMBIA		5-0	Sao Paulo	
	Ademir Menezes 2,					
	Orlando Pingo de Ouro,					
	Tesournha, Canhoteiro					
17.04.49	URUGUAY	v BOLIVIA	(0-0)	2-3	Rio de Janeiro	
	Moll, Suarez					
20.04.49	CHILE	v COLOMBIA		1-1	Rio de Janeiro	
	P Lopez	*F Verdugo*				
20.04.49	PERU	v ECUADOR	(2-0)	4-0	Rio de Janeiro	
	J E Salinas, Bermego own goal,					
	F Castillo, V Pedroza					
20.04.49	PARAGUAY	v URUGUAY	(0-1)	1-2	Sao Paulo	
	D Arce	*J Garcia 2*				

24.04.49	BRAZIL Jair R Pinho 2, Simao, Augusto, Arce own goal, Orlando Pingo de Ouro, Ademir Menezes	v PERU JE.Salinas	(4-1)	7-1	Rio de Janeiro
24.04.49	URUGUAY R Martinez, Ayala	v COLOMBIA L Castelbondo, A Perez	(0-1)	2-2	Sao Paulo
27.04.49	PARAGUAY Arce 3, Benitez	v CHILE A Cremaschi, U Ramos		4-2	Sao Paulo
27.04.49	PERU R Drago 2, G Heredia penalty	v BOLIVIA	(1-0)	3-0	Sao Paulo
30.04.49	PERU A Mosquera 2, F Castillo	v CHILE	(1-0)	3-0	Sao Paulo
30.04.49	BRAZIL Jair R Pinto 2, Danilo Alvim, Tesourinha, Zizinho	v URUGUAY R Castro	(3-1)	5-1	Rio de Janeiro
??.05.49	PARAGUAY D Benitez 4, D Arce 2, P Fernandez	v BOLIVIA		7-0	Rio de Janeiro
03.05.49	ECUADOR	v COLOMBIA N Perez		4-1	Rio de Janeiro
04.05.49	URUGUAY Moll, R Castro, Ayala	v PERU A Mosquera, F Castillo, C Gomez 2	(0-2)	3-4	Rio de Janeiro
06.05.49	BOLIVIA	v COLOMBIA		4-0	Rio de Janeiro
08.05.49	URUGUAY Ayala	v CHILE R Infante 2, 1 penalty, A Cremaschi	(0-1)	1-3	Belo Horizonte
08.05.49	BRAZIL Tesourinha	v PARAGUAY E Avalos, D Benitez		1-2	Rio de Janeiro
11.05.49	BRAZIL Ademir Menezes 3, Jair R Pinto 2, Tesourinha 2	v PARAGUAY		7-0 po	Rio de Janeiro Championship play off

Brazil	7	6	0	1	39-7	12
Paraguay	7	6	0	1	21-6	12
Peru	7	5	0	2	20-13	10
Bolivia	7	4	0	3	13-24	8
Uruguay	7	2	1	4	14-20	5
Chile	7	2	1	4	10-14	5
Ecuador	7	1	0	6	7-21	2
Colombia	7	0	2	5	4-23	2

1953 (OFFICIAL)

Champions PARAGUAY, in PERU

			H/T	F/T	Venue	Attend
??.02.53	PARAGUAY	v ECUADOR		0-0	Lima	
??.02.53	URUGUAY	v ECUADOR		6-0	Lima	
22.02.53	PERU	v BOLIVIA Calderon own goal	(0-0)	0-1	Lima	
25.02.53	PARAGUAY A Berni, R Fernandez 2	v CHILE		3-0	Lima	
25.02.53	URUGUAY O Mendez 2	v BOLIVIA	(1-0)	2-0	Lima	
28.02.53	PERU C Gomez	v ECUADOR	(0-0)	1-0	Lima	
??.03.53	PARAGUAY Romerito, A Berni penalty	v BOLIVIA		2-1	Lima	
??.03.53	ECUADOR	v BOLIVIA		1-1	Lima	
01.03.53	URUGUAY Morel, Puentez	v CHILE F Molina 3	(0-1)	2-3	Lima	
01.03.53	BRAZIL Julinho I 4, Pinga I 2, Rodrigues II 2	v BOLIVIA		8-1	Lima	
04.03.53	PERU	v CHILE		0-0	Lima	

08.03.53	PERU *A Terry, E Villamares*	v PARAGUAY *R Fernandez, A Berni*	(1-1)	2-2	Lima
12.03.53	URUGUAY *Pelaez, Romero*	v PARAGUAY *A Lopez, A Berni*		2-2	Lima
12.03.53	BRAZIL *Ademir Menezes, Claudio C Pinho*	v ECUADOR		2-0	LIMA
15.03.53	URUGUAY	v BRAZIL *Ipojucan*	(0-0)	0-1	Lima
19.03.53	CHILE *F Molina 2, A Cremaschi*	v ECUADOR		3-0	Lima
19.03.53	PERU *L Navarrete*	v BRAZIL	(0-0)	1-0	Lima
23.03.53	BRAZIL *Baltazar I, Julinho I, Zizinho*	v CHILE *F Molina 2*		3-2	Lima
27.03.53	PARAGUAY *A Lopez, P Leon*	v BRAZIL *Nilton Santos*		2-1	Lima
28.03.53	CHILE *G Diaz 2*	v BOLIVIA *Brown, Alcon*		2-2	Lima
28.03.53	PERU	v URUGUAY *Puentez 3*	(0-2)	0-3	Lima
01.04.53	PARAGUAY *A Lopez, M Gavilan, R Fernandez*	v BRAZIL *Baltazar 2*		3-2 po	Lima Championship play off

Paraguay	6	4	2	0	10-4	8
Brazil	6	4	0	2	15-6	8
Uruguay	6	3	0	3	13-5	6
Chile	6	2	2	2	10-10	6
Peru	6	2	2	2	4-6	6
Bolivia	6	1	1	4	6-15	3
Ecuador	6	0	2	4	1-13	2

1955 (OFFICIAL)

Champions ARGENTINA, in CHILE

			H/T	F/T	Venue	Attend
27.02.55	CHILE *E Hormazabal 3, G Diaz 2, R Melendez, J Robledo*	v ECUADOR		7-1	Santiago	
01.03.55	ECUADOR	v PARAGUAY *M Rolon 2*		0-2	Santiago	
03.03.55	ARGENTINA *A Labruna, R Bonelli, C Cecconato, R Michelli, E Grillo*	v PARAGUAY *M Rolon, S Villalba, J.Parodi*	(2-1)	5-3	Santiago	
06.03.55	CHILE *J Robledo 2, M Munoz, E Hormazabal, J.Ramirez*	v PERU *F Castillo, G Barbadillo, C Heredia penalty, O Gomez*	(2-1)	5-4	Santiago	
09.03.55	URUGUAY *O Miguez 2, C Borges*	v PARAGUAY *M Rolon*	(2-1)	3-1	Santiago	
09.03.55	ARGENTINA *R Bonelli, E Grillo, R Michelli, J Borello*	v ECUADOR	(1-0)	4-0	Santiago	
13.03.55	ECUADOR *Matute 2*	v PERU *O Gomez 2, Gonzaby own goal, M Mosquera*	(1-3)	2-4	Santiago	
13.03.55	CHILE *M Munoz, E Hormazabal*	v URUGUAY *Galvan 2*	(1-2)	2-2	Santiago	
16.03.55	ARGENTINA *E Grillo, C Cecconato*	v PERU *O.Gomez 2*	(2-1)	2-2	Santiago	
20.03.55	CHILE *R Melendez 2, M Munoz 2, E Hormazabal penalty*	v PARAGUAY		5-0	Santiago	
23.03.55	PERU *A Terry*	v PARAGUAY *M Rolon*	(1-0)	1-1	Santiago	

161

SOUTH AMERICAN CHAMPIONSHIPS

23.03.55	ECUADOR	v URUGUAY	(1-2)	1-5	Santiago
	J C Abbadie 2, Galvan, O Miguez,				
	J Perez				
27.03.55	ARGENTINA	v URUGUAY		6-1	Santiago
	A Labruna 3, R Michelli 2, J Borello	O Miguez			
30.03.55	PERU	v URUGUAY	(1-0)	2-1	Santiago
	R Castillo, O Gomez	Morel			
30.03.55	CHILE	v ARGENTINA	(0-0)	0-1	Santiago
		R Michelli			

Argentina	5	4	1	0	18-6	9
Chile	5	3	1	1	19-8	7
Peru	5	2	2	1	13-11	6
Uruguay	5	2	1	2	12-12	5
Paraguay	5	1	1	3	7-14	3
Ecuador	5	0	0	5	4-22	0

1956 (UNOFFICIAL-EXTRAORDINARIOS)

Champions URUGUAY, in URUGUAY

			H/T	F/T	Venue	Attend
21.01.56	URUGUAY	v PARAGUAY	(3-0)	4-2	Montevideo	
	Escalada 2, O Miguez, Roque	M Rolon, A R Gomez				
22.01.56	ARGENTINA	v PERU	(1-0)	2-1	Montevideo	
	R Michelli, F Vairo	R Drago				
24.01.56	BRAZIL	v CHILE		1-4	Montevideo	
	Maurinho	E Hormazabal 2, R Melendez,				
	L Sanchez					
28.01.56	URUGUAY	v PERU	(1-0)	2-0	Montevideo	
	Escalada, O Miguez					
29.01.56	ARGENTINA	v CHILE	(0-0)	2-0	Montevideo	
	A Labruna 2					
29.01.56	PARAGUAY	v BRAZIL		0-0	Montevideo	
01.02.56	BRAZIL	v PERU		(1-1)	Montevideo	
	Alvaro, Zezinho	R Drago				
01.02.56	PARAGUAY	v ARGENTINA	(0-0)	0-1	Montevideo	
		R Bonelli				
05.02.56	PARAGUAY	v PERU	(0-0)	1-1	Montevideo	
	M Rolon	C Lazon				
05.02.56	BRAZIL	v ARGENTINA		1-0	Montevideo	
	Luizinho					
06.02.56	URUGUAY	v CHILE	(0-0)	2-1	Montevideo	
	O Miguez, C Borges	J Ramirez				
09.02.56	CHILE	v PERU	(2-1)	4-3	Montevideo	
	E Hormazabal, J Fernandez,	F Castillo, M Mosquera, O Gomez				
	M Munoz, L.Sanchez					
10.02.56	URUGUAY	v BRAZIL		0-0	Montevideo	
12.02.56	PARAGUAY	v CHILE		0-2	Montevideo	
		E Hormazabal, J Ramirez				
15.02.56	URUGUAY	v ARGENTINA	(1-0)	1-0	Montevideo	
	J Ambrois					

Uruguay	5	4	1	0	9-3	9
Brazil	5	3	2	0	7-2	8
Argentina	5	3	0	2	5-3	6
Chile	5	2	0	3	8-11	4
Paraguay	5	0	2	3	3-8	2
Peru	5	0	1	4	6-11	1

SOUTH AMERICAN CHAMPIONSHIPS

1957 (OFFICIAL)

Champions ARGENTINA, in PERU

				H/T	F/T	Venue	Attend
07.03.57	URUGUAY	v	ECUADOR		5-2	Lima	
	J Ambrois 4, J F Sasia						
10.03.57	PERU	v	ECUADOR	(1-1)	2-1	Lima	
	A Terry 2		*Cantos*				
13.03.57	ARGENTINA	v	COLOMBIA	(4-2)	8-2	Lima	
	H Maschio 5, J Sanfilippo, O Cruz,		*D Gamboa penalty, Valencia*				
	O Corbatta						
13.03.57	BRAZIL	v	CHILE		4-2	Lima	
	Didi 3, Pepe		*J Ramirez, J Fernandez*				
16.03.57	PERU	v	CHILE	(0-0)	1-0	Lima	
	M Mosquera						
17.03.57	ARGENTINA	v	ECUADOR	(3-0)	3-0	Lima	
	A Angelillo 2, E O Sivori						
17.03.57	URUGUAY	v	COLOMBIA	(0-1)	0-1	Lima	
	C Arango						
20.03.57	ARGENTINA	v	URUGUAY	(1-0)	4-0	Lima	
	H Maschio 2, A Anelillo,						
	J Sanfilippo						
21.03.57	COLOMBIA	v	CHILE		2-3	Lima	
	J Gutierrez, A Carrillo		*C Verdejo 2, S Espinoza*				
21.03.57	BRAZIL	v	ECUADOR		7-1	Lima	
	Joel 2, Evaristo 2, Zizinho, Pepe,						
	Didi						
23.03.57	BRAZIL	v	COLOMBIA		9-0	Lima	
	Evaristo 5, Didi 2, Zizinho, Pepe						
23.03.57	PERU	v	URUGUAY	(1-2)	3-5	Lima	
	A Terry, J Seminario, M Mosquera		*J Ambrois 3, Carranza, Campero*				
24.03.57	CHILE	v	ECUADOR		2-2	Lima	
	J Ramirez 2						
27.03.57	PERU	v	COLOMBIA	(3-0)	4-1	Lima	
	A Terry, M Rivera 2, J Bassa		*C Arango*				
28.03.57	ARGENTINA	v	CHILE	(2-2)	6-2	Lima	
	A Angelillo 2, H Maschio 2,		*J.Fernandez 2*				
	E O Sivori, O Corbatta						
28.03.57	URUGUAY	v	BRAZIL	(1-0)	3-2	Lima	
	J Ambrois, Campero 2		*Evaristo, Didi*				
31.03.57	PERU	v	BRAZIL	(0-0)	0-1	Lima	
			Didi penalty				
01.04.57	COLOMBIA	v	ECUADOR		4-1	Lima	
	D Gamboa 2, Alvarez, J Gutierrez						
01.04.57	URUGUAY	v	CHILE		2-0	Lima	
	Pippo, J Ambrois						
03.04.57	ARGENTINA	v	BRAZIL	(1-0)	3-0	Lima	
	H Maschio 2, O Cruz						
06.04.57	PERU	v	ARGENTINA	(1-0)	2-1	Lima	
	M Mosquera, A.Terry		*E O Sivori*				

Argentina	6	5	0	1	25-6	10
Brazil	6	4	0	2	23-9	8
Uruguay	6	4	0	2	15-12	8
Peru	6	4	0	2	12-9	8
Colombia	6	2	0	4	10-25	4
Chile	6	1	1	4	9-17	3
Ecuador	6	0	1	5	7-23	1

SOUTH AMERICAN CHAMPIONSHIPS

1959 (OFFICIAL)

Champions ARGENTINA, in Argentina

Date			H/T	F/T	Venue	Attend
07.03.59	ARGENTINA *P Manfredini 2, J Pizzutti 2, E Calla, J Belen*	v CHILE *E H Alvarez*		6-1	Buenos Aires	90,000
08.03.59	URUGUAY *C Borges 2, D Perez, V H Guaglianone*	v BOLIVIA *Escalada, J F Sasia 2*	(3-0)	7-0	Buenos Aires	
10.03.59	BRAZIL *Pele, Didi*	v PERU *J Seminario 2*	(1-1)	2-2	Buenos Aires	35,000
11.03.59	ARGENTINA *O Corbatta, J Pisutti*	v BOLIVIA	(1-0)	2-0	Buenos Aires	
11.03.59	PARAGUAY *Aveiro 2*	v CHILE *L Sanchez penalty*		2-1	Buenos Aires	75,000
14.03.59	PERU *M Loayza 3, O Gomez, J Joya*	v URUGUAY *Demarco, D Douksas, J.F.Sasia*	(4-2)	5-3	Buenos Aires	40,000
15.03.59	PARAGUAY *C Re 3, I Sanabria, Aveiro*	v BOLIVIA		5-0	Buenos Aires	40,000
15.03.59	BRAZIL *Pele 2, Didi*	v CHILE		3-0	Buenos Aires	40,000
18.03.59	ARGENTINA *E Calla, O Corbatta penalty, R Sosa*	v PERU *A Terry*	(1-1)	3-1	Buenos Aires	100,000
19.03.59	PARAGUAY *Aveiro*	v URUGUAY *Demarco, D Douksas, J F Sasia*	(0-1)	1-3	Buenos Aires	100,000
21.03.59	BRAZIL *Pele, Paulo Valentim 2, Didi*	v BOLIVIA *Santos, Aramayo*		4-2	Buenos Aires	30,000
21.03.59	PERU *M Loayza*	v CHILE *M Moreno*		1-1	Buenos Aires	30,000
22.03.59	ARGENTINA *O Corbatta, L Cap, A Nardiello*	v PARAGUAY *I Sanabria*	(1-1)	3-1	Buenos Aires	55,000
26.03.59	CHILE *J Soto 2, M Soto 2, L Sanchez*	v BOLIVIA *Alcocer 2*		5-2	Buenos Aires	65,000
26.03.59	BRAZIL *Paulo Valentim 3*	v URUGUAY *Escalada*	(0-1)	3-1	Buenos Aires	65,000
29.03.59	PERU	v BOLIVIA		0-0	Buenos Aires	35,000
29.03.59	BRAZIL *Pele 3, Chinezinho*	v PARAGUAY *S Parodi*		4-1	Buenos Aires	35,000
29.03.59	ARGENTINA *J Belen 2, R Sosa 2*	v URUGUAY *Demarco*	(1-0)	4-1	Buenos Aires	75,000
02.04.59	PARAGUAY *Aveiro 2*	v PERU *O Gomez*	(1-0)	2-1	Buenos Aires	1,000
03.04.59	CHILE *M Moreno*	v URUGUAY	(0-0)	1-0	Buenos Aires	1,000
04.04.59	ARGENTINA *J Pizutti*	v BRAZIL *Pele*	(1-1)	1-1	Buenos Aires	100,000

Argentina	6	5	1	0	19-5	11
Brazil	6	4	2	0	17-7	10
Paraguay	6	3	0	3	12-12	6
Chile	6	2	1	3	9-14	5
Peru	6	1	3	2	10-11	5
Uruguay	6	2	0	4	15-14	4
Bolivia	6	0	1	5	4-23	1

1959 (UNOFFICIAL-EXTRAORDINARIOS)

Champions URUGUAY, in ECUADOR

				H/T	F/T	Venue	Attend
05.12.59	BRAZIL	v	PARAGUAY		3-2	Guayaquil	
	Paulo 2, Ze de Mello		*S Parodi, G Benitez*				
06.12.59	ECUADOR	v	URUGUAY	(0-2)	0-4	Guayaquil	
			Silveira, Escalada, M Bergara, D Perez				
09.12.59	ARGENTINA	v	PARAGUAY		4-2	Guayaquil	
	J Sanfilippo 3, R Sosa		*E Insfran, Cabral*				
12.12.59	ECUADOR	v	ARGENTINA	(1-0)	1-1	Guayaquil	
	R Sosa						
12.12.59	URUGUAY	v	BRAZIL	(0-0)	3-0	Guayaquil	
	Escalada, J F Sasia 2						
16.13.59	URUGUAY	v	ARGENTINA	(3-0)	5-0	Guayaquil	
	Silveira 2, M Bergara 2, J F Sasia						
19.12.59	ECUADOR	v	BRAZIL		1-3	Guayaquil	
			Ze de Mello, Paulo, Geraldo II				
22.12.59	URUGUAY	v	PARAGUAY		1-1	Guayaquil	
	J F Sasia		*S Parodi*				
22.12.59	ARGENTINA	v	BRAZIL	(2-1)	4-1	Guayaquil	
	J Sanfilippo 3, O Garcia		*Geraldo II*				
27.12.59	ECUADOR	v	PARAGUAY		3-1	Guayaquil	
			R Gomez own goal				

Uruguay	4	3	1	0	13-1	7
Argentina	4	2	1	1	9-9	5
Brazil	4	2	0	2	7-10	4
Ecuador	4	1	1	2	5-9	3
Paraguay	4	0	1	3	6-11	1

1963 (OFFICIAL)

Champions BOLIVIA, in BOLIVIA

				H/T	F/T	Venue	Attend
10.03.63	BOLIVIA	v	ECUADOR		4-4	La Paz	
	Lopez, Castillo, Camacho, Alcocer		*C Raffo, Raimondo, Gando, Bolanes*				
10.03.63	ARGENTINA	v	COLOMBIA	(2-2)	4-2	Cochabamba	
	M Savoy 2, J Vasquez, E Fernandez		*Campilla, G Aceros*				
10.03.63	BRAZIL	v	PERU	(1-0)	1-0	Cochabamba	
	Flavio II						
14.03.63	ARGENTINA	v	PERU	(0-0)	1-2	Cochabamba	
	M Savoy		*E Tenemas, V Segarra*				
14.03.63	PARAGUAY	v	ECUADOR		3-1	La Paz	
	Zarate, C Cabrera, O Quinonez		*C Raffo*				
14.03.63	BRAZIL	v	COLOMBIA		5-1	Cochabamba	
	Flavio II 2, Osvaldo, Marco Antonio, Fernando		*D Gamboa*				
17.03.63	BOLIVIA	v	COLOMBIA		2-1	Cochabamba	
	Alcocer, Lopez		*Botero*				
17.03.63	PERU	v	ECUADOR	(2-1)	2-1	La Paz	
	P Leon, N Mosquera		*C Raffo*				
17.03.63	PARAGUAY	v	BRAZIL		2-0	Cochabamba	
	Ayala, Arambulo						
20.03.63	PARAGUAY	v	COLOMBIA		3-2	La Paz	
	C Cabrera, Aramburu, Valdez		*Campilla, D Gamboa*				
20.03.63	ARGENTINA	v	ECUADOR	(1-1)	4-2	Cochabamba	
	M Savoy 2, M Rodriguez, R Zarate		*Pineda, Palacios*				

21.03.63	BOLIVIA	v PERU	(1-1)	3-2	La Paz
	Camacho, Alcocer, Garcia	A Gallardo, P Leon			
24.03.63	PERU	v COLOMBIA	(1-1)	1-1	La Paz
	Gallardo	G Gonzalez			
24.03.63	ARGENTINA	v BRAZIL		3-0	Cochabamba
	M Rodriquez, M Savoy, M Juarez				
24.03.63	BOLIVIA	v PARAGUAY		2-0	La Paz
	Castillo, Garcia				
27.03.63	PARAGUAY	v PERU	(4-0)	4-1	Cochabamba
	Zarate 2, C Cabrera, C Martinez	A Gallardo			
27.03.63	BRAZIL	v ECUADOR		2-2	Cochabamba
	Osvaldo, Flavio	Gando, Raffo			
28.03.63	BOLIVA	v ARGENTINA	(2-2)	3-2	La Paz
	Garcia, Castillo, Alcocer	M Rodriquez 2			
31.03.63	BOLIVIA	v BRAZIL		5-4	
	Jorge own goal, Camacho	Flavio II 2, Marco Antonio, Almir			
	Garcia, Alcocer, Ugarte penalty				
31.03.63	ARGENTINA	v PARAGUAY	(0-1)	1-1	La Paz
	C Lallana	C Cabrera			
31.03.63	ECUADOR	v COLOMBIA		4-3	Cochabamba
	C Raffo 2, Bolanos, Azon	D Gamboa, M Coll, Salla			

Bolivia	6	5	1	0	19-13	11
Paraguay	6	4	1	1	13-7	9
Argentina	6	3	1	2	15-10	7
Brazil	6	2	1	3	12-13	5
Peru	6	2	1	3	8-11	5
Ecuador	6	1	2	3	14-18	4

1967 (OFFICIAL)

Champions URUGUAY, in CHILE

Preliminary round			**H/T**	**F/T**	**Venue**	**Attend**
30.11.66	CHILE	v COLOMBIA	(3-0)	5-2	Santiago	69,066
	P Araya, I Prieto, O Castro 2, 1 pen	D Gamboa, L Moreno				
	M Saavedra					
11.12.66	COLOMBIA	v CHILE		0-0	Bogota	35,000
22.12.66	ECUADOR	v PARAGUAY		2-2	Quito	
	J C Rojas, Apodaca					
29.12.66	PARAGUAY	v ECUADOR		3-1	Asuncion	
	C Mora 2, Del Puerto					
13.01.67	URUGUAY	v BOLIVIA	(2-0)	4-0	Montevideo	12,500
	P Rocha, J M Castillo, Oyarbide,					
	Troncoso own goal					
18.01.67	CHILE	v VENEZUELA	(2-0)	2-0	Montevideo	12,325
	R Marcos 2					
18.01.67	ARGENTINA	v PARAGUAY	(1-0)	4-1	Montevideo	12,325
	O Mas, L Bernao, R Albrecht pen,	C Mora				
	L Artime					
21.01.67	URUGUAY	v VENEZUELA	(1-0)	4-0	Montevideo	6,634
	J Urrezmendi, M Viera, H Salve,					
	P Rocha					
22.01.67	CHILE	v PARAGUAY	(2-1)	4-2	Montevideo	4,778
	J Gallardo 2, P Araya 2	Riveros, Apodaca				
23.01.67	ARGENTINA	v BOLIVIA	(0-0)	1-0	Montevideo	4,778
	L Bernao					
25.01.67	PARAGUAY	v BOLIVIA	(1-0)	1-0	Montevideo	2,116
	Del Puerto					
25.01.67	ARGENTINA	v VENEZUELA	(2-0)	5-1	Montevideo	2,116
	L Artime 4, R Cardona	Santana				
26.01.67	URUGUAY	v CHILE	(1-2)	2-2	Montevideo	16,718
	P Rocha penalty, Oyarbide	J Gallardo, R Marcos				

28.01.67	VENEZUELA	v BOLIVIA		(0-0)	3-0	Montevideo	14,352
	A Ravello 2, Santana						
29.01.67	ARGENTINA	v CHILE		(1-0)	2-0	Montevideo	14,352
	C Sarnari, O Mas						
29.01.67	URUGUAY	v PARAGUAY		(1-0)	2-0	Montevideo	12,431
	J Urruzmendi 2						
01.02.67	CHILE	v BOLIVIA			0-0	Montevideo	360
01.02.67	PARAGUAY	v VENEZUELA		(4-2)	5-3	Montevideo	360
	C Mora, R Colman,	*Mendoza, Santana, Scovino*					
	J C Rojas 2, 1 penalty, A Gonzalez						
02.02.67	URUGUAY	v ARGENTINA		(0-0)	1-0	Montevideo	70,000
	P Rocha						

Uruguay	5	4	1	0	13-2	9
Argentina	5	4	0	1	12-3	8
Chile	5	2	2	1	8-6	6
Paraguay	5	2	0	3	9-13	4
Venezuela	5	1	0	4	7-16	2
Bolivia	5	0	1	4	0-9	1

Name changed to Copa America

1974 **Independiente** (Argentina)

1980 **Nacional** (Uruguay)

1965 **Independiente** (Argentina)

COPA AMERICA

**Name changed from South American Championships
(Home and away matches)**

1975

Champions PERU

				H/T	F/T	Venue	Attend
16.07.75	CHILE	v	PERU	(1-0)	1-1	Santiago	
	J Crisosto		*P Rojas*				
20.07.75	BOLIVIA	v	CHILE	(0-1)	2-1	Oruro	
	Mezza 2, 1 penalty		*M A Gamboa*				
20.07.75	COLOMBIA	v	PARAGUAY	(0-0)	1-0	Bogota	
	E Diaz						
24.07.75	ECUADOR	v	PARAGUAY		2-2	Guayaquil	
			H Kiese 2				
27.07.75	ECUADOR	v	COLOMBIA	(1-1)	1-3	Quito	
	Polo Carrera		*W Ortiz, E Retat, F Castro*				
27.07.75	BOLIVIA	v	PERU	(0-1)	0-1	La Paz	
			O Ramirez				
30.07.75	VENEZUELA	v	BRAZIL	(0-1)	0-4	Caracus	
			Romeu, Danival, Palinha 2				
30.07.75	PARAGUAY	v	COLOMBIA	(0-1)	0-1	Asuncion	
			E Diaz				
03.08.75	VENEZUELA	v	ARGENTINA	(1-3)	1-5	Caracus	8,000
	Irairte		*L Luque 3, M Kempes, C Cardenas*				
06.08.75	BRAZIL	v	ARGENTINA	(1-1)	2-1	Belo Horizonte	
	Nelhinho 2		*L Asad*				
07.0.8.75	PERU	v	BOLIVIA	(2-0)	3-1	Lima	
	O Ramirez, C Cueto penalty, J C Oblitas		*Mezza penalty*				
07.08.75	COLOMBIA	v	ECUADOR	(1-0)	2-0	Bogota	
	E Diaz, O Calero						
10.08.75	PARAGUAY	v	ECUADOR	(2-0)	3-1	Asuncion	
	C Baez, C Rolon 2		*Castaneda*				
10.08.75	ARGENTINA	v	VENEZUELA	(4-0)	11-0	Rosario	
	M Killer 3, M Kempes 2, A J Gallego, O Ardiles, M Zanabria 2, J Boveda, L Luque						
12.08.75	BRAZIL	v	VENEZUELA	(3-0)	6-0	Belo Horizonte	30,000
	Batata 2, Nelhinho, Danival, Campos, Palinha						
16.08.75	ARGENTINA	v	BRAZIL	(0-1)	0-1	Rosario	
			Danival				
17.08.75	CHILE	v	BOLIVIA		4-0	Santiago	
	S Ahumada, L Araneda 2, M A Gamboa						
20.08.75	PERU	v	CHILE	(3-0)	3-1	Lima	
	P Rojas, J C Oblitas, T Cubillas		*C Reinoso*				
Semi-finals							
21.09.75	COLOMBIA	v	URUGUAY	(0-0)	3-0	Bogota	
	E Diaz 2, E Angulo, W Ortiz						
30.09.75	BRAZIL	v	PERU	(0-1)	1-3	Belo Horizonte	
	Batata		*T Cubillas, E Cassareto 2*				
01.10.75	URUGUAY	v	COLOMBIA	(1-0)	1-0	Montevideo	65,000
	F Moreno						

COPA AMERICA

				H/T	F/T	Venue	Attend
04.10.75	PERU	v BRAZIL		(0-1)	0-2	Lima	
		Ze Carlos, Campos					
Final							
16.10.75	COLOMBIA	v PERU		(1-0)	1-0	Bogota	60,000
	F Castro						
22.10.75	PERU	v COLOMBIA		(2-0)	2-0	Lima	43,000
	J C Oblitas, O Ramirez						
28.10.75	PERU	v COLOMBIA		(1-0)	1-0	Caracus	Playoff
	H Sotil*						

* suspended half-time, awarded to Colombia

```
Group One
Brazil          4   4   0   0   13-1   8
Argentina       4   2   0   2   17-4   4
Venezuela       4   0   0   4   1-26   0

Group Two
Peru            4   3   1   0   8-3    7
Chile           4   1   1   2   7-6    3
Bolivia         4   1   0   3   3-9    2

Group Three
Colombia        4   4   0   0   7-1    8
Paraguay        4   1   1   2   5-5    3
Ecuador         4   0   1   3   4-10   1
```

Semi Finals
Peru v Brazil 3-1 0-2
Colombia v Uruguay 3-0 0-1
Final
Peru v Colombia 2-0 0-1 1-0

1979 (OFFICIAL)

Champions PARAGUAY

				H/T	F/T	Venue	Attend
18.07.79	BOLIVIA	v ARGENTINA		(1-1)	2-1	La Paz	30,000
	Reynaldo 2	*C Lopez*					
26.07.79	BOLIVIA	v BRAZIL		(1-1)	2-1	La Paz	
	Aragones 2, 1 penalty						
01.08.79	VENEZUELA	v COLOMBIA			0-0	San Cristobal	40,000
02.08.79	BRAZIL	v ARGENTINA		(1-1)	2-1	Rio de Janeiro	
	Zico, Tita	*R A Dias*					
08.08.79	ARGENTINA	v BOLIVIA		(2-0)	3-0	Buenos Aires	
	D Passerella, J Gaspari,						
	D Maradona						
08.08.79	VENEZUELA	v CHILE		(0-0)	1-1	San Cristobel	
	Carvajal	*J Peredo*					
15.08.79	COLOMBIA	v CHILE			1-0	Bogota	
16.08.79	BRAZIL	v BOLIVIA		(0-0)	2-0	Sao Paulo	
	Tita, Zico						
22.08.79	COLOMBIA	v VENEZUELA		(1-0)	4-0	Bogota	
	A Iguaran 2, Chaparro, J Moron						
23.08.79	ARGENTINA	v BRAZIL		(1-1)	2-2	Buenos Aires	
	D Passerella, R A Diaz	*Socrates 2, 1 penalty*					
28.08.79	ECUADOR	PARAGUAY		(0-2)	1-2	Quito	
	Torres Carcas penalty	*H Talavera, Solaline*					
29.08.79	CHILE	v VENEZUELA		(3-0)	7-0	Santiago	
	J Peredo 2, C Rivas 2, L Veliz,						
	M Soto, P Yanez						
05.09.79	Ch. ?	v COLOMBIA		(1-0)	2-0	Santiago	80,000
	CC ely, J Peredo						

05.09.79	ECUADOR	v URUGUAY	(2-0)	2-1	Guayaquil	
	B Tenorio, Alarcon	*V Victorino penalty*				
13.09.79	PARAGUAY	v ECUADOR		2-0	Asuncion	
	J Osario, T Garces own goal					
17.09.79	URUGUAY	v ECUADOR	(1-0)	2-1	Montevideo	
	Bica, V Victorino penalty	*Klinger*				
20.09.79	PARAGUAY	v URUGUAY		0-0	Asuncion	
26.09.79	URUGUAY	v PARAGUAY	(2-0)	2-2	Montevideo	25,000
	Millar, R Pas	*E Morel 2*				

Semi-final

17.10.79	PERU	v CHILE	(1-1)	1-2	Lima	
	R Mosquera	*C Caszely 2*				
24.10.79	PARAGUAY	v BRAZIL	(2-0)	2-1	Asuncion	
	E Morel, H Talavera	*Palinha*				
24.10.79	CHILE	v PERU		0-0	Santiago	
31.10.79	BRAZIL	v PARAGUAY	(1-1)	2-2	Rio de Janeiro	
	Falcao, Socrates	*M Morel, J C Romero*				

Final

28.11.79	PARAGUAY	v CHILE	(2-0)	3-0	Asuncion	
	J C Romero 2, M Morel					
05.12.79	CHILE	v PARAGUAY	(1-0)	1-0	Santiago	
	C Rivas					
11.12.79	CHILE	v PARAGUAY		0-0	Buenos Aires	

Group One

Chile	4	2	1	1	10-2	5
Colombia	4	2	1	1	5-2	5
Venezuela	4	0	2	2	1-12	2

Group Two

Brazil	4	2	1	1	7-5	5
Bolivia	4	2	0	2	4-7	4
Argentina	4	1	1	2	7-6	3

Group Three

Paraguay	4	2	2	0	4-1	6
Uruguay	4	1	1	2	3-3	4
Ecuador	4	1	0	3	4-7	2

Semi Finals
Brazil v Paraguay 2-2 1-2
Peru (holders) v Chile 1-2 0-0

Final
Paraguay v Chile 3-0 0-1 0-0

1983 OFFICIAL

Champions URUGUAY

			H/T	F/T	Venue	Attend
10.08.83	ECUADOR	v ARGENTINA	(0-1)	2-2	Quito	45,000
	Vazquez, Vega	*J Burruchaga 2*				
14.08.83	BOLIVIA	v COLOMBIA	(0-1)	0-1	La Paz	50,000
		A Valderama				
17.08.83	ECUADOR	v BRAZIL	(0-1)	0-1	Quito	45,000
		Roberto				
17.08.83	PERU	v COLOMBIA	(0-0)	1-0	Lima	20,000
	F Navarro					
21.08.83	BOLIVIA	v PERU	(0-0)	1-1	La Paz	50,000
	Romero	*F Navarro*				

24.08.83	ARGENTINA *R Gareca*	v BRAZIL	(0-0)	1-0	Buenos Aires	57,000
28.08.83	COLOMBIA *M Prince, Fiorillo*	v PERU *E Malasquez 2 1 penalty*	(0-1)	2-2	Bogota	45,000
31.08.83	COLOMBIA *A Valderrama, N Molina pen*	v BOLIVIA *Melgar, Rojas*	(1-0)	2-2	Bogota	
01.09.83	URUGUAY *L Acevdeda, F Morena penalty*	v CHILE *J C Orellana*	(1-0)	2-1	Montevideo	
02.09.83	BRAZIL *Renato, Roberto 2, Eder, Tita*	v ECUADOR	(1-0)	5-0	Goiania	
04.09.83	PERU *G Leguia, J Caballero*	v BOLIVIA *Paniagua*	(2-0)	2-1	Lima	
04.09.83	URUGUAY *W Cabrera, F Morena penalty,* *A Luzardo*	v VENEZUELA	(2-0)	3-0	Montevideo	
07.09.83	ARGENTINA *V Ramos, J Burruchaga penalty*	v ECUADOR *Quinones, Maldonado penalty*	(0-1)	2-2	Buenos Aires	
07.09.83	CHILE *J Aravena 2, O Arriaza, R Dubo,* *R Espinoza*	v VENEZUELA	(3-0)	5-0	Santiago	
11.09.83	CHILE *R Dubo, J C Letelier*	v URUGUAY	(1-0)	2-0	Santiago	50,000
14.09.83	BRAZIL	v ARGENTINA		0-0	Rio de Janeiro	60,000
18.09.83	VENEZUELA *Febles*	v URUGUAY *v Santelli, C Aguilera*	(0-0)	1-2	Caracas	
21.09.83	VENEZUELA	v CHILE		0-0	Caracas	2,000

Semi-finals

23.10.83	PARAGUAY *Morel*	v BRAZIL *v Eder*	(0-0)	1-1	Asuncion	
13.01.83	PERU	v URUGUAY *C Aguilera*	(0-0)	0-1	Lima	
20.10.83	BRAZIL	v PARAGUAY		0-0	Uberlandia	75,000
20.10.83	URUGUAY *W Cabrera*	v PERU *E Malasquez*	(0-1)	1-1	Montevideo	70,000

Final

27.10.83	URUGUAY *E Francescoli, V Diogo*	v BRAZIL	(1-0)	2-0	Montevideo	65,607
04.11.83	BRAZIL *Jorginho*	v URUGUAY *C Aguilera*	(1-0)	1-1	Salvador	76,704

Group One

Uruguay	4	3	0	1	7-4	6
Chile	4	2	1	1	8-2	5
Venezuela	4	0	1	3	1-10	1

Group Two

Brazil	4	2	1	1	6-1	5
Argentina	4	1	3	0	5-4	5
Ecuador	4	0	2	2	4-10	2

Group Three

Peru	4	2	2	0	6-4	6
Colombia	4	1	2	1	5-5	4
Bolivia	4	0	2	2	4-6	2

Semi Finals
Paraguay (holders) v Brazil 1-1 0-0
Peru v Uruguay 0-1 1-1

Final
Uruguay v Brazil 2-0 1-1

1987 (OFFICIAL)

Champions URUGUAY, in ARGENTINA

				H/T	F/T	Venue	Attend
27.06.87	ARGENTINA	v	PERU	(0-0)	1-1	Buenos Aires	28,000
	D Maradona		L Reyna				
28.06.87	BRAZIL	v	VENEZUELA	(2-0)	5-0	Cordoba	10,000
	Edu, Morovic own goal, Careca,						
	Nelsinho, Romario						
28.06.87	PARAGUAY	v	BOLIVIA		0-0	Cordoba	2,000
30.06.87	CHILE	v	VENEZUELA	(1-1)	2-1	Cordoba	532
	J C Letelier, J Contreras, S Salgado		P Acosta penalty				
01.07.87	COLOMBIA	v	BOLIVIA	(1-0)	2-0	Rosario	500
	C Valderrama, A Iguaran						
02.07.87	ARGENTINA	v	ECUADOR	(0-0)	3-0	Buenos Aires	20,000
	C P Caniggia, D Maradona 2, 1 pen						
03.07.87	CHILE	v	BRAZIL	(1-0)	4-0	Cordoba	15,000
	I Basay 2, J C Letelier 2						
04.07.87	PERU	v	ECUADOR	(0-0)	1-1	Buenos Aires	5,000
	E La Rosa		H E Cuvi				
05.07.87	COLOMBIA	v	PARAGUAY	(2-0)	3-0	Rosario	5,000
	A Iguaran 3						

Semi-finals

				H/T	F/T	Venue	Attend
08.07.87	CHILE	v	COLOMBIA	(0-0)	2-1 aet	Cordoba	10,000
	F Astengo, J Vera		B Redin penalty				
09.07.87	URUGUAY	v	ARGENTINA	(0-0)	1-0	Buenos Aires	75,000
	A Alzamendi						
11.07.87	ARGENTINA	v	COLOMBIA	(0-2)	1-2	Buenos Aires	5,000
	C P Caniggia		G J Gomez, J J Galeano				

Final

				H/T	F/T	Venue	Attend
12.07.87	CHILE	v	URUGUAY	(0-0)	0-1	Buenos Aires	20,000
			P J Bengoechea				

Group One
Argentina	2	1	1	0	4-1	3
Peru	2	0	2	0	2-2	2
Ecuador	2	0	1	1	1-4	1

Group Two
Chile	2	2	0	0	7-1	4
Brazil	2	1	0	1	5-4	2
Venezuela 2	0	0	2	1-8	0	

Group Three
Colombia	2	2	0	0	5-0	4
Bolivia	2	0	1	1	0-2	1
Paraguay	2	0	1	1	0-3	1

Semi Finals
Chile v Colombia 2-1
Uruguay (holders) v Argentina 1-0

3/4 Place
Colombia v Argentina 2-1

Final
Uruguay v Chile 1-0

COPA AMERICA

1989 (OFFICIAL)

Champions BRAZIL, in BRAZIL

Date	Home		Away	H/T	F/T	Venue	Attend
01.07.89	BRAZIL	v	VENEZUELA	(2-0)	3-1	Salvador	16,000
	Bebeto, Geovani penalty, Baltazar		*C Maldonado*				
01.07.89	PARAGUAY	v	PERU	(2-1)	5-2	Salvador	2,000
	A Canete 2, G Neffa, A Mendoza,		*J Hirano, F Manassero*				
	J G Del Solar own goal						
02.07.89	URUGUAY	v	ECUADOR	(0-0)	0-1	Goiania	40,000
			E Benitez				
02.07.89	ARGENTINA	v	CHILE	(0-0)	1-0	Goiania	45,000
	C P Caniggia						
03.07.89	BRAZIL	v	PERU		0-0	Salvador	25,000
03.07.89	VENEZUELA	v	COLOMBIA	(0-1)	2-4	Salvador	10,000
	C Maldonado 2		*R Higuita penalty, A Iguaran 2,*				
			A De Avila				
04.07.89	URUGUAY	v	BOLIVIA	(2-0)	3-0	Goiania	10,000
	S J Ostolaza 2, R Sosa						
04.07.89	ARGENTINA	v	ECUADOR		0-0	Goiania	12,000
05.07.89	PERU	v	VENEZUELA	(1-1)	1-1	Salvador	2,250
	F Navarro		*C Maldonado*				
05.07.89	COLOMBIA	v	PARAGUAY	(0-0)	0-1	Salvador	3,000
			A Mendoza				
06.07.89	ECUADOR	v	BOLIVIA		0-0	Goiania	4,500
06.07.89	CHILE	v	URUGUAY	(0-1)	0-3	Goiania	4,500
			R Sosa, A Altamendi, E Francescoli				
07.07.89	BRAZIL	v	COLOMBIA		0-0	Salvador	15,000
07.07.89	PARAGUAY	v	VENEZUELA	(1-0)	3-0	Salvador	10,000
	G Neffa, B Ferreira 2						
08.07.89	BOLIVIA	v	CHILE	(0-2)	0-5	Goiania	5,000
			J Olmis, J Ramirez, F Astengo,				
			J Pizzaro, O Reyes				
08.07.89	URUGUAY	v	ARGENTINA	(0-0)	0-1	Goiania	15,000
			C P Caniggia				
09.07.89	BRAZIL	v	PARAGUAY	(0-0)	2-0	Recife	55,000
	Bebeto 2						
09.07.89	COLOMBIA	v	PERU	(1-1)	1-1	Receife	50,000
	A Iguaran		*J Hirano*				
10.07.89	CHILE	v	ECUADOR	(1-0)	2-1	Goiania	15,000
	J Olmis, J C Letelier		*A Aguinoga*				
10.07.89	ARGENTINA	v	BOLIVIA		0-0	Goiania	
12.07.89	URUGUAY	v	PARAGUAY	(1-0)	3-0	Rio de Janeiro	110,000
	E Francescoli, A Alzamendi, R Paz						

2nd round

Date	Home		Away	H/T	F/T	Venue	Attend
12.07.89	BRAZIL	v	ARGENTINA	(0-0)	2-0	Rio de Janeiro	115,000
	Bebeto, Romario						
14.07.89	BRAZIL	v	PARAGUAY	(1-0)	3-0	Rio de Janeiro	70,000
	Bebeto 2, Romario						
14.07.89	ARGENTINA	v	URUGUAY	(0-1)	0-2	Rio de Janeiro	70,000
			Rubin Sosa 2				
16.07.89	BRAZIL	v	URUGUAY	(0-0)	1-0	Rio de Janeiro	148,000
	Romario						
16.07.89	ARGENTINA	v	PARAGUAY		0-0	Rio de Janeiro	110,000

Group A						Group B						Final Round					
Brazil	4	2	2	0	5-1	6	Argentina	4	2	2	0	2-0	6	Brazil	3	3	0	0	6-0	6
Paraguay	4	3	0	1	9-4	6	Uruguay	4	2	0	2	6-2	4	Uruguay	3	2	0	1	5-1	4
Colombia	4	1	2	1	5-4	4	Chile	4	2	0	2	7-5	4	Argentina	4	0	1	2	0-4	1
Peru	4	0	3	1	4-7	3	Ecuador	4	1	2	1	2-2	4	Paraguay	4	0	1	2	0-6	1
Venezuela	4	0	1	3	4-11	1	Bolivia	4	0	2	2	0-8	2						

SUMMARY - OFFICIAL

27 Official Championships held

	participation	P	W	D	L	F-A	Winners
ARGENTINA	24	105	65	19	21	260-100	9
URUGUAY	24	110	66	19	34	256-133	9
CHILE	21	102	33	20	49	166-196	0
PARAGUAY	21	104	46	18	40	174-177	2
BRAZIL	18	93	50	17	26	230-124	4
PERU	17	87	33	23	31	137-141	1
BOLIVIA	14	68	13	13	42	71-196	1
ECUADOR	13	65	3	15	47	59-186	0
COLOMBIA	9	51	15	10	26	60-105	0
VENEZUELA	6	23	1	4	18	15-87	0

UNOFFICIAL (EXTRAORDINARIOS)

		P	W	D	L	F-A	Winners
ARGENTINA	8	32	24	4	4	87-31	4
URUGUAY	8	32	21	3	8	73-26	4
CHILE	7	28	10	2	16	42-55	0
BRAZIL	6	26	14	5	7	56-34	0
PARAGUAY	4	17	4	4	9	26-31	0
PERU	3	12	2	1	9	13-21	0
ECUADOR	3	14	1	2	11	13-57	0
BOLIVIA	1	5	0	0	5	4-23	0
COLOMBIA	1	6	1	1	4	7-25	0

1979 **Olimpia** (Paraguay)